GREAT AVIATORS AND EPIC FLIGHTS

SMITHSONIAN
NATIONAL AIR AND SPACE MUSEUM

GREAT AVIATORS

AND EPIC FLIGHTS

VON HARDESTY

HUGH LAUTER LEVIN ASSOCIATES, INC.

Great Aviators and Epic Flights

ISBN: 0-88363-526-7

PROJECT EDITOR: Ellin Yassky

BOOK DESIGNER: Kevin Osborn, Research & Design, Ltd.
Arlington, Virginia

ILLUSTRATIONS EDITOR: Charles O. Hyman

ASSISTANT ILLUSTRATIONS EDITOR: Lawrence DiRicco

COPYEDITOR: Deborah T. Zindell

DISTRIBUTED BY PUBLISHERS GROUP WEST

PRINTED IN CHINA

(PAGE 1)

*A Blériot-type monoplane
at Hippodrome race track,
St. Petersburg, Russia, ca. 1912.*

(PAGES 2–3)

U.S. Air Force F-117
Nighthawk *stealth fighters
in flight.*

(OPPOSITE)

The Gossamer Albatross
in flight.

(PAGE 6)

*Looking forward from the
pilot's seat in the Bell X-1*
Glamorous Glennis, *flown
by Chuck Yeager.*

(PAGE 264)

*A group photo taken at the
conclusion of the Archbold
expedition, with expedition
members and locals
atop the* Guba II.

CONTENTS

FOREWORD
FATEFUL CHOICES

PIONEERING aviators, both men and women, shaped the course of aviation in the twentieth century. *Great Aviators and Epic Flights* evokes this world. "Courage mounteth with occasion," William Shakespeare once wrote, suggesting that the human potential for heroic action comes with opportunity. The saga of human flight has given meaning to the Bard's prescient remarks. No sooner had the Wrights made their first tentative flights at Kitty Hawk, North Carolina, in December 1903 than they were joined by a host of intrepid aviators in the quest to fly faster, farther, and higher.

Great Aviators and Epic Flights draws selectively on this rich history, a core sample drawn from the layered history of the air age. Between the covers of this anthology one will encounter not only the celebrated pilots of the past such as Louis Blériot, Charles Lindbergh, and Chuck Yeager; but lesser known figures, who—sadly and inexplicably—have slipped into the fog of history. No less important, the whole gamut of flying machines can be found in this book—fabric and wood biplanes, fighters and bombers in two world wars, gliders, amphibians, jets, experimental aircraft, dirigibles, balloons, and helicopters. As an anthology, *Great Aviators and Epic Flights* cannot claim to be coextensive with the history of aviation, but through the selective content of the book the reader gains a sense of aviation's rapid development in the first century of human flight. We see how the airplane has dazzled us, set new milestones in human achievement, become a devastating weapon of war, linked continents even as it has altered our notions of time and space, and transformed modern life in countless ways.

Famed French aviator Jean Mermoz in many ways caught the animating spirit of the fast-paced air age with his preference for the blue skies over any terrestrial pursuit. He once remarked that death in a bed would be a real misfortune, but in a plane it would be perfectly acceptable. A pilot for *L'Aeropostale* (later Air France), Mermoz knew first hand the high risks associated with flying. His flight log was filled with stunning aerial feats—flying air mail at night, navigating across the sun-baked Sahara desert, crossing the storm-tossed South Atlantic, and traversing the high Andes. His fellow pilot, Antoine de Saint-Exupery, captured the extraordinary bravery of Mermoz in his literary classic *Wind, Sand, and Stars*. Fittingly, fate allowed Mermoz to encounter death at the controls of his airplane: he disappeared on a flight across the South Atlantic in 1936.

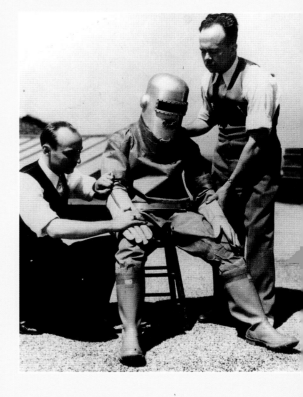

(ABOVE)

Wiley Post is fitted for his special high-altitude flight suit, July 1934.

(OPPOSITE)

Steve Fossett in the Spirit of Freedom *completed a 13-day, 12-hour aerial trek around the globe in August 2002.*

Like sports, aviation has its official records and pantheon of heroes. Also like sports, the story of aviation is punctuated with debates—most beyond resolution—on what constitutes real human or technical achievement. Air museums face this dilemma in designing an exhibit; fateful choices have to be made in the selection of every artifact, event, or personality to illustrate a historical theme.

And so it is with this particular book: if you mention Jean Mermoz as an exemplar of the intrepid aviator, why not his fellow airman, Henry Guillaumet, who crashed and survived a six-day ordeal in the Andes? If you devote a chapter to the London-to-Australia flight of Amy Johnson, why not look at other worthy women pilots? If you cover the crossing of the English Channel by Louis Blériot, why not the transcontinental aerial trek of Cal Rodgers in the *Vin Fiz*? If the *Voyager* around-the-world flight strikes us as a benchmark, why not mention the Douglas World Cruisers of 1924? If Eddie Rickenbacker suggests certain classic attributes of the ace, why not examine World War II, which became an arena for another generation of aces to achieve extraordinary numbers of air victories? Certainly, a Chuck Yeager or a Scott Crossfield mirror the boldness of test flying, so why not some reference to Jimmy Doolittle or Wiley Post? And if you speak of the helicopter rescue flights when Saigon fell to the North Vietnamese in 1975, how can you ignore the even more dramatic helicopter flights at Chernobyl in 1986, dropping sand to suppress the fires in the nuclear reactor and evacuating over 100,000 people to safety?

Any poll of aviation enthusiasts will prompt myriad lists of notable aviators and famous flights. Such diversity of opinion merely points to the rich and often untapped drama of aviation history. When the chapter outline for

Great Aviators and Epic Flights was shown to one curator at the National Air and Space Museum, he remarked, "The problem is who and what to omit!" Such an observation genuinely haunted all of us who designed and worked on this book.

While we have endeavored to recapture some of the "lost" stories in aviation history, we are keenly aware of our omissions. One could point to the 1933 flight of two Westland PV3s over the Himalayas as one of the great air adventures of all time. Sir Douglas Douglas-Hamilton and David F. Macintyre piloted these open-cockpit biplanes across the top of world at an altitude of six miles and with the outside temperature hovering at nearly minus 70 degrees Fahrenheit. Only primitive heated flying suits and supercharged radial engines sustained them in this most dangerous passage. Commercial airliners have offered moments of high drama as well: we remember the improvisational skills of Al Haynes and the cockpit crew of United Flight 232 at Sioux City in 1989, when they landed a DC-10 airliner after a catastrophic engine explosion had destroyed all the redundant hydraulic control systems.

Of course, human flight possesses its own momentum. Even as *Great Aviators and Epic Flights* sped to press, we were reminded that the quest for aerial milestones is relentless: Steve Fossett made his solitary flight around the world in his balloon, the *Spirit of Freedom*. His flying exploits have not lacked drama: he survived five earlier failed attempts, including a perilous descent into the Coral Sea on his fourth try. We have included one photo of Fossett's balloon, just to suggest that record-breaking flights persist into the twenty-first century.

Our ensemble of stories may be viewed as a celebration of flight on one level. Certainly, the trajectory of flight has been

Jimmy Doolittle with his Curtiss R3C2 shortly after he flew the aircraft to win the Schneider Cup in 1925.

Amelia Earhart stands next to a 1936 Cord convertible and her Lockheed Electra 10E, the same aircraft she flew on her ill-fated around-the-world flight in 1937.

(TOP)
Francis Gabreski (right) stands in the cockpit of his P-47D on the occasion of his 11th air victory. Gabreski is greeted by pilot Sylvester Burke, January 1944.

(BOTTOM)
Cal Rodgers, first to fly coast to coast in 30 days or less, with his distinctive cigar, ca. 1912.

fueled by personal risk taking, often against formidable odds. Aviators, quite appropriately, have been viewed in the popular mind as an heroic elite, many possessing that unique blend of skill and courage popularized by the writer Tom Wolfe as the "Right Stuff." This same quality of flying prowess has spilled over into the space age.

But we are equally aware that the airplane possesses a mixed legacy, on the one hand transporting millions around the globe in safety, but also serving as a decisive weapon of war. To acknowledge this reality, *Great Aviators and Epic Flights* has included three distinctly military chapters, one on the genesis of the ace in World War I, another on how the B-29 Superfortress, flying the second atomic mission to Nagasaki, helped to usher in the nuclear age, and finally a look at stealth technology in the Gulf war, a fascinating hint of modern air warfare in the twenty-first century.

The story of aviation is punctuated with both triumph and tragedy. When Charles Lindbergh made his successful solitary passage across the Atlantic in May 1927, he prompted a number of pilots to attempt transoceanic flights. That same summer 40 pilots attempted high-risk ocean crossings, with 21 losing their lives. A decade later, Amelia Earhart, then one of most renowned woman aviators, disappeared in a flight across the Pacific Ocean.

A century now separates us from the Wright brothers, who inaugurated the air age with their first successful flight of a powered heavier-than-air flying machine. *Great Aviators and Epic Flights* is a modest effort to show this remarkable phenomenon in all its drama and historical significance.

Von Hardesty
Smithsonian National Air and Space Museum

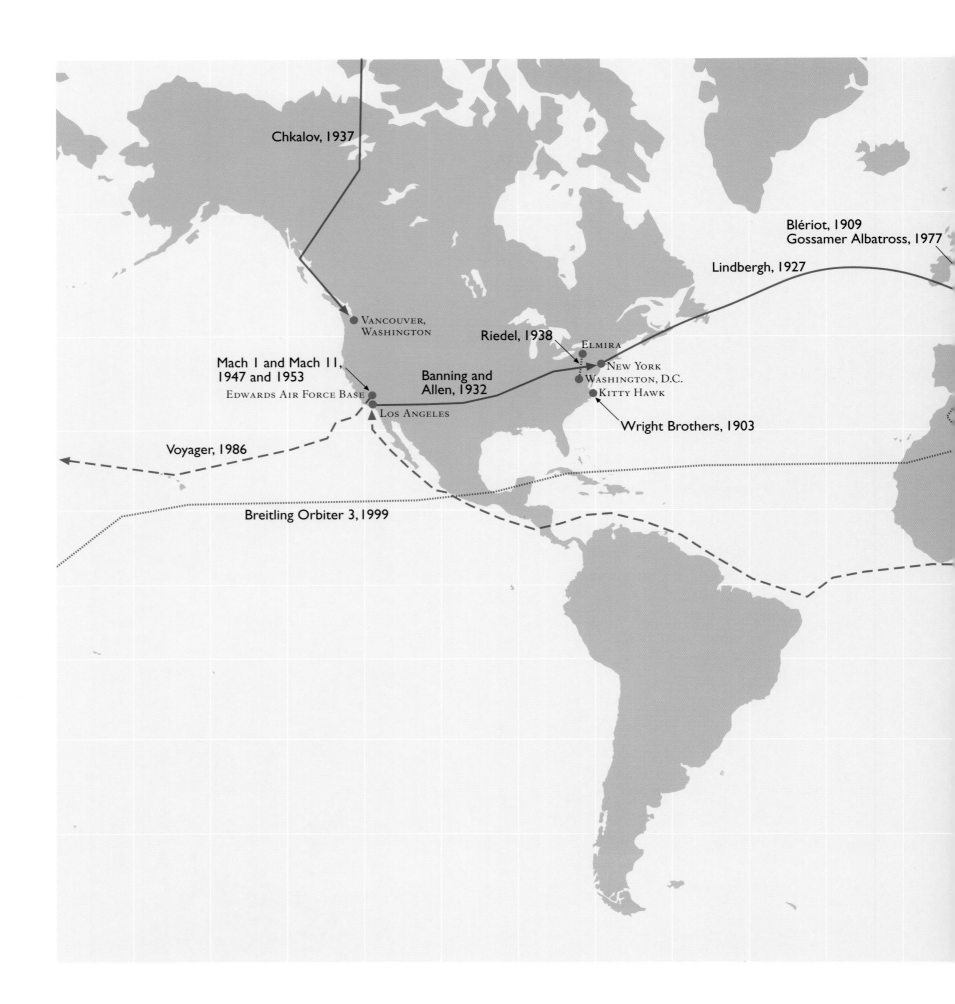

Chkalov, 1937

Blériot, 1909
Gossamer Albatross, 1977

Lindbergh, 1927

Vancouver,
Washington

Riedel, 1938

ELMIRA

Mach 1 and Mach 11,
1947 and 1953

NEW YORK
WASHINGTON, D.C.

Banning and
Allen, 1932

KITTY HAWK

EDWARDS AIR FORCE BASE

LOS ANGELES

Wright Brothers, 1903

Voyager, 1986

Breitling Orbiter 3, 1999

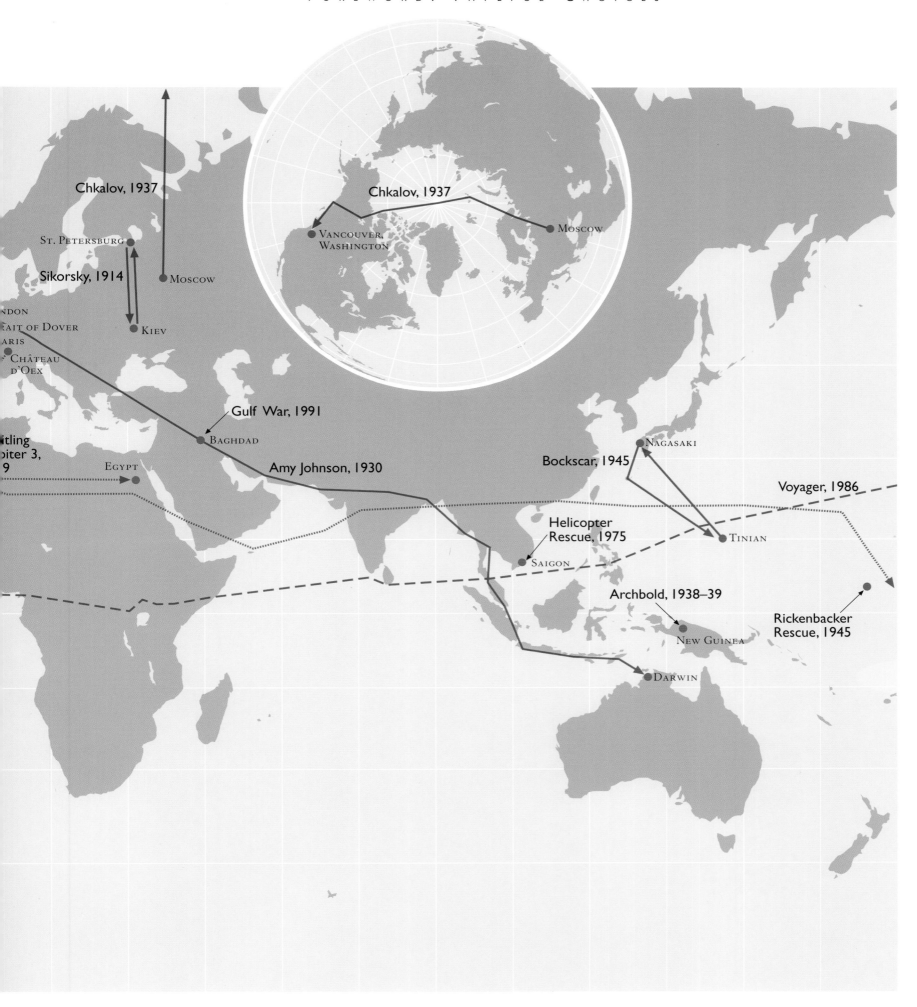

Chkalov, 1937

Chkalov, 1937

VANCOUVER,
WASHINGTON

MOSCOW

ST. PETERSBURG

Sikorsky, 1914

MOSCOW

NDON

RAIT OF DOVER

ARIS

CHÂTEAU
D'OEX

KIEV

Gulf War, 1991

itling
piter 3,
9

EGYPT

BAGHDAD

Amy Johnson, 1930

NAGASAKI

Bockscar, 1945

Voyager, 1986

Helicopter
Rescue, 1975

TINIAN

SAIGON

Archbold, 1938–39

Rickenbacker
Rescue, 1945

NEW GUINEA

DARWIN

THE WRIGHTS
ORVILLE AND WILBUR LAUNCH THE AIR AGE

THE AIR AGE began at wind-swept Kitty Hawk, North Carolina, on December 17, 1903—a flying machine, crafted by Orville and Wilbur Wright, lifted into the air under its own power, moved forward without any loss of speed, and landed on ground as high as that from where it had taken off. The extraordinary aerial trek lasted a mere 12 seconds, covering a distance of 120 feet. The Wright Flyer made four flights that memorable day, one lasting an awe-inspiring 59 seconds. With each incremental advance in performance, the Wright Flyer suggested the vast potential for humans to conquer the skies, to fly as the birds.

The Wrights were part of an era filled with stunning technological breakthroughs: electric lighting, the telegraph, photography and cinema, the wireless, the electrified trolley, and the automobile. The airplane appeared as the most improbable invention of them all, a metaphor for human progress and the fulfillment of an ancient human dream to fly.

Orville and Wilbur Wright managed to build a successful heavier-than-air flying machine in a remarkably short time frame, from their initial work in 1899 to their triumph at Kitty Hawk in 1903. In the popular mind, the two brothers are often trivialized—and quite unfairly—as untutored bicycle mechanics who somehow fashioned a flying machine. Indeed, they did build bicycles and for that matter, ran a printing press in Dayton, Ohio. They possessed no advanced degrees or special technical training. But their design of the Flyer represented a genuine engineering triumph, one based on careful research, systematic testing, and an empirical grasp of the mechanics of flight. They were highly practical in their approach, always seeking the most simple and effective solution to any problem. When accurate data on airfoils was lacking, they fashioned their own wind tunnel to generate the necessary information. They took full advantage of the fact that lightweight internal combustion engines had become available for the first time at the end of the nineteenth century. And they equipped their flying machine with propellers of optimal design to provide necessary thrust to sustain flight. All these factors—and many others—came together in the integrated design of the Wright Flyer.

The Wright brothers belonged to a close-knit family in Dayton, Ohio. They were the sons of Milton and Susan Wright, the father being a bishop in the United Brethren

(ABOVE)

Orville (left) and Wilbur Wright launched the air age in December 1903 with the successful flight of the first powered heavier-than-air flying machine.

(OPPOSITE)

Today, the historic Wright Flyer hangs in the Milestones of Flight Gallery at the National Air and Space Museum, Washington, D.C.

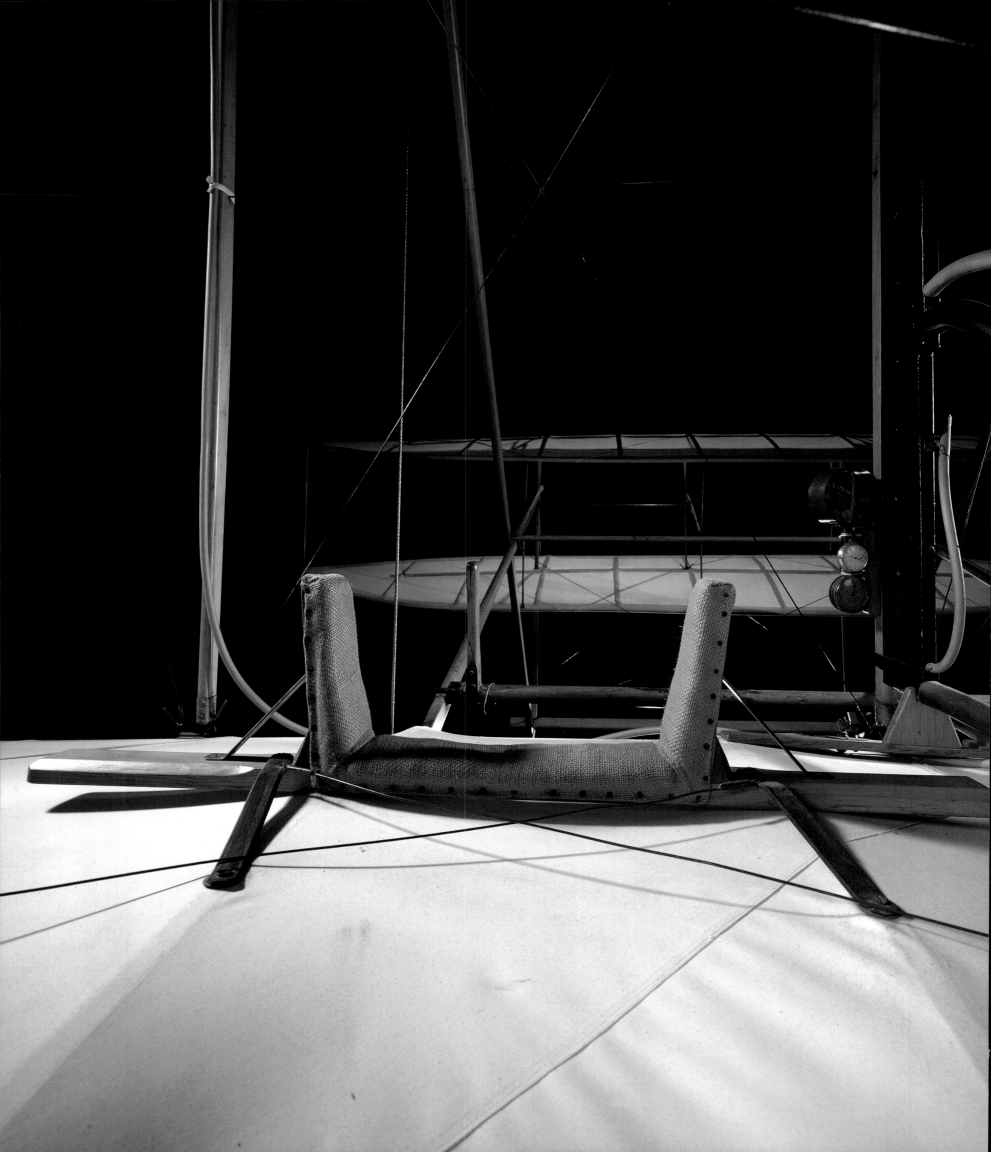

Looking forward from the pilot's position on the Wright Flyer. The pilot lay in a prone position in the u-shaped upholstered cradle, visible in the center of the wing.

The canard at the forward edge controlled the pitch of the aircraft. The engine for the Flyer is visible at the right.

in Christ Church. Their young sister, Katharine, took a keen interest in her brothers' flying experiments. As individuals, both Orville and Wilbur were strong-willed and relentless in their quest to design a flying machine, an aspiration that some have traced to a childhood gift from their father: a rubber-band-powered toy helicopter. Critical for their success, even apart from their innate intelligence, was their work ethic: they read widely in science and engineering; they possessed impressive analytical skills; and through self study, they acquired a thorough grasp of mathematics.

The Wrights began their odyssey by requesting literature on the theory of flight from the Smithsonian Institution. They corresponded with Octave Chanute, who had written a pioneering book, *Progress in Flying Machines.* Both Wilbur and Orville were keenly interested in the flying exploits of Otto Lilienthal, a German who made pioneering glider flights and conducted aerodynamic research before his untimely death in a flying mishap in 1896. There was also the towering figure of Samuel P. Langley, the secretary of the Smithsonian, who had received congressional funding in 1898 to develop a flying machine. The last decade of the nineteenth century, in fact, was fertile with speculation on the theory of flight, not only in America, but even in distant Australia, where Lawrence Hargrave had constructed box kites that caught the attention of the Wrights. For the Wrights, a meaningful path to explore the mystery of flight included kites and gliders.

A key factor in the ultimate success of the Wrights was their decision to concentrate their labors on solving the problem of control. Getting into the air was a challenge requiring both power and lift, but once any future aviator left the ground there was the more daunting task of

maintaining balance and directional control. Much of the
Wrights' experimentation centered on this pivotal question
of control. They sought to master the three axes of
control—pitch (nose up or down), yaw (nose to the right or
to the left), and roll (banking the wing up or down). In the
end, the Wrights conquered all three dimensions with the
use of moveable elevators and the so-called wing-warping
technique, which involved the twisting or flexing of the
wing. During flight this induced more lift on one side
than the other, forcing the airplane to bank. The Wrights
ultimately designed their airplane with a canard, a forward
set of elevators, which dampened any violent pitching
movement (the very uncontrolled movement that had
led to the death of Lilienthal). The pilot controlled the
yawing motion of the airplane with the aft vertical
rudders. Building the Wright Flyer involved a methodical
program of design, testing, and redesign—the brothers
from Dayton wished to fly, not to produce a treatise on
the theory of flight.

For their flight testing, the Wrights needed a place
where the winds were steady and powerful, to allow
sustained flight of a glider. The Great Lakes area was one
option, but they sought a more suitable place. In November
1899, they sent off a letter to the U.S. Weather Bureau
seeking a recommendation. Eventually they learned of
Kitty Hawk, North Carolina, on the Outer Banks, offering
hills and consistently strong winds. For the next four years,
they traveled to this remote spot each summer and into late
fall. To reach Kitty Hawk, the brothers had to transport
their gear and supplies by boat across the Albemarle Sound,
since at the time there was no bridge connecting the area
to the mainland. Their camp site was at Kill Devil Hill,

The historic first flight of the Wright Flyer at Kitty Hawk, North Carolina, December 17, 1903. Orville is at the controls of the Flyer, with his brother Wilbur to the right.

(TOP)

The engine for the Wright Flyer was built by Charles Taylor. The water-cooled engine powered two propellers by means of a chain drive.

(MIDDLE)

Octave Chanute visits the Wright Brothers at their work shed at Kill Devil Hill (Kitty Hawk) in 1901.

(BOTTOM)

The Wright Flyer positioned in front of the work shed on November 24, 1903, three weeks before its first flight.

situated 100 feet above sea level. Living in tents and improvised wooden structures, the Wrights contended with mosquitoes, high winds, violent rain storms, and, with the onset of winter, bone-chilling cold. Kitty Hawk, with its striking beauty and austere conditions, offered the Wrights the optimal place to conduct their historic program of flight testing.

They first arrived in Kitty Hawk in September 1900. On this initial outing they flew their first biplane glider. They returned the following year with a new biplane glider fitted with a forward elevator, but the new design did not necessarily surpass the performance of their first glider. Modifications were made to the wing to allow better flights. They learned that by lying prone on the wing, they dramatically reduced the drag on the glider. Experiments were also conducted with a moving hip cradle, a device that allowed the pilot to warp the wings for right and left banks—a maneuver the Wrights discovered posed certain dangers. There were some successes, but the 1901 glider failed to provide the breakthrough the Wrights had anticipated. Further tests would be required to solve the problem of control.

Upon their return to Dayton, Orville and Wilbur decided to design a new glider, one that would be based on their own data, not that of earlier pioneers. They measured lift and drag coefficients with models mounted on a bicycle. They also built their own wind tunnel to test various airfoils and wing models. Soon they had developed their own aerodynamic tables, which became a major piece of empirical data on flight. From this energetic interlude of ground testing, the Wrights came up with the design of their new 1902 glider. The new design was a biplane glider

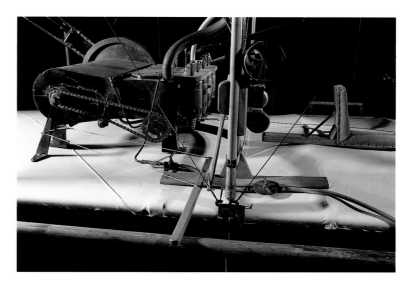

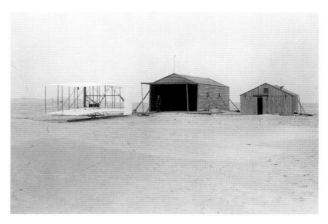

with a wingspan of 32 feet and weight of 260 pounds, equipped with redesigned forward and rear control surfaces. The wings were long and narrow, allowing for maximum lift.

The 1902 glider was first flown at Kitty Hawk on September 19, 1902. In the weeks that followed, approximately 1,000 flights were made with the new glider, a process punctuated by modifications, such as a moveable rudder for the fixed vertical tail. The rudder was linked to the wing warping controls, so that whenever the pilot warped the wings, the rudder moved in a coordinated way to achieve proper control.

For the first time, the Wrights had achieved effective control of their glider in all three axes, a monumental breakthrough. With the success of the 1902 glider, the Wrights began to think about the next fateful step— mounting an engine to their flying machine.

Having mastered the science and technique of flight, the Wrights turned to a talented machinist in Dayton, Charles Taylor, to develop a special Wright-designed engine for their flying machine. Taylor quickly went about building this reliable lightweight gasoline engine, arguably the most essential component for their success. Without such an engine, the many breakthroughs of the Wrights in understanding the nature of aerodynamics and controlled flight would have come to naught. They would have been restricted to the sphere of soaring. Indeed, if the brothers had been born in the eighteenth century, or had begun their work even a half century earlier, there would have been no workable propulsion system available to them, except a steam engine, which would have been too heavy and impractical. The Wrights thus were beneficiaries of

(LEFT)
A Wright Model B aircraft makes a historic flight over Paris early in the 20th century.

(OPPOSITE)
The Wright Flyer quickly became a part of popular culture, as evident in the 1909 Collier's *magazine cover and a 1912 children's book entitled* The Flight Brothers.

advances in engine design and performance dating back to the pioneering work of Nicolaus Otto, who fashioned the modern four-stroke cycle engine in the 1870s. By the turn of the twentieth century, such engines were accessible, and they soon became the vital breakthrough to allow both automobiles and airplanes to transform modern life.

The Wrights equipped the Flyer with two propellers linked to the engine by a chain drive system. This proved to be another area in which research and testing by the Wrights proved decisive. They learned that the propeller functioned as a rotating wing, not an air screw as some might think in comparing it to a maritime propeller. An aerial propeller generates thrust or horizontal force. They worked diligently to understand the optimal form of a propeller for powered flight, and once they had made this breakthrough, they carefully fashioned wooden propellers made from laminated spruce.

Orville and Wilbur worked on the construction of their flying machine in the summer of 1903. Toward the end of September, they were ready and set out for Kitty Hawk. They arrived in a confident mood, determined to make their dream of powered flight a reality. When they arrived at the base camp, a violent wind storm hit the Outer Banks, nearly destroying their shed. There were also technical challenges at this critical stage, from the uneven performance of their engine to broken steel propeller shafts. But they persisted as the winter set in along the North Carolina coast.

On December 14, the day of their first flight attempt, a coin was tossed and Wilbur won the right to steer the Flyer into the air. The Flyer was set on a track, heading down a small incline. Once the engine started, Wilbur steered the craft down the track, only to pitch upwards, stall, and then land unceremoniously some 60 feet from the starting point. The whole flight had lasted a mere four seconds.

Repairs were necessary, but by December 17, a cold and windy day, they were ready once again to attempt a powered flight. They were joined by members of the Kill Devil Hill Life Saving Station, who assisted in setting up the track for the historic flight. At 10:35 a.m. Orville rode the Flyer down the track and into history. Wilbur jogged at the side of the Flyer as it lifted away, climbing into the air. The flying machine remained airborne under its own power for 12 seconds, and then landed in the soft sand. Later, Wilbur took the controls on the fourth flight, covering some 852 feet in 59 seconds.

The air age had been born.

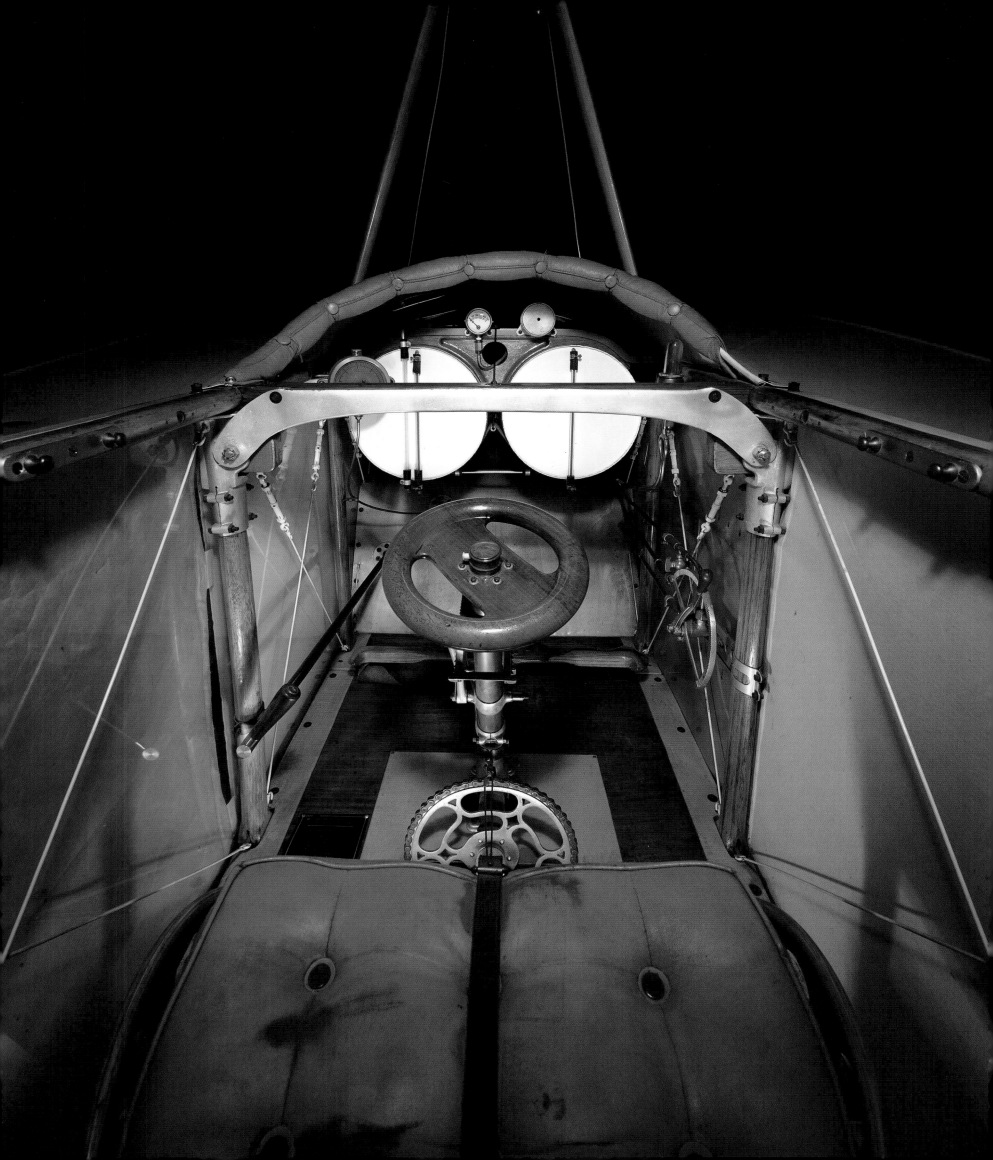

BLÉRIOT
AIR BRIDGE TO ENGLAND

NEWS of the epic flight found its way to *The New York Times* with the headline, "Blériot Flies Over the Channel!" In Europe there was a vast outpouring of enthusiasm for the new air hero, Louis Blériot. Flying a monoplane of his own design, Blériot had made the first crossing of the English Channel in an airplane on July 25, 1909. The distance covered was 23 miles, in $36\frac{1}{2}$ minutes, from a takeoff on the dunes at Les Baraques near Calais to a dramatic landing in a field at Dover on the south coast of England.

Less than six years separated the first Channel hop from the Wrights' tentative first powered flight in 1903. Blériot's contemporaries were awestruck by this aerial leap across the storm-tossed English Channel. They celebrated Blériot as an epochal figure. England remained an island only in a geographical sense: the airplane now compromised the insularity and security of the island nation.

Others viewed Blériot's fragile monoplane as the harbinger of a whole new form of transportation that would link all nations. Blériot himself reveled in the fact that he had surpassed all his competitors to win the $5,000 award offered by Lord Northcliffe to the first person to make a cross-Channel flight from either side.

By the turn of the twentieth century, Louis Blériot had become a wealthy entrepreneur, the manufacturer of brass acetylene lamps for automobiles. His fortune assured, Blériot turned his attention to fixed-wing flying machines, designing gliders as early as 1905. He belonged to a small group of talented aviation enthusiasts then working in France—Alberto Santos-Dumont, Gabriel Voisin, and Henri Farman among them. After Wilbur Wright demonstrated their airplane in France on August 8, 1908, Blériot decided to engage in some pioneering endeavors of his own.

Competition among aviators to make the first crossing of the English Channel dominated the aviation world in Europe in the remarkable summer of 1909. Three pilots vied for the honor. The Comte de Lambert, a Russian aristocrat with established ties to France, had been trained by Wilbur Wright, and even owned two Wright airplanes, but his interest in the competition was more informal than others. Hubert Latham, a French resident with English roots and education, was the odds-on favorite with his sleek Antoinette IV monoplane. Finally, there was Louis Blériot, whose bourgeois lifestyle stood in sharp contrast to the flamboyant Latham's.

(ABOVE)

Louis Blériot in leather flying gear at the controls of his Blériot XI in 1909.

(OPPOSITE)

The cockpit of a Blériot XI, exhibited by the National Air and Space Museum, Washington, D.C. This cockpit is similar to that in the aircraft flown by Louis Blériot in his historic flight across the English Channel in 1909.

A scale model of the Blériot XI in the collection of the National Air and Space Museum, Washington, D.C.

Latham caught the attention of the public with his good looks, checkered cap, and ivory cigarette holder. He reflected the lifestyle of the wealthy sportsman adventurer of the era—a person with leisure time to engage in big game hunting, racing motor boats off Monaco, and tinkering with the newly invented airplane. He worked with his red-bearded technical assistant, Leon Levavasseur, to perfect the design of the Antionette IV airplane—a birdlike flying machine of polished wood with a 42-foot wingspan and a tapered fuselage of 38 feet, powered by a 50-horsepower V-8 engine. The Antoinette IV was not only a beautiful design, it possessed rudimentary ailerons and performance qualities that seemed to make it ideal for the English Channel crossing. Latham held the French flight endurance record of one hour and seven minutes, an impressive, if not a world record for that era. Sustained flight in those days was problematical because aero engines on the average ran for only 15 minutes before there was some sort of mechanical breakdown. Learning to fly was hazardous as well, with 139 people worldwide reportedly killed in training in 1911 alone. Even for veteran pilots, flying brought many perils, and the attrition rate among aviators remained high in this formative period of the air age.

Blériot, for his part, combined the technical skills of an engineer with a strong will, critical traits that set him apart from others, in particular his more glamorous rival Latham. A graduate of the Ecole Centrale des Arts and Manufactures, Blériot sported a distinctive handlebar mustache and was a dedicated family man with six children. His airplane, the Blériot XI monoplane, was one of his more successful designs. The airplane had made its

(ABOVE)

Louis Blériot stands in the cockpit of his Type XI monoplane, ca. 1909.

(ABOVE, RIGHT)

Children watch a Blériot-type monoplane in flight. Early flying machines such as the Blériot prompted great public interest in aviation.

(RIGHT)

Blériot after his historic landing at North Foreland meadow near Dover Castle, at 5:12 p.m. on July 25, 1909.

debut at a Paris aeronautical exhibition in December 1908
and was then flown successfully the following month.
Much of the success of the design was due to the work of
Blériot's assistant, Raymond Saulnier, and the powerplant,
the 25-horsepower Anzani engine. On July 4, Blériot made
an endurance flight of 50 minutes and 8 seconds, a
welcome harbinger of success for him and his team.

Given its shifting weather and strong winds, the
English Channel held many challenges for any pilot. At
the narrowest point, the passage between Calais and Dover,
there were frequent gusts of wind and heavy fog. The
weather could change abruptly, making the crossing by a
fragile wood and fabric airplane difficult, if not impossible.

The gray-green waters of the English Channel had
served as a sort of moat for England through the centuries,
providing protection from such external enemies as the
Spanish Armada and Napoleon's armies. While a
formidable barrier, it was nevertheless true that
individuals had made balloon crossings of the Channel,
beginning as early as 1785 with the flight of Jean-Pierre
François Blanchard and John Jeffries. Over the decades
that followed, some 53 people had made balloon crossings.
But these uncontrolled, wind-driven passages across the
Channel were significantly different in kind from the
heavier-than-air competition of 1909: Latham and
Blériot were attempting the passage in powered and
controllable flying machines, and, if successful, such
a crossing would indeed demonstrate the formidable
potential of the airplane.

Latham made the first attempt to cross the Channel on
July 19. At Sangatte, outside Calais, he waited for days for
the rain and fog to clear for the flight across to Dover. His

*Louis Blériot is greeted by
enthusiastic countrymen in 1909.
Blériot became one of the first
celebrated air heroes of the
twentieth century.*

A Blériot XI, piloted by a man named Salmet, flies low over enthusiastic spectators at an air meet in Margate, England, in August 1913.

anticipated crossing attracted huge crowds on both sides of the English Channel, with many observers waiting in small boats positioned along the coasts of France and England to see Latham make the historic flight. With Levavasseur giving the signal to take off from a French destroyer off shore, Latham took to the air as the destroyer fired two salvoes. His takeoff required a death-defying leap from the short runway over the bluffs at Sangatte. His Antoinette quickly gained an altitude of 1,000 feet on a direct flight path to England. The Antoinette, however, developed engine trouble at the seven-mile mark over the Channel. The engine first began to run erratically and then stopped. The intrepid Latham then guided his stricken airplane to a pancake landing in the churning waters. He was smoking a cigarette and seated in the cockpit of his partially submerged Antoinette when his French rescuers arrived to pluck him from the Channel.

Now there was a chance for one of Latham's rivals to attempt a crossing. The Comte de Lambert moved slowly to exploit his opportunity, spending precious time checking out potential landing sites on the English coast. Then, to his great disappointment, he wrecked one of his Wright airplanes in a test flight. This mishap also involved some minor personal injuries that were nonetheless serious enough to remove him from the competition for Lord Northcliffe's prize. By contrast, Blériot moved rapidly to set up an improvised hangar at Les Baraques, a small village outside Calais. Could he launch his flight before Latham reorganized his team at Sangatte and equipped another airplane for a Channel hop?

While alert to the calendar and acting with all deliberate speed, Blériot's own situation was not ideal.

(ABOVE, LEFT)

A Blériot XI, piloted by Jean Olieslager, flies near Oran, Algeria, ca. 1913.

(ABOVE, RIGHT)

A Blériot-type XI-2, fitted with pontoons, is shown here taxiing on the Seine River near St. Cloud, France, in October 1913.

(LEFT)

Salmet pilots his Blériot XI above a beach near Nice, France, in January 1914.

(OPPOSITE)

A Blériot XII rounds the pylon at an air meet in Reims, France, in August 1909.

(TOP)

Louis Blériot's historic Channel-crossing monoplane on exhibition at the Grande Palais in Paris in October 1909.

(BOTTOM)

A poster depicting a Blériot XI to showcase a forthcoming air meet on Staten Island, New York.

Earlier he had burned his foot in a freak flying accident: the asbestos covering on the exhaust pipe on the engine broke away and the hot pipe severely injured his foot. As a result, he could barely walk. For Blériot, however, there was no option. He would have to fly as soon as the weather permitted, even if the use of the foot controls for the rudder would involve no small amount of pain.

The Blériot XI airplane lacked the rakish beauty of Latham's Antoinette: the Blériot machine, in fact, appeared to be awkwardly designed for flight, with its partially covered box fuselage and snub nose. Blériot sat in an open cockpit on a leather seat, tenuously held in place by a seat belt. Unlike the Antoinette, the Blériot used the wing warping mechanism for lateral control.

Still, the Blériot airplane possessed one distinct advantage over the Antoinette: it was equipped with the sturdy and relatively reliable 25-horsepower Anzani engine. Designed by Alessandro Anzani, the cast-iron engine was a rough and ready power plant, with holes punched in the bottoms of the cylinders to allow the vetting of exhaust gases. The Anzani engine was loud and discharged oil back on the pilot in a regular and uncontrolled way. Flying the Blériot XI was a daunting task—even in excellent weather.

Six days after Latham's crash in the Channel, Blériot made his move. The morning of July 25 offered him a break in the weather, not ideal but sufficiently calm to warrant a try at flying the Channel. Blériot alerted the French destroyer *Escopette* to set out to sea in anticipation of his flight. The Blériot XI was started up by the ground crew and Blériot donned blue coveralls and a helmet for the flight. Still feeling the injuries to his foot, Blériot had

Flying
International Aviation Meet
The Great Flyers will participate
Cross Country Races
Military Aeroplane Demonstration
Aerial Sharpshooting
Balloonatic Race
1000 Foot Aeroplane Glide
Columbus Day Oct. 13th
Aeronautical Society Aerodrome
Oakwood Heights
Staten Island

(ABOVE)

Landing was often more difficult than flying, as John Moisant discovered in the crash of his Blériot during an air meet in October 1910 at Belmont Park, Long Island, New York.

(LEFT)

Famed American aviator Harriet Quimby, seated in her Blériot XI on the eve of her flight across the English Channel from Dover to Hardelet, France, April 1912.

Blériot XIs leave the Blériot factory in Levallois, France, for service in the French army, ca. 1913.

The Imperial Russian air service and navy also purchased Blériot aircraft, as seen on this book cover showing a Blériot type in flight with the Russian fleet, ca. 1912.

his crutches attached to the side of the airplane—if he made it to Dover, he wanted to be able to move about on land. Even as he began his final preparations, there was an anxious glance toward the Latham camp at Sangatte, to see if they would attempt a crossing that day. The view through binoculars revealed no activity—Latham had not been yet awakened.

Blériot took off amid great excitement, clearing the nearby telegraph wires and flying confidently over the dunes. As he moved out to sea, he quickly overtook the *Escopette*, already in place and ready to come to Blériot's rescue if he was forced to ditch in the Channel. Blériot's wife, Alice, by arrangement with the French navy, had boarded the *Escopette* to observe the flight. By this time the sun had risen and Blériot was on his way toward the distant English shore, which remained out of sight.

The weather was excellent. There were hardly any wind gusts to contend with as Blériot moved slowly in a northwest direction at around 40 miles per hour. He flew just a few hundred feet above the water. The calm air meant there was no need to counter cross winds with the rudder or make elaborate moves to keep the airplane on a level flight. Best of all, the Anzani engine continued to run in its loud but reassuring way.

At mid-point over the Channel, Blériot was well beyond visual contact with the *Escopette* and all those onboard were curious as to his fate. Blériot's situation was optimal. Alone and above the Channel in his fragile airplane, Blériot experienced a sense of euphoria, a growing confidence that he was going to make it after all. Looking at the far horizon, he still could not see the Dover cliffs. Around him there was the wide expanse of

the Channel, with no ships in view. For 10 minutes he flew in this isolation.

Then the English coast appeared, just visible above the horizon. Blériot's sense of excitement mounted as he approached the coastline. Ahead, finally, he saw the distinctive white cliffs of Dover, a beckoning landmark for the French aviator who now was so close to his intended destination. Three ships came into view, and as Blériot flew over them the crews waved and cheered.

Having reached the area of the white chalk cliffs, Blériot feared that he could not fly over them. He could only fly parallel to the cliffs and seek out the intended spot for his landing, a small trough in the cliffs opening to a plateau. No small amount of anxiety overcame Blériot as he sought out this little valley near Dover Castle.

Suddenly, Blériot saw a man waving a French tricolor flag at the edge of an opening between the cliffs. This was the North Foreland meadow, the predetermined landing site. Blériot turned his airplane toward the open and welcoming green field. His landing proved to be less than expert, a rough maneuver in which Blériot cut the engine ignition at 20 meters and glided to the ground. The impact of the landing shattered the landing gear and the propeller. A small group of enthusiastic onlookers— some soldiers, a policeman, and a French photographer— rushed to greet Blériot. The "French invader" himself appeared exhilarated, if disheveled, eyes bloodshot, soaked with perspiration and spattered with oil.

Blériot soon found himself draped in the French flag. He had one question: What about Latham? Was his rival still at Sangatte? When he was informed that Latham

had not even taken off, Blériot was overjoyed; he had made the historic crossing of the English Channel ahead of his competition. Latham soon sent his congratulations to Blériot in a cable. It was later reported that Latham expressed his profound disappointment silently with tears in his eyes as he stood next to his Antoinette airplane that same day at Sangatte. Latham did attempt to fly the English Channel two days later, on July 27, but fate treated him cruelly again: he was forced to make another water landing, one that resulted in some minor injuries when his head struck the fuselage upon hitting the water. The famed Latham died in 1912, gored to death by a wounded buffalo in the French Sudan while on a big game hunting trip to Africa.

By contrast, Blériot lived on for several decades, and he would be in Paris in 1927 to greet Charles Lindbergh after his epic transatlantic crossing. The Blériot monoplane became one of the more widely used flying machines in the era of early flight. In fact, the awestruck Grand Duke Alexander Mikhailovich arranged for the Russian government to purchase a Blériot XI airplane in 1911. This acquisition was the genesis of Russia's air force.

Blériot had entered the pantheon of air heroes. In 1909, he enjoyed a unique status as a national and international celebrity. His achievement received accolades as "epic" and "historic," and stood as a symbol of how aeronautical technology had reduced the size of the planet. In the words of Sir Alan Cobham, the Blériot flight "marked the end of our insular safety, and the beginning of the time when Britain must seek another form of defense besides its ships."

*An original Blériot XI, still flown
regularly at air shows at the Old
Rhinebeck Aerodrome, in
Rhinebeck, New York.*

SIKORSKY
ACROSS THE RUSSIAN EXPANSE

RUSSIAN-AMERICAN Igor Sikorsky occupies a prominent place in the pantheon of aviation pioneers as the designer of amphibians, a successful industrialist, and the inventive genius behind the VS–300, the prototype for modern helicopters, all accomplished in the United States. Less known is Igor Sikorsky's first career in Tsarist Russia, where he made one of the most remarkable flights in the formative years of the air age flying his giant four-engine airplane, the *Il'ya Muromets*, from St. Petersburg to Kiev in 1914.

Sikorsky's *Il'ya Muromets* amazed his contemporaries as a true technological marvel. The prototype for this behemoth biplane, the *Grand*, established a host of records, taking bold passengers aloft for leisurely flights above the palaces of the imperial capital of St. Petersburg. Many experts warned Sikorsky that such a huge multiengine aircraft ran a high risk of crashing: aero engines were notorious for breaking down and the loss of one or more engines would mean a rapid, perhaps uncontrolled, descent to the ground. Sikorsky rejected these dire predictions. He knew from flight tests and what he called his own "intuition" that the *Il'ya Muromets* was a safe flying machine.

Sikorsky demonstrated the reliability of the *Il'ya Muromets* in the summer of 1914 when he made an extraordinary flight from St. Petersburg to Kiev and back. Each leg of the journey consisted of 800 miles. To the amazement of all, Sikorsky flew nonstop for five hours or more between refueling stops. Unlike other aircraft of the time, the *Il'ya Muromets* was equipped with a glass-enclosed cockpit, which allowed for maximum visibility while shielding the pilot from the wind. The futuristic *Il'ya Muromets* appeared to many awestruck onlookers as something out of a Jules Verne saga.

Flying the *Il'ya Muromets* from St. Petersburg to Kiev represented a new milestone in aviation: no aircraft had ever flown so far. For Sikorsky and the Russian aeronautical community, there was great pride in the achievement of the *Il'ya Muromets*. But Sikorsky soon learned that his remarkable aircraft had become a victim of bad timing: the flight had taken place in late June and early July 1914, just a few weeks before the outbreak of World War I. Consequently, press coverage of the war quickly overshadowed Sikorsky's achievement. In fact, only a few notices of the flight actually reached the West in August 1914 as the European powers, including Sikorsky's native Russia, entered what became known as the Great War. This same war ultimately brought military defeat and a cataclysmic revolution to Russia. The new revolutionary context, in particular the

(ABOVE)

Legendary aviation pioneer Igor Sikorsky, ca. 1914.

(OPPOSITE)

Breakthrough over Kiev, painted by James Dietz in 1989, depicts the descent of the Il'ya Muromets *over the Kiev Pechersk Monastery, the dramatic end to Igor Sikorsky's epic flight from St. Petersburg to Kiev in July 1914.*

triumph of Lenin's Bolsheviks, prompted Sikorsky to emigrate to the United States.

As the decades unfolded, the Communist regime studiously ignored Sikorsky's achievement, even expunging his name from histories. Because Sikorsky's feats in Russia slipped into this Orwellian "memory hole," there has been no small amount of difficulty in reconstructing the story of the *Il'ya Muromets.*

We do know that Sikorsky was at work as an aircraft designer in his late teens, experimenting with a design for a helicopter as early as 1908. Sikorsky was only 23 years old when he won a state-sponsored aircraft design competition with his biplane, the S-6-A. This achievement, in turn, won Sikorsky financial patronage for the construction of a new multiengine aircraft, which he dubbed the *Grand* (the prototype for the *Il'ya Muromets*). Sikorsky's four-engine experimental airplane prompted no small amount of skepticism. Many aviation experts of the time were openly doubtful about whether such a huge airplane would actually fly. Their skepticism was well placed, since at the time little was known about the aerodynamics of large aircraft, and many assumed that the unreliable engines of the era—known for their minimal horsepower and frequent breakdowns—were not capable of lifting such a huge flying machine.

Yet, Sikorsky's *Grand* flew safely, setting new records for sustained flight and passenger comforts. To the amazement of the citizens of St. Petersburg, the huge flying machine cruised effortlessly at 65 miles per hour and remained aloft for hours. The passengers on board sat in an enclosed cabin on wicker chairs, viewing the squares, broad boulevards, and palaces of the imperial capital from a unique and breathtaking perspective. News of Sikorsky's remarkable feat reached the

West in fragmentary notices, but few took seriously the stories of the remarkable flying machine. As a youth, Sikorsky had been an avid reader of Jules Verne, and the *Grand* appeared to capture the futuristic trajectory of aviation. No less important, the Russian military took a keen interest in this strange giant of the air, inviting Sikorsky to fly the *Grand* to Krasnoe Selo, near St. Petersburg, for summer army maneuvers in 1913. Here Sikorsky gave Emperor Nicholas II a tour of the parked *Grand.*

When the *Grand* was destroyed in a freak accident (while parked at the aerodrome in St. Petersburg, an engine from a passing airplane broke lose and crashed through the port wing), Sikorsky decided to build a more advanced version of his multiengine aircraft. He called the new variant the *Il'ya Muromets*, after a legendary figure in Russian folklore. The aircraft quickly established new benchmarks in flying in the spring of 1914, once Sikorsky took aloft 16 people and his pet dog for a leisurely cruise over St. Petersburg. At one point, and with no small risk, Sikorsky took five members of Russia's Duma, or parliament, for a breathtaking aerial trek over St. Petersburg—a demonstration flight that happily ended without incident. England's *Flight* magazine that year also took note of Sikorsky's "aerial bus," alerting the wider aeronautical community to Russia's new air achievement.

Now at the apogee of his young career as an aircraft designer, Sikorsky planned another aerial spectacular, an unprecedented one that would require the airplane to master the vast Russian landscape: the aforementioned round-trip flight from St. Petersburg to Kiev, his hometown. No airplane had ever crossed the vast expanse of European Russia. Sikorsky realized the dangers of such an undertaking, even for his remarkable *Il'ya Muromets.* The air age was just a

(LEFT)

Igor Sikorsky, second from the right, is pictured with his three crewmen who made the historic flight from St. Petersburg to Kiev in July 1914.

(BELOW)

While en route to Kiev from St. Petersburg, Sikorsky made one refueling stop at the city of Orsha. This is the only surviving image of that event, where townsmen gathered to push the huge Il'ya Muromets *aircraft down a long incline for takeoff.*

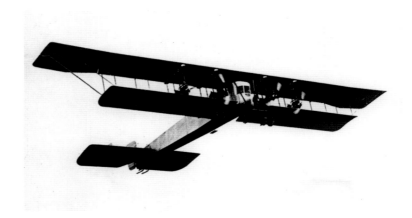

The Il'ya Muromets *in flight.
In honor of Sikorsky's long-distance
flight, Tsar Nicholas II named the
aircraft the* Il'ya Muromets Kievsky.

decade old. Flying machines were primitive at best:
the typical airplane was constructed of wood and fabric,
powered with temperamental and unreliable aero engines,
and austerely equipped with only a few instruments, mostly
tachometers and altimeters.

The selection of an able crew became an important
priority for Sikorsky. Each person selected brought skill and
resourcefulness to the aerial jaunt to Kiev. For the critical
position of mechanic, Sikorsky chose his long-time associate
V. S. Panasiuk, a man intimately acquainted with the design
and operation of the *Il'ya Muromets*—and a person known for
his fearless approach to flying. Turning to the Russian
military, Sikorsky recruited a copilot and a navigator, Captain
K. F. Prussis and Lieutenant G. I. Lavrov, respectively. The
entire crew had flight experience and all shared a deep and
abiding respect for the young designer from Kiev.

As if on some interplanetary journey, Sikorsky took
special pains to stock his huge aircraft with essential supplies.
There would be no network of aerodromes and emergency
fields to support the effort—only vast stretches of forest,
swamps, rivers, and the steppe. Containers for additional fuel
and oil with a special fuel pump were set up in the main
cabin. Extra parts, including a spare propeller and tools, also
were packed into the *Il'ya Muromets*. Food and drink—all
carefully rationed—were added to the payload of the now
overloaded plane.

Sikorsky departed on June 29, 1914, at 1:00 a.m. from
Komendantsky airfield on the northern edge of St. Petersburg.
At this hour there were minimal winds. In the predawn
darkness Sikorsky took great pains to start and warm the
Il'ya Muromets's four engines. With a flashlight in hand, he
monitored the four tachometers in the forward cockpit.

Outside, 20 men stood ready behind the wings awaiting the
signal to push the plane forward once the takeoff run started.
Finally, Sikorsky began—throttles at full power—to move
the behemoth aircraft down the dark corridor of the grass
runway. While it was impossible for Sikorsky to see the
ground, the horizon was clearly visible, allowing a slow
ascent into the air. Once above the trees, he found it difficult
to goad the overloaded aircraft upward, reaching only
500 feet after 15 minutes of flight.

In June, the so-called white nights of St. Petersburg
meant only four hours of darkness; the sun stayed below the
horizon only briefly in these short and balmy weeks of the
summer season. By 2:00 a.m., the sky grew brighter around
the aircraft, and as the fuel was consumed, it slowly acquired
altitude, reaching 2,000 feet. So far, the trip had been
smooth and carefree, with the pilots alternating at the
controls every half hour. Sikorsky, writing in his memoir,
The Story of the Winged S, recorded that on this journey he
periodically would walk out on the platform on the lower
wing to inspect the engines on both the port and starboard

Igor Sikorsky equipped his Il'ya Muromets *with skis for winter operations at St. Petersburg, Russia, ca. 1914. In this historic photograph, two crewmen are visible holding onto the platform's rails atop the aircraft's fuselage.*

sides of the *Il'ya Muromets.* Such wing walking—in the midst of loud engine noise and buffeting winds—brought a "strange feeling" to Sikorsky, as if he were standing on an "apparently motionless wing in the smooth, clear, and cool air of the morning."

By 7:00 a.m., with St. Petersburg behind them over the horizon, the *Il'ya Muromets* cruised at the optimal speed of 65 miles per hour and at an altitude of 5,000 feet. While Captain Prussis took the controls, Sikorsky joined his crew for a meal in the central compartment of the plane. The airmen sat on wicker chairs around a table covered elegantly with a tablecloth for a breakfast of fruit, sandwiches, and hot coffee. From the windows, Sikorsky and his crew could see the passing landscape below. In addition to the comforts of the main cabin, the *Il'ya Muromets* had interior lights, a heating system, and an observation platform on top of the fuselage. Such luxuries anticipated the airliner, which would become a reality only decades later.

Navigation was by "pilotage," the eyeballing of prominent landmarks, rivers, and towns with maps. The first milestone was Vitebsk, a city Sikorsky reached at around 8:00 a.m. As the *Il'ya Muromets* passed slowly over the city, Sikorsky recorded that he could see clearly the grid of streets, houses, and the distinctive churches with their golden domes. At Vitebsk, two letters were dropped in an aluminum tube sealed at both ends by corks with a bright cloth streamer. One message was addressed to Sikorsky's home, the other to the factory in St. Petersburg where the *Il'ya Muromets* had been built. Money was included for postage, with a tip; Sikorsky learned later that both letters reached their destinations.

(TOP)
Tsar Nicholas II inspects the four-engine Grand, *the prototype for the* Il'ya Muromets. *To inspect the huge aircraft, the tsar climbed into the forward balcony by ladder, where Igor Sikorsky explained the design and operation of the aircraft.*

(BOTTOM)
Igor Sikorsky seated at the controls of his four-engine behemoth, the Grand.

One hour out of Vitebsk the crew looked anxiously toward the horizon for the city of Orsha. Here an open field had been marked for a scheduled landing and refueling. Sikorsky then took the controls and began a gradual descent over the city. At 2,000 feet, the air became quite turbulent, but he found the field, where a large crowd had gathered to watch the huge bird from St. Petersburg land. The landing proved relatively easy, with Sikorsky taxiing to one end of an improvised air strip where local air enthusiasts, by prearrangement, had stacked barrels of gasoline for the refueling of the *Il'ya Muromets.*

Over 400 gallons of fuel were required. The process of refueling proved to be slow and tedious because the gasoline pumps were few in number and not all that effective. Meanwhile, Sikorsky and Lavrov managed to break away from the crowd to take a closer look at the field and to plan for the takeoff. The grass strip itself was spacious, 150 feet wide and 1,200 feet long, but it sloped downward at an angle toward the Dnieper River at one end. In fact, the sloping field ended abruptly above a 100-foot precipice to the river below. Beyond the river, on the opposite shore, they could see clearly the city of Orsha. Sikorsky estimated that six hours of flying remained to complete the final leg of the trip to Kiev—one that would follow the meandering Dnieper River. Could this final leg be completed before darkness fell?

At around 2:00 p.m., Sikorsky decided to attempt to take off down the sloping grass strip toward the precipice below. If for any reason the overloaded *Il'ya Muromets* failed to climb after clearing the edge of the precipice, Sikorsky and his crew faced a fiery death at the river bottom. To assist the *Il'ya Muromets* in gaining speed for the takeoff run, Sikorsky picked some 50 young men out of the crowd to help push the

(TOP)
Sikorsky standing next to the Grand, *which was destroyed in a freak accident in 1913: an engine from a passing airplane broke loose and fell through the port wing of the parked* Grand.

(BOTTOM)
The remains of the engine are visible below the shattered port wing of the Grand.

aircraft down the incline. Whatever the result, he realized the margin would be narrow, a real white-knuckle experience for all. Once underway, Sikorsky pushed the control yoke forward to gain maximum speed and to keep the airplane on course. Only when the undercarriage of the lumbering giant reached the edge of the precipice did he rotate the nose upward. Slowly and cautiously the sure-handed Sikorsky guided his plane upward—there would be no descent into rocky shoals below. And as the aircraft moved toward the opposite shore and the city of Orsha, he made a shallow bank. The Dnieper River suddenly came into view, the winding path of the river pointing south toward Kiev.

The passage to Kiev proved to be the most dangerous phase of the trip. No sooner had the *Il'ya Muromets* cleared the boundaries of Orsha than another tense moment ensued, only the first of several emergencies that would plague Sikorsky and his crew. The *Il'ya Muromets*, topped off with fuel and supplies, resisted all Sikorsky's efforts to ascend. The aircraft doggedly held to an altitude of 250 feet, but no more. The air was very turbulent at this height, and the buffeting winds made control of the aircraft difficult, although Sikorsky managed to hold course. The *Il'ya Muromets* then hit a pocket of air with a powerful downdraft.

The altitude suddenly dropped to little over 100 feet and Sikorsky found himself at treetop level. He responded quickly, ordering his crew to throw overboard three cans of water and a can of oil. The emergency maneuver appeared to work, and in a few minutes the *Il'ya Muromets* managed to achieve an altitude of about 400 feet.

Within minutes, a new crisis caught the beleaguered Sikorsky's attention: Panasiuk, the mechanic, rushed to the forward cockpit and pointed to the far starboard engine.

SIKORSKY - 1917

(TOP)

A head-on view of an Il'ya Muromets *Type G provides a clear image of the nose section, where lavish use of windscreens offered the pilot maximum visibility.*

(BOTTOM)

The view from the cockpit of an Il'ya Muromets *Type G. This particular variant of the* Il'ya Muromets *flew as a bomber in World War I for the Imperial Russian Air Force.*

The gasoline line to the carburetor had broken, spewing a steady stream of fuel into the air stream. The engine was at full power and its exhaust quickly ignited the fuel. Sikorsky looked on in horror as a 12-foot flame emerged from the trailing edge of the starboard wing.

Sikorsky immediately steadied the aircraft, allowing Lavrov and Panasiuk to climb out on the lower wing to suppress the fire. In the midst of engine noise and flames, the two men edged cautiously out to the stricken engine. Lavrov boldly reached around the stream of fire and closed off the value feeding the fuel to the engine. Both men then beat the flames with their overcoats to extinguish the fire. All these maneuvers were done almost instinctively in the airstream, as the *Il'ya Muromets* cruised at 65 miles per hour. Finally, they subdued the fire. Only a small harmless stream of smoke gave evidence of the crisis they had passed through. With only three engines operating, the *Il'ya Muromets* held course at 400 feet.

What next? Looking at the blackened struts and burned portion of the wing, Sikorsky decided to land and make repairs. There were tools and parts on board to fix the severed gasoline line and restart the fourth engine. Finding a large narrow strip of land near the river, Sikorsky guided his *Il'ya Muromets* to a safe stop. As at Orsha, the field had a sloping contour leading to a stretch of marshy fields. It was decided to take off down this field, regardless of wind direction, once repairs were made.

Panasiuk quickly repaired the fuel line, but darkness had now descended. Sikorsky decided to stay the night. By this time a large crowd had gathered around the *Il'ya Muromets*. Many of the curious onlookers were peasants who had never seen an airplane before and looked on the strange

(TOP)

Russian military officers stand on the rear fuselage of the Il'ya Muromets.

(MIDDLE)

Igor Sikorsky stands on the fuselage balcony of the first Il'ya Muromets *in 1914.*

(BOTTOM)

A wartime sketch of the Il'ya Muromets *bomber in air combat with German fighters.*

flying machine as a visitor from another world. The crew found themselves besieged with questions. How did the airplane flap its wings? Could they land in a tree or on a smokestack? Only dinner at the home of the local police chief gave Sikorsky an interlude of relaxation. Staying overnight at the field meant sleeping in the *Il'ya Muromets*, with Sikorsky making use of the one sleeping cabin and his crew occupying the cabin and cockpit. A rain storm pelted the airplane throughout the dark hours of the night, giving way to an overcast morning of low clouds.

Despite the miserable weather and a wet field, Sikorsky opted to chance a takeoff. The *Il'ya Muromets* was still heavy with fuel and there was a strong possibility that it might get mired in the soft improvised runway. The takeoff run, as it turned out, was easy. All engines started quickly and roared to full power. The flying machine slowly gained speed down the slope of the field and leaped into the air. Now on course again, Sikorsky moved through broken layers of clouds at normal cruising speed as he looked southward to the horizon and beyond to Kiev.

This carefree interlude proved to be shortlived: the weather worsened, with a steady rain and turbulent air. Sikorsky found himself flying blind through the clouds. At best, the *Il'ya Muromets* was a difficult machine to control in rough air. With only a compass, Lavrov pointed to the direction to follow as Sikorsky maintained level flight. The rain only increased, prompting great anxiety that the engines, with their exposed magnetos and wires, might shut down. But the engines continued to purr as Sikorsky maintained an altitude of 2,500 feet.

Hoping to escape the enveloping clouds, Sikorsky used full power to climb to 3,000 feet. The turbulent air tossed the huge airplane up and down. Sikorsky managed to gain a few hundred feet of precious altitude, only to lose it. Suddenly a powerful wind tipped the port wing down. Next the nose appeared to dip down as well. Denied any reference point on the ground or the horizon by the clouds, Sikorsky struggled to maintain level flight. There was no artificial horizon or turn and bank indicator on the airplane to provide a clear instrument reading of the position of the *Il'ya Muromets.* When the compass needle made several complete turns, Sikorsky and the crew— holding on for dear life—realized they were in a spin.

The apparent loss of 1,000 feet of altitude only confirmed the grim set of circumstances. As he had spiraled downward, Sikorsky wisely neutralized the controls and let the airplane slowly pick up speed and level out on its own. Another 1,200 feet had been lost in this maneuver. For Sikorsky, the spin had been his first, a novel experience for him and one for which he possessed no knowledge on the best recovery method. Instinct prompted him to pull the yoke back as a way to pull out. But he resisted such a move or any frantic efforts to manipulate the controls, allowing the airplane to correct itself. Only later, once he had learned more about the phenomenon of spins, did he fully appreciate how close he and his crew came to a catastrophe that day.

Having survived the spin and now faced with another gauntlet of rain and air turbulence, Sikorsky decided to seek sanctuary above the foul weather. However, this meant an arduous climb through the clouds and another risky interlude of blind flying. With Lavrov, his navigator, at his side watching the altimeter and compass, Sikorsky cautiously pushed the *Il'ya Muromets* up through the

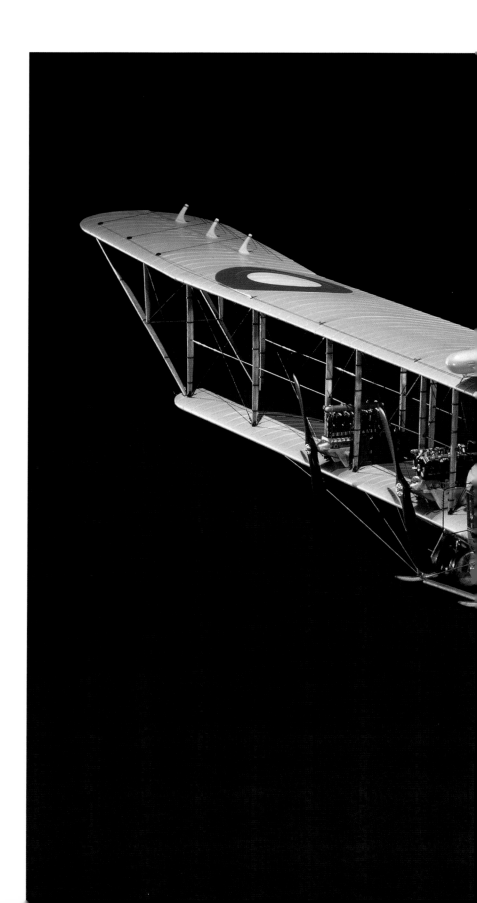

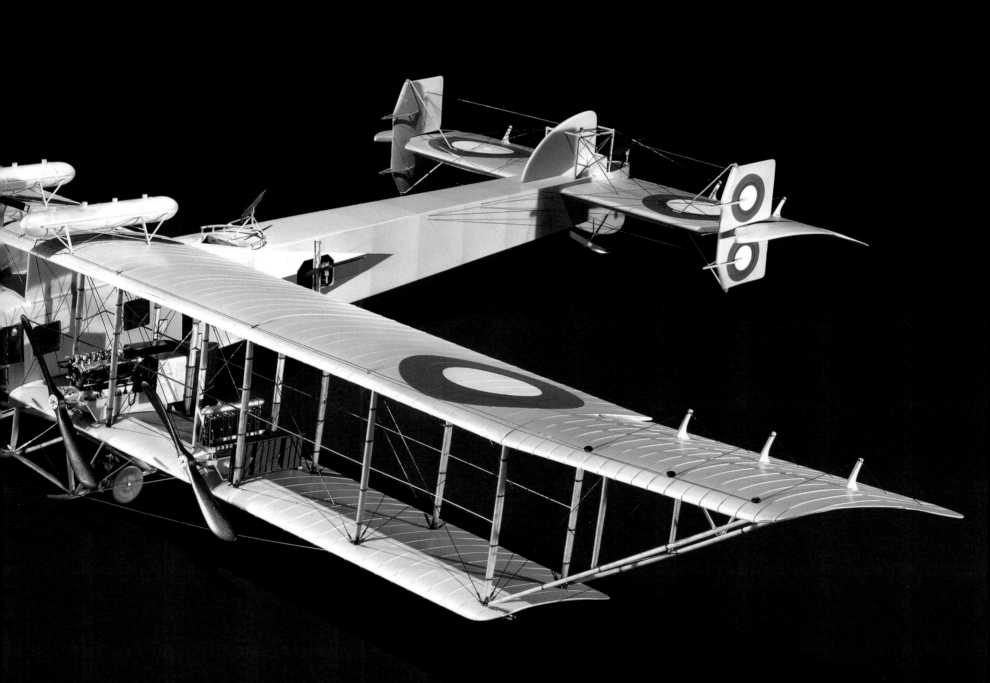

(LEFT AND BELOW)

Once the new Bolshevik government assumed power in revolutionary Russia in 1917, they mobilized the Il'ya Muromets *bomber for service in* the new Red Air Force. These two *photos show an* Il'ya Muromets *with the distinctive red star of the Red Air Fleet.*

expanse of clouds. The reading on the altimeter showed 3,000 feet, and the airplane steady on course.

At 4,000 feet the rain began to taper off, but there was no escape from the enveloping clouds. A few minutes passed. Sikorsky continued his upward trajectory to 5,000 feet. At this elevation the clouds suddenly gave way to calm air, allowing the *Il'ya Muromets* to cruise smoothly toward Kiev. Where before there had been darkness and limited visibility, Sikorsky and his crew now found themselves in a vast heavenly sphere, above the clouds and with a blue sky and a bright sun overhead. The *Il'ya Muromets* now appeared to be above the weather, as if on the top of the world. They would only descend when Lavrov signaled that the *Il'ya Muromets* was over Kiev.

Giving Captain Prussis the controls, Sikorsky moved to the upper platform above the center fuselage. Standing alone and firmly holding on to the rail, he saw the wide expanse of the wings of the *Il'ya Muromets*, the turning propellers, and the white sea of clouds below stretching to the horizon. For Sikorsky, this exhilarating moment endured in memory for the remainder of his life.

"All around me," he recorded later, "there was a fairyland, formed by clouds. . . . From time to time the plane would pass close to a strange-looking mountain. Next there would be a gigantic mushroom several hundred feet high. When we passed close to it, the cloud motion below its huge head would become apparent and a few bumps would be noticeable. For a long time, I stayed alone on the platform admiring the wonderful panorama—the strange beauty of which I will never forget." One can search in vain in the chronicles of early flight to find a moment equal to this one.

The remainder of the flight, at least for Igor Sikorsky, became anticlimatic. Lavrov gave the signal to descend just at the right moment, a testimony to his extraordinary skills as a navigator. When the *Il'ya Muromets* broke through the lower edge of the cloud bank, Sikorsky found himself above the Dnieper River and the historic city of Kiev. Beyond the river he saw the golden domes of the ancient Kiev-Pechersk Monastery. Upon landing at the Kourenev airfield, Sikorsky took note of the fact that he had completed the aerial trek from St. Petersburg to Kiev in 12 hours and 57 minutes of flying time. The reaction of Sikorsky's native city was unprecedented, with thousands of Kiev's residents coming to the airfield to see the remarkable *Il'ya Muromets*. One gala event included the attendance of Peter Nesterov, another Russian air hero who had performed the first-ever aerial loop.

The return flight to St. Petersburg took some 30 hours, but this leg proved to be less dramatic and challenging. There were no onboard fires, spins, or emergency landings—just the steady passage of the *Il'ya Muromets* home. Upon arriving in St. Petersburg, Sikorsky was again fêted with public acclaim. Nicholas II expressed his high regard for Sikorsky's achievement by giving the airplane a new name—*Il'ya Muromets Kievsky*. At the conclusion of his epic aerial trek to Kiev, Sikorsky owned a total of nine world records in various categories of distance, duration, and altitude.

It would be an unanticipated quirk of fate that before news of Igor Sikorsky's aerial trek reached the outside world, Europe would find itself caught up in the Great War in August 1914. This cruel war obscured one of the most remarkable achievements in early flight even as it set Igor Sikorsky on a course that would lead to his new life in the United States.

RICKENBACKER
THE CULT OF THE ACE

WORLD WAR I gave birth to a new hero, the military pilot. The ultimate measure of heroism in aerial warfare was the "ace." A pilot achieved the exalted status of ace with five or more air victories. In a war largely fought in trenches, with a grim toll of 10 million casualties, the airplane alone offered a real measure of movement and an arena for personal heroism. Military pilots soared above the stalemate of the trenches, becoming transcendent figures.

Still, air combat was a high-risk endeavor in which the life expectancy for pilots at the front could be very short, sometimes as brief as two weeks for the new recruits. Airmen of that era flew primitive flying machines fashioned of wood and fabric, powered by engines notorious for mechanical breakdowns. Most pilots entered the lethal realm of air combat without parachutes. For the public on both sides of the Great War, the aces were the knights of the air and national heroes—René Fonck of France, William Bishop of the British Empire, Manfred von Richthofen of Germany.

For the United States, Eddie Rickenbacker emerged in that war as a towering figure, the exemplar of personal heroism. Moreover, his entire life also suggests the influential role some air heroes came to play in the larger life of their country. Rickenbacker's war service set the stage for an extraordinary career, from organizing an automobile manufacturing firm to building a major airline. As a public figure Rickenbacker carved out his own niche as a spokesman on many issues, domestic and foreign. Always independent, he nevertheless found avenues to serve presidents on special missions, as he did for President Franklin Roosevelt. His 22-day ordeal at sea, lost in the Pacific during World War II, only reinforced his legendary survival skills in the face of adversity. America's "Ace of Aces" became a powerful and controversial figure in twentieth-century America.

Born of Swiss-German parents in Columbus, Ohio, on October 8, 1890, Edward Vernon Rickenbacker was one of eight children. As a youth, Rickenbacker displayed a self-reliance and rugged independence that would characterize his entire life. He was smoking cigarettes at the age of five. In school, he established a reputation for toughness. His father died when he was in his teens, prompting the young Rickenbacker to seek out a series of jobs to support his family, including work in a glass factory, a steel casting plant, and a brewery.

(ABOVE)

Captain Eddie Rickenbacker stands next to his Nieuport 28 fighter, with the distinctive insignia of the "Hat-in-the-Ring" 94th Aero Squadron.

(OPPOSITE)

A close-up of the cockpit of a SPAD XIII fighter. This particular aircraft was flown by Raymond Brooks and is part of the aircraft collection of the National Air and Space Museum, Washington, D.C.

The National Air and Space Museum's SPAD XIII, an Allied fighter aircraft that won considerable fame in World War I.

Early on, Rickenbacker became infatuated with autos, in particular racing cars. He loved the thrill and danger of the dirt racetrack circuit, racing for early auto racing pioneers such as Lee Frayer and Fred Duesenberg. At one point, Rickenbacker decided to race independently, forming his own race team. In 1914, he set a record at Daytona, achieving a speed of 134 miles per hour. By 1916, the year before the United States entered World War I, Rickenbacker was an established race driver, winning over $60,000 that year in prize money.

The war in Europe sparked Rickenbacker's deeply felt patriotism and sense of duty. He joined the American Expeditionary Force (AEF) in May 1917. Initially, he was assigned to General John Pershing, commander of the AEF, as his chauffeur, a logical position for one of America's most talented race car drivers. Rickenbacker, however, found the job boring, routine, and devoid of the high risks of actual combat. He yearned to test his skills in aviation, to become a pilot and engage the enemy in aerial combat. In fact, before he was assigned to duty in Europe, Rickenbacker had supported the idea of a special squadron to be composed of former race car drivers, arguing that these professional auto racers possessed the fast reflexes and the daring to be effective military pilots. Rickenbacker's duties as a staff chauffeur eventually brought him into contact with General Billy Mitchell of the fledgling Army Air Service, who arranged for the irrepressible Rickenbacker to be admitted to a flight training school at Issoudon, France. He did well and soon was assigned to the 94th Aero Pursuit Squadron, posted near Toul, France.

The 94th became known as the "Hat-in-the-Ring" squadron, and at the time of Rickenbacker's arrival, Major

Raoul Lufbery was the commander. Lufbery came to his command with considerable experience, having served first with the French Air Service and the Lafayette Escadrille, the latter a special air unit composed of American volunteer pilots flying for the French. Lufbery was a high-ranking American ace with 17 victories. Initially, Rickenbacker's blunt manner, outspoken ways, and reputation as a loner resulted in a certain degree of isolation for him within the squadron. However, Rickenbacker's personal aggressiveness and manifest talents as a combat pilot eventually won the day, earning him the respect of his fellow squadron mates. His first air victory came on May 7, 1918. But this triumph was overshadowed by the combat death of Lufbery three days later. By September, Rickenbacker himself assumed command of the 94th Aero Squadron.

By this late juncture in World War I, popular fascination with the aces had reached a new intensity: in a war of stalemate and unparalleled carnage, the fabled aces embodied a personal nobility that stood apart from the anonymity of the ground action. The war created its own pantheon of heroic aces: Germany's Manfred von Richthofen and Oswald Boelcke; France's René Fonck, Charles Nungesser, and Georges Guynemer; Britain's Edward Mannack and Albert Ball; and Canada's Billy Bishop and William Barker. Some aces, such as Richthofen, the so-called Red Baron, towered over their contemporaries; prior to his death in aerial combat, Richthofen scored an astounding 80 air victories.

The Red Baron's exploits became legendary. But the work of lesser-known aces, such as Canadian William Barker, with his 52 victories, established a high standard for Allied pilots. In fact, Barker emerged as one of the more efficient aces on the Allied side just prior to Rickenbacker's assignment to the 94th Aero Squadron.

The airplane itself had undergone rapid technical refinements during the four years of the Great War, becoming an effective weapon of war. When Rickenbacker reached the front in 1918, the last year of the war, Allied pilots were flying fast and highly maneuverable pursuit planes such as the SPAD XIII and the Nieuport 28; the Germans were deploying the lethal and equally maneuverable Fokker D.VIIs and Albatros fighters. These fighter aircraft stood in sharp contrast to the fragile and slow-moving types used in the opening months of the war. Aerial photography, arguably the most important contribution of air power to the war, also had evolved in a dramatic way as the war progressed.

Among the fabled aces, Barker exemplified the flying skills and personal aggressiveness that had made the ace a pivotal symbol of the war by 1918. As a late arrival to air combat that year, Rickenbacker mirrored Barker's style and exploits. Billy Bishop, also a Canadian air hero, called Barker "the greatest fighter pilot the world has ever known." Such an appellation may be more descriptive than hyperbole. As a youth, the lanky Barker preferred hunting and horseback riding to schoolwork. His skill as a marksman would later be useful in aerial combat in the Great War.

Like Rickenbacker, Barker was something of a loner, intense and independent. He could be sullen and seemed always on the edge of rebellion when it came to contact with external authority. He did not drink, carouse, or even engage in any of the pranks and frivolity associated with military life, and he approached war with high seriousness. Barker's squadron mates marveled at his extraordinary bravery and

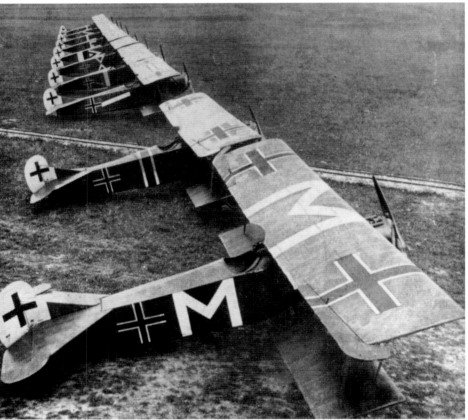

(TOP)

Famed German ace Manfred Freiherr von Richthofen (aka the Red Baron) scored 80 air victories in World War I.

(MIDDLE)

Colorfully marked German Fokker D.VIIs await the next patrol. The Fokker D.VII was considered one of the most effective German fighters to see service in World War I.

(BOTTOM)

German ace Oswald Boelcke earned fame as an innovator of air combat tactics. Many of his tactics were used in "dogfights" during both World War I and World War II.

skills as a pilot, even if his superiors rankled in the face of his blunt manner and thinly veiled aversion to the routine demands of military discipline. His first taste of battle as a pilot in the Royal Flying Corps came in the rear seat of a B.E. 2d aircraft, downing a German fighter in August 1916.

As a combat pilot, Barker possessed impressive skills at maneuver and marksmanship, but the fearless Canadian also entered the arena of air combat with another trait, arguably the most critical: the eagle-eyed perception of the entire sky in which he flew. He displayed an uncanny sense of place in the sky, along with a capacity to see enemy aircraft at long distances—even when hidden in the clouds or flying through haze. His keen eyes monitored the whole realm of the skies, catching faint images of airplanes flying at any altitude. His mastery of gunnery came with an impeccable sense of timing as he waited for a chance to fire short bursts at close range. Barker was a hunter. Few could rival his proficiency in air combat.

Barker's most extraordinary aerial feat came just a few days before the armistice of November 11, 1918, which finally ended the war. Alone, he encountered a large group of German aircraft, estimated at between 50 and 60 planes. The bold Canadian downed four of the airplanes in an uneven air battle. Severely wounded and barely conscious, Barker was able to escape his pursuers and return to his air base. For his bravery, he won the prestigious Victoria Cross.

While he was a relentless and merciless hunter, Barker also possessed a sportsman's sense of fairness, an abiding conviction that air combat should be a duel of equals. This notion haunted Barker in the aftermath of an attack on a manned observation balloon. Such sorties were typically dangerous, requiring Barker to run a gauntlet of enemy

(TOP)

Hydrogen-filled German observation balloons with their suspended observer's basket offered tempting targets to Allied fighter pilots, even with protection from antiaircraft batteries and German escort fighters.

(BOTTOM)

The spectacular results of a successful "balloon busting" attack by Allied pilots using incendiary bullets.

ground fire. One day Barker attacked an observation balloon with a two-man crew dangling precariously in a basket below the towering gas bag. Firing his Vickers gun from his Sopwith Camel, Barker's aim was deadly accurate, setting the balloon on fire. As the doomed balloon fell into a series of contortions and began to lose its buoyancy, the two observers parachuted. Barker circled as the two men began their descent; he did not seek to interfere with their passage to safety. But then suddenly the gas balloon—now a flaming streamer in a rapid free fall—enveloped the two observers. The burning mass of balloon and humanity fell to the ground in a heap. Barker was greatly troubled by this "slaying" of an observation balloon and he vowed he would never again attack a balloon, concluding that such combat was unequal and unworthy. In the future he decided to fight against only those who could fight back.

Such "knightly" sensibilities were not unique to Barker. Rickenbacker and his American squadron mates also mirrored these notions of honor in combat, although in the heat of battle not all airmen adhered to the unwritten code. Fighter pilots became a sort of flying cavalry, dashing and animated by a certain notion of chivalry that stood in sharp contrast to the brutality and carnage associated with the ground war. British Prime Minister Lloyd George echoed the popular adoration of the "sky pilots" of the Great War when he stated these airborne warriors evoked "the legendary days of chivalry, not merely by the daring of their exploits but by the nobility of their spirit." These pilots flew over a 400-mile line of trenches and defensive fortifications, a battle zone of barbed wire, mud, poison gas, lice, and wholesale slaughter that would consume millions of the youth on both sides between 1914 and 1918.

(TOP)

Famed Royal Flying Corps ace Albert Ball, who disappeared in a combat sortie in May 1917.

(MIDDLE)

A Sopwith 7F.1 Snipe, flown by William G. Barker of the Royal Flying Corps.

(BOTTOM)

Canadian William G. Barker emerged as one of the most effective pilots on the Allied side, flying with the Royal Flying Corps on the Italian front. A master of air combat tactics, Barker won the Victoria Cross for his bravery in combat.

The fighter pilot enjoyed an exalted reputation and exemption from the rigors of the trenches, even living in the relative luxury of barracks. With this lifestyle, even with its manifest dangers, pilots fought as individuals against the enemy. As Cecil Lewis put it, flying alone gave "a sense of mastery over mechanism, mastery indeed over space, time, and life itself." Most were young, around 20 years old, and many fell victim to the high attrition rate associated with combat flying. They often flew without parachutes, in open cockpits where, at combat altitude, the temperature dropped below zero even in the summer. Enemy fire offered constant danger, but fragile aircraft with unreliable engines came with their own set of peculiar hazards. Only the most skilled survived, but even the best could fall to the angel of death: Manfred von Richthofen was killed in combat, as was his Allied counterpart Albert Ball, the most celebrated RFC ace.

Later in life, Rickenbacker reflected that a fighter pilot had to be cautious in any encounter with the enemy, but never timid. He felt that boldness such as that shown by William Barker and others often assured survival in aerial combat. He always insisted on getting close to an adversary in the air, and only then firing—so close to be able to, in his own words, "hit him with a baseball bat." One had to be bold at the right moment, and part of the ultimate success of the fighter pilot, in Rickenbacker's mind, was self-knowledge and personal discipline. During his combat tour Rickenbacker estimated that he engaged in 134 air battles, in which he scored 26 air victories, becoming America's top-ranking ace.

Rickenbacker's air triumphs came in the last year of the war, occurring in the narrow time frame between May and November 1918. A typical example of Rickenbacker's boldness came one day in the skies over Verdun, when he

downed two enemy aircraft. On patrol that day, he spotted two LVG reconnaissance planes en route to the frontlines. Above and to their rear were five Fokker fighters flying escort. Flying from altitude and out of the sun to gain surprise, Rickenbacker dove on the last escort fighter, firing at close range: the Fokker fell away and crashed. Rickenbacker's aggressive attack prompted the enemy to scatter in confusion.

Rickenbacker then attacked the LVG airplanes below, zooming down and then climbing beneath the tail of one LVG to avoid the fire of the rear gunner. The pilot of the LVG then turned to give his rear gunner a better vantage point to fire. Rickenbacker later recalled a stream of bullets coming so close to the cockpit that he could have reached out and caught them. Now above his adversary, Rickenbacker sideslipped his SPAD toward the two LVGs, banked, and then opened fire. The nearest LVG flew into Rickenbacker's stream of bullets and burst into flames, falling to the ground with a long trail of black smoke. The four remaining Fokker escorts then attacked, seeking revenge. But Rickenbacker's speedy SPAD managed to carry him home safely that memorable day.

By his own account, Rickenbacker's narrowest escape came in an afternoon sortie over the Meuse River. He was patrolling alone, in what had been a long period of inaction over the front. German airplanes typically did not fly into this sector in the afternoon hours, so his own vigilance was relaxed. Ahead, an Allied balloon drifted lazily in the air. As he approached this friendly object in the sky, it suddenly burst into flames: the fiery end of the balloon alerted Rickenbacker to the fact that one or more German fighters were nearby. He anxiously scanned the sky and horizon in the distance.

(TOP)

French ace Georges Guynemer stands next to his SPAD VII fighter. Guynemer scored 53 air victories, emerging in the war as one of the top Allied aces.

(MIDDLE)

American ace Frank Luke, the sole American aviator in World War I to earn the Congressional Medal of Honor.

(BOTTOM)

Born in France of an American father, Raoul Lufbery became a mechanic in the French Air Service and later joined the famed American volunteer Lafayette Escadrille. He scored 17 air victories before his death in aerial combat.

Eddie Rickenbacker stands in front of a German Hannover CLII, an enemy aircraft he shot down with squadron mate Reed Chambers.

Rickenbacker acted quickly, deciding to fly toward the enemy lines, anticipating that the German fighter or fighters would eventually turn for home. Once he was in place and at high altitude, he reasoned, he would enjoy superior position and would have the option of attacking. No sooner had he turned toward the enemy trenches than he came under fire, with a stream of tracers passing near him. No time to seek altitude, he was now the prey as two German airplanes closed in on him.

Rather than dive–the maneuver his adversaries would no doubt anticipate–Rickenbacker pulled the stick backward and began a tortuous climb, in a sort of corkscrew maneuver. As he ascended, his attackers were descending—so close, Rickenbacker later remembered, he could see their faces and

the distinctive red noses of their Fokker airplanes. The red markings revealed his pursuers were part of Richthofen's legendary air unit, the "Flying Circus."

Reaching altitude, Rickenbacker quickly discovered a new peril: two additional German fighters were waiting for him. They had assumed the higher altitude to fly cover. The enemy renewed the attack, now from two areas of the sky. Caught in this vice, the smart thing for Rickenbacker no doubt was to attempt an escape from this highly uneven challenge, escape being the better part of valor when outnumbered. Instead, he zigzagged and maneuvered violently to elude his enemy, two attacking from above and two attacking from below, while he looked for an opening. As the Fokkers closed in on him, Rickenbacker saw his chance. For an instant, one of the Fokkers flying beneath him came too close and Rickenbacker turned and dove on him, firing a burst ahead into the flight path of the Fokker. The German pilot, not anticipating this maneuver, flew into the stream of fire, which hit the gas tanks of the Fokker, causing it to burst into flames. This unexpected triumph offered a momentary respite for the beleaguered Rickenbacker, who then looped to engage his remaining pursuers. Startled by the sudden aggressiveness of their prey, the Germans turned away and headed for home.

Rickenbacker, in the tradition of Richthofen and Barker, never lacked boldness in the face of unexpected opportunity. He knew his SPAD was faster than the Fokkers, so he decided to give chase. Slowly he narrowed the distance with the Fokkers. At this point, he was some three miles behind enemy lines and flying at an altitude of merely 1,000 feet. Rickenbacker opened fire, hitting one of the Fokkers. The intense, close-in burst of fire had a devastating effect:

A downed Fokker D.VII. This particular German fighter aircraft was so feared by the Allies that it was explicitly banned by the Treaty of Versailles, which followed World War I.

the enemy airplane nosed over, dove into the ground, and burst into flames. Rickenbacker was now at 500 feet altitude, at which time German guns opened fire, forcing a quick retreat. That day Rickenbacker narrowly escaped death. His resourcefulness and bravery had carried the day.

Rickenbacker emerged from World War I as a national hero and the winner of numerous awards, including the Congressional Medal of Honor. In 1921, he organized his own automobile company, using his name as the marque for a whole new line of automobiles. The Rickenbacker car was an advanced design for its day, even sporting four-wheel brakes. But the whole enterprise failed in the highly competitive auto market of the 1920s. While caught in debt, Rickenbacker doggedly refused to declare bankruptcy, vowing to pay off his creditors.

Over time, Rickenbacker reemerged as a successful entrepreneur, purchasing the Indianapolis Motor Speedway (he would sell it in 1947) and a new airline, which later became Eastern Air Lines. Both enterprises were lucrative, with Rickenbacker exercising tight management over all his business ventures. Being America's "Ace of Aces," he inspired the *Ace Drummond* comic strip, which later was serialized on film. Eventually Rickenbacker became an outspoken figure in American political life, serving as a consultant to the United States government in World War II. His outspoken views on many political issues of the day made Rickenbacker a colorful, if controversial, figure.

Life as a civilian brought new challenges. In 1941, as a passenger on a DC-3 airliner, Rickenbacker narrowly survived a crash near Atlanta, Georgia. In the crash, the pilot, the copilot, and eight passengers died. Rickenbacker's injuries were severe, but he managed to recover after many months of recuperation.

(TOP)

Eddie Rickenbacker shakes hands with former foe, German ace Ernst Udet. With his 62 air victories, Udet was the highest scoring German ace to survive the war. The two famed airmen met at the National Air Races during the 1930s.

(BOTTOM)

Eddie Rickenbacker poses in a Peugeot racing car. Before the war, he had been a successful motorcycle and auto racer.

However, the most harrowing experience for the intrepid aviator came in October 1942. That month Rickenbacker agreed to make a trip to Port Moresby in New Guinea to deliver a special message from War Department secretary Henry L. Stimson to General Douglas MacArthur. After crossing the Pacific to Hawaii in a Pan American clipper, Rickenbacker joined eight other men in a Boeing B-17D for the long flight to General MacArthur's headquarters in New Guinea. Their first destination was Canton Island in the Gilbert Islands, a small, low, narrow atoll surrounded by a large shallow lagoon. Canton Island was a small dot of land in the vast Pacific, located some 1,800 miles from Hawaii. Navigation, as Rickenbacker later recalled, was a "reasonable guess," with no established weather stations or even landmarks across the watery expanse to gauge their progress. On the approach to the Canton base, the radio operator on the B-17 called and asked for a bearing, only to be told that Canton Island lacked such navigation equipment; it was learned later that the equipment had arrived in crates at the Canton base several weeks before and remained unpacked in the confusing first months of the war in the Pacific. Soon it became apparent to Rickenbacker and the eight men on board the B-17 that they had overshot the Canton Island airfield and were lost at sea.

The ditching of the B-17 went well, a soft landing that allowed the passengers to evacuate quickly from the slowly sinking bomber and board three rafts. They hurriedly drew the three rafts together with ropes and prepared for a long wait for rescue planes to arrive. As it turned out, they spent 22 days floating on the ocean surface before rescue. For Rickenbacker, this episode became another narrow encounter with death in his storied life.

A U.S. Navy Vought OS2U Kingfisher observation floatplane at work retrieving a group of downed personnel in the Pacific war. A Kingfisher was the first rescue plane to reach Rickenbacker and his crew, who had been lost at sea in World War II.

Eddie Rickenbacker climbs down from a U.S. Navy Consolidated PBY flying boat shortly after his rescue at sea.

Crowded on the rafts, the eight men faced a scorching daytime sun and dehydration. They possessed only a few rations, a cache that included chocolate bars, some small oranges, and a limited supply of water, all strictly apportioned during the ordeal. Occasional rain storms punctuated their life at sea, always a welcome event to replenish their small reservoirs of water. They were able to catch small fish, which supplemented the meager diet. Each raft had aluminum paddles, but these were frequently ineffectual when facing 12-foot swells. Danger also lurked nearby, as sharks circled them, often brushing up against their inflated rafts. With time, all the men acquired sores and blisters, which were a source of great pain and discomfort. Trapped in small rafts, menaced by the circling dark shadows of sharks, and seemingly beyond discovery by Navy rescue planes, the men experienced frequent periods of depression and anger. The indomitable Rickenbacker, if technically a civilian, played a key role in their survival with his aggressive style and discipline.

After two weeks, it was decided to allow the rafts to drift apart, in the hope that one of the rafts would catch the eye of a passing airplane. Eventually a Navy plane did spot one of the rafts, and a concerted rescue effort was launched to find the survivors. Another of the drifting rafts reached an uninhabited island, where the men were discovered by a missionary. Rickenbacker and the men in his raft were also picked up.

When rescued, Rickenbacker had lost some 60 pounds, but he soon displayed remarkable recuperative powers in a military hospital. After a short interlude, he was able to make it to New Guinea and meet with General MacArthur.

LINDBERGH
ALONE ACROSS THE ATLANTIC

ROOSEVELT FIELD, Long Island, New York, May 14–15, 1927: a huge crowd gathered to take in the so-called Transatlantic Derby—a competition to be the first to fly from New York to Paris nonstop and win the Orteig prize of $25,000. Raymond Orteig, a French-American hotel magnate, had made the offer in 1919, but no one had yet claimed it. Richard Byrd and Clarence Chamberlin occupied center stage as the two main contenders for the Orteig prize. Both aviators possessed impressive portfolios as long-distance flyers. Byrd, a lieutenant commander in the U.S. Navy, had flown round trip to the North Pole in 1926. Flying his Fokker Trimotor, *America*, Byrd and his crew hoped to be the first to make it across the storm-tossed North Atlantic. That same year, Chamberlin, with Bert Acosta, set a world record in a Wright Bellanca by staying aloft for over 51 hours. This extraordinary feat revealed the durability of the Wright Whirlwind engine, which had revolutionized duration flying, even suggesting that vast expanses of ocean could now be conquered by aviators. The press monitored closely the scene on Long Island, anticipating that one of these legendary men would lead the way to win the Orteig prize.

The previous Thursday, largely unnoticed, another contender had landed at nearby Curtiss Field, determined to compete for the Orteig prize against these more famous rivals. His name: Charles Lindbergh. A former air mail pilot, Lindbergh had flown into Long Island in his *Spirit of St. Louis*, having made a record-breaking transcontinental flight from San Diego. Both the press and the milling crowds largely ignored the new entry that weekend. And Lindbergh's determination to fly the Atlantic alone had generated no small amount of skepticism. Some in the press labeled Lindbergh the "Flying Fool." Few took his challenge to Byrd and Chamberlin as a serious one.

Lindbergh's silver monoplane was built in a record 60 days at the Ryan Airlines factory in San Diego—just in time for the young Minnesotan aviator to enter the Transatlantic Derby. The *Spirit of St. Louis* was designed at Ryan by Donald Hall, a man who translated into reality Lindbergh's vision of a single-engine airplane capable of flying 4,000 miles nonstop. The *Spirit* seemed to mirror the sleek silhouette of the Ryan M-1 and M-2 monoplanes of the era, but in most respects it was a radical new design, featuring an enlarged wingspan, reinforced chassis to carry the weight of 450 gallons of fuel, and fitted with the latest Wright Whirlwind engine, the J-5-C, a nine-piston radial engine with 223 horsepower. It was a streamlined airplane with extraordinary range.

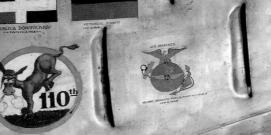

A dramatic close-up of the nose section of the Spirit of St. Louis *as it appears today in the National Air and Space Museum, Washington, D.C. The insignia, including the national flags, was attached to the cowling of the aircraft after Lindbergh completed his tour of Central America and the Caribbean in 1928 to promote aviation.*

Charles Lindbergh was not well known in the spring of 1927 except among a small coterie of aviators. He grew up in Little Falls, Minnesota, and was the son of a congressman. As a youth, Lindbergh displayed little interest in formal education, even flunking out of the University of Wisconsin. He did display a keen interest in flying, however, and earned his pilot's license, purchased his own war surplus plane, and entered the rough and tumble world of aerial barnstorming in the early 1920s. Later he earned his wings in the United States Army Air Service reserves. Prior to his entry into the transatlantic competition, he served as an air mail pilot, arguably the most perilous of all flying professions. When Lindbergh arrived at Roosevelt Field he thus possessed an impressive background in flying and was a man known for his personal discipline and coolness in any flight emergency.

Popular interest in the Orteig prize had been fueled in part by tragedy: A week before, newspaper headlines blazoned that two French aviators, Charles Nungesser and François Coli, had disappeared mysteriously over the Atlantic. Also, two American aviators, Noel Davis and Stanton Wooster, were killed while testing their Atlantic racer, the *Keystone Pathfinder*, in an abortive attempt to prepare for the Orteig competition. And participants were still haunted by the memory of French World War I ace Rene Fonck, who had attempted to fly out of Roosevelt field to Paris the previous September in his Sikorsky-built S-35; an abortive takeoff ended in a flaming crash that killed two of his crewmen.

No one minimized the real dangers awaiting anyone venturing across the Atlantic, in particular the 2,000 miles of open water between Newfoundland and Ireland. Mariners told of the stormy conditions that often sweep

Lindbergh (at right), garbed in suit and fedora, inspects the newly built Spirit of St. Louis *at San Diego in April 1927.*

By the evening of May 19, Lindbergh received word of a sudden arrival of mild weather over the northern latitudes of the Atlantic, and he decided, even with minimal sleep, to depart on the morning of May 20. To his surprise, he flew alone that day: Clarence Chamberlin had been grounded by a legal suit and Richard Byrd decided to move deliberately, calling for additional tests of his airplane before any departure. Quite inexplicably, the dark horse, Charles Lindbergh, was airborne on that memorable day, even as his rivals—as a consequence of circumstance or poor judgment—stayed put.

Lindbergh's departure from Roosevelt Field showcased the inherent dangers for all transoceanic flyers of that era. To traverse a great ocean required an airplane equipped with an elaborate system of auxiliary fuel tanks. Rene Fonck's crash in 1926 revealed the perils associated with takeoff runs in an overladen aircraft. On the morning of May 20, Lindbergh's *Spirit of St. Louis* was topped off with 450 gallons of fuel, meaning a payload of around 5,000 pounds. The passage down the rain-soaked runway at Roosevelt Field proved to be a dangerous one, but Lindbergh managed to clear the obstacles at the end of the runway by some 20 feet.

Once airborne, Lindbergh followed a curving trajectory over New England and Newfoundland to reach the North Atlantic and ultimately Paris. This flight path was the so-called great circle route, the shortest distance on a sphere, a passage of just over 3,600 miles. Lindbergh elected to fly alone and in an austerely equipped single-engine airplane. Unlike Fonck or Byrd, Lindbergh believed large and heavily laden tri-motor aircraft offered greater chances of engine failure or some other en route disaster. For the *Spirit of St. Louis*, Lindbergh placed his trust in the reliability of his

across the North Atlantic. Any aviator following the siren call to make a transoceanic crossing could expect—even in the spring season—shifting winds, sudden and violent storms, fog and heavy rain, even icebergs. In addition, flying through or around cloud formations involved the high risk of icing. The Atlantic posed a formidable natural barrier for all air travelers.

As it turned out, no one flew out of Roosevelt Field on the weekend of May 14–15, to the disappointment of thousands of onlookers. The weather bureau reports on the North Atlantic were grim, suggesting to all the competitors a prudent delay. As the days passed, the contenders remained grounded, awaiting a shift in the weather.

(TOP)

Lindbergh selected the Wright J-5C Whirlwind radial engine, a state-of-the-art engine known for its power and dependability, for the Spirit of St. Louis.

(BOTTOM)

The original aluminum spinner for the Spirit of St. Louis, *autographed by Ryan Aircraft workers in San Diego, California. The swastika in the center was a symbol of good luck popular at the time, before Adolf Hitler appropriated the symbol for his Nazi movement.*

Wright Whirlwind engine, which had revolutionized long-distance flying in the 1920s. The only real question for Lindbergh, the one that sparked so much skepticism about his chances, was whether a man could stay awake for the duration of the long flight, perhaps as long as 40 hours.

His transatlantic passage was laid out on navigation charts in a curving black line, divided into 100-mile segments. By the third hour, he was over Cape Cod, setting the stage for his first leg of open water, which separated New England from Nova Scotia. He passed over the vast emptiness of Nova Scotia in the sixth and seven hours, followed by a 200-mile leg to reach Newfoundland, which represented a real milestone in his flight. Beyond Newfoundland was a 2,000-mile stretch of open ocean, to be encountered on the night of May 20–21. To let the world know that he had reached this initial milestone, Lindbergh diverted from the black line on his navigation chart to make a low-level pass over St. Johns before he headed across the North Atlantic. At this juncture, he had flown 1,100 miles.

The middle leg across the Atlantic proved to be the most perilous for Lindbergh. Flying at night offered a unique challenge to the young Minnesotan. He realized that any en route mishap—an engine failure, icing, or a violent storm—meant ditching at sea, with little chance of survival; he would experience the same fate as Nungesser and Coli.

Darkness enveloped the *Spirit of St. Louis* at around 8:15 p.m., New York time. Even as the shadows lowered, Lindbergh noticed more than one iceberg floating ominously below. Cloud formations, like towering mountains, stretched from the ocean surface into the sky,

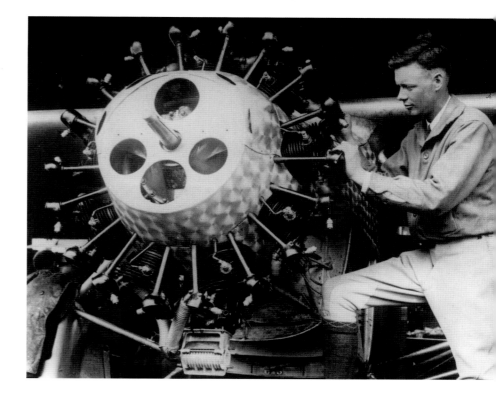

(BELOW)

A rare and informal photo of a pensive Charles Lindbergh, taken by a young woman at Roosevelt Field just days before Lindbergh made his epic transatlantic flight.

(RIGHT)

The Spirit of St. Louis *flies low over the water on a test flight.*

dwarfing Lindbergh and his small plane. For Lindbergh to make it to distant Paris would require no small amount of personal discipline and fortitude.

Flying through the night sky, around and through scattered cloud formations, Lindbergh was slow to realize that he was facing an icing situation. He was tired and showing the effects of sleep deprivation, being caught up with the cockpit routine of monitoring his compass heading and periodically shifting the petcocks that controlled the steady flow of fuel to the engine.

When he took a flashlight to examine the underside of the wing, he detected no icing. But further inspection revealed evidence of icing on the strut. This meant a layer of ice was accumulating on the forward edge of the wing, which was out of sight. He then determined that the airplane was cruising at five miles per hour less than normal, the result of increased drag from the icing.

The icing problem, if not corrected, could have led to a disaster. But Lindbergh managed to lessen the problem by steering the airplane around the moisture-filled pillars of clouds, diving into narrow passageways to keep in the clear night sky. As the ice problem dissipated, Lindbergh found himself in more open and clear skies. When he reached his 15th-hour milestone, he was delighted with the clearing weather and the passing of a crisis that could have ended his flight. Cruising at 10,500 feet, he then faced a malfunction with his compass, forcing him to continue his night flight unaided by its vital readings.

Over the next few hours, even with the daybreak, Lindbergh struggled with the most pressing danger—his body's demand for sleep. He discovered that his mental control over this powerful urge only weakened with time,

A close-up of the cockpit of the Spirit of St. Louis, *taken from the port window. Visible at the top left is the extended periscope, which was fitted to the airplane to compensate for the absence of a forward wind screen (eliminated to accommodate a fuel*

tank). The airplane was austere, equipped with instruments mounted on a thin, lightweight plywood panel. Petcocks at the bottom of the instrument panel controlled the flow of fuel to the engine.

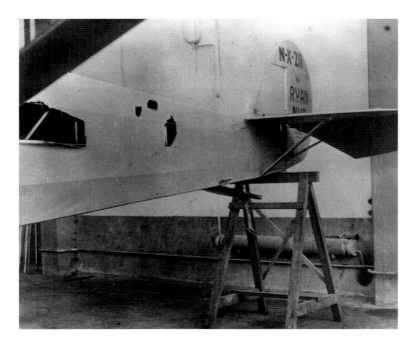

(TOP)

Banner headlines in The New York Times *heralded Lindbergh's triumphant arrival in Paris on May 21, 1927.*

(MIDDLE)

Gendarmes hold back the Parisian crowd at Le Bourget Airport on the night of Lindbergh's arrival.

(BOTTOM)

Souvenir seekers tore small patches of fabric from the fuselage of the Spirit of St. Louis.

prompting a sort of semiconsciousness. One aid in his heroic striving to stay alert was the *Spirit of St. Louis* itself, an airplane that had been shrewdly designed to be unstable in flight. Only constant attention by Lindbergh to the stick and the rudder pedals kept the airplane in level flight and on course. The slightest relaxation of the controls prompted the *Spirit* to climb or to make a diving turn. As Lindbergh slowly slipped into a state of drowsiness, the plane veered off course, awakening him. This coordinated move and countermove helped Lindbergh overcome his urge to sleep. For this reason, in part, Lindbergh later described his passage across the Atlantic in terms of "we," the joint effort of man and machine.

When morning arrived, Lindbergh was still at mid-Atlantic, with nearly a thousand miles separating him from his first land fall, the coast of Ireland. He pressed on with renewed vigor and in remarkably improved weather. Along the way he saw birds and porpoises, but for the longest time, he saw no evidence of humans. Finally, in the 27th hour of his flight, Lindbergh spotted several fishing boats ahead and to the south of his flight path. He banked to intercept the boats, but failed to get the waving fishermen to point the way to Ireland, to confirm he was on track.

So Lindbergh resumed his relentless passage eastward, and after the passing of an hour, he caught a glimpse of landfall on the northeast horizon. Flying directly toward the coastline in the distance, he discovered he was over Cape Valentia and Dingle Bay on the Irish coast. A quick calculation revealed that he was now 2,500 miles from New York. More remarkable, he was just two miles off his intended flight path.

The passage over Ireland and then Cornwall and southwest England brought an epiphany to the fatigued

(LEFT)

Lindbergh buzzes a huge crowd at Croydon airport, near London, in June 1927.

(TOP)

Mayor Jimmie Walker's yacht (lower left) led a flotilla of well-wishers for Lindbergh when he arrived in New York City.

(BOTTOM)

Lindbergh's stunning transatlantic crossing prompted a tumultuous ticker-tape parade down Broadway.

aviator. The strain and exhaustion of the long trek across the Atlantic, the storms and fog, the long wrestling with the urge to sleep—all gave way to a sense of anticipation, the feeling that his landing at Le Bourget was now plausible.

At the 32nd hour, May 21, Lindbergh crossed the English Channel and reached Cherbourg, France, his anticipated gateway to Paris. Night was approaching, and 200 miles separated him from Paris. There were beacons along the Seine, used to direct airplanes flying between London and Paris, and they offered Lindbergh an assured pathway through the night sky to Paris. At around 10:00 p.m., local time, the lights of Paris came vividly into view, as Lindbergh banked around the Eiffel Tower and headed northeast of the city for Le Bourget Airport.

On his approach to Le Bourget, Lindbergh noticed that the roads leading into the airport were aglow with automobile headlights. He had no way of knowing that word of his arrival had reached the French capital and tens of thousands of people were crowding the highway to reach the airport in time to see the American aviator land. Over 100,000 enthusiastic Parisians greeted him that night, the first of many enthusiastic welcomes Lindbergh would encounter in Europe and America. He landed at 10:21 p.m., local time, having flown some 3,610 miles in 33 hours and 29 minutes.

Lindbergh had won the Orteig prize in a stunning fashion, catapulting the 25-year-old aviator into unparalleled global celebrity. The "Lone Eagle" had won the high-stakes Atlantic competition with a blend of tenacity and bravery. He had flown a superbly designed airplane, the *Spirit of St. Louis*. And throughout the long journey, the dependable Wright Whirlwind engine had maintained a constant roar, assuring his success.

Lindbergh's aerial spectacular ignited a firestorm of popular acclaim, one that drastically and irreversibly altered his life. Evidence of his celebrity was apparent in Europe even before he returned home to be greeted by wildly enthusiastic crowds in Washington, D.C., and New York City. While in Paris he dined with the president of France, was awarded the Cross of the Legion of Honor, and met the legendary aviator Louis Blériot, who had flown over the English Channel in 1909. Flying the *Spirit of St. Louis* on to Brussels, Lindbergh was greeted by King Albert and enthusiastic crowds. His next stop in London offered him a chance to meet King George of England and again to be received as the air hero of the age.

The clamor for him to return to the United States became so intense that President Coolidge sent the cruiser *Memphis* to England to pick up Lindbergh and his plane. Upon his return, he was awarded the Distinguished Flying Cross, and later Congress voted to award him the Congressional Medal of Honor. Later, in the summer and fall of 1927, Lindbergh flew on a 48-state tour in his celebrated *Spirit of St. Louis*, traveling over 22,000 miles. Shortly after the conclusion of this historic aerial tour, Lindbergh flew to Central America, the Panama Canal Zone, and the Caribbean, also to bring attention to aviation.

Lindbergh's heroics and popularization of aviation did much to promote the airplane as a safe mode of transportation. This cause dominated the Lone Eagle, who revealed himself to be a highly serious man, in no way a typical stunt pilot of his era. After his marriage to Anne Morrow, the so-called First Couple of the Skies went on several survey flights to lay out future commercial airline routes, for Lindbergh the cutting edge of modernity for society. They flew to the North Pacific, Japan, and China

The Spirit of St. Louis *on display at the National Air and Space Museum, Washington, D.C.*

in 1931, a journey that later became the basis for Anne Morrow Lindbergh's best-seller, *North to the Orient* (1935). Other survey flights took them to Newfoundland, northern Europe, and South America. At home, Charles Lindbergh associated himself with TAT (the forerunner to TWA) and worked with Juan Trippe in the development of Pan American World Airways. In the decade after his historic transatlantic flight, Lindbergh emerged as the ubiquitous face of aviation.

Lindbergh lived a long and active life; for nearly a half century he was a prominent and controversial figure (he died in August 1974 at the age of 72). The kidnapping and death of his firstborn son, Charles Augustus Lindbergh, Jr., became a defining moment in the American experience, and led to legislation making kidnapping a federal offense. In many ways, this tragic episode stood as a cautionary tale on the perils of celebrity.

Perhaps his most controversial years came in the late 1930s, when he made several inspection tours of aviation facilities in Nazi Germany. This work was done at the behest of the American government, to gather intelligence data on the Luftwaffe, but Lindbergh's own selected praise of aspects of the "New Germany" and his opposition to war led to controversy and for a period of time, his ostracism in America.

Throughout his life, Charles Lindbergh yearned for privacy, but his promotion of causes and ideas—aviation, the invention of an artificial heart, rocketry, nonintervention into World War II, and advocacy in later life of conservation—inevitably kept him in the public spotlight. Few American heroes have enjoyed such a sustained place in the American consciousness. It all began with his sudden appearance on the world stage in 1927. He has remained a paradoxical figure, the symbol of both inspiration and controversy.

ZEPPELIN

AIR VOYAGERS ACROSS OCEANS

THE STORY is told that during the California Gold Rush of 1848, when thousands of easterners clamored to find a quick passage to the gold fields in faraway California, an enterprising con artist in New York City advertised the invention of an "airship" that would soon carry passengers to the West Coast in days, not months. In fact, the new flying machine boasted cross-country aerial treks of a mere seven days. No small number of impatient travelers attempted to book passage on this extraordinary flying machine.

While the story may be apocryphal, one can only imagine the appeal of such a scam to the countless adventurers responding to the siren call of the gold rush. Such an airship—as a magic carpet—would have conquered both time and space. At that time, there was no speedy link between the eastern seaboard and America's Pacific coast—no transcontinental railroad, no Panama Canal, or for that matter, no highway for horse-drawn wagons. The only option—and a time-consuming one—was to sail around the tip of South America to distant California.

The mythical airship of the gold rush days possessed an appeal because of the popular interest in a practical lighter-than-air flying machine in the nineteenth century. This mania took various forms, and later Jules Verne would do much to provide imaginative detail for such a futuristic craft, one that would allow humans to travel leisurely between distant geographical points in the same style and comfort as an ocean-going vessel.

The invention of the hot-air balloon by the Montgolfiers in 1783 had allowed humans to become airborne, but aeronauts still awaited an efficient means of propulsion. There had been experiments to transform the balloon into a true flying machine, with the use of sails, wooden paddles, even flapping wings, but none of these devices proved workable. Steam engines were available, but they were impractical and heavy. Only at the end of the nineteenth century did a practical gasoline engine emerge to solve the problem.

Alberto Santos-Dumont, a Brazilian, became the first to fashion the first practical airship, a motorized lighter-than-air machine. With Santos-Dumont's breakthrough, the airship technology took form and direction, a new mode of flying that would include in the future both nonrigid airships (blimps) and rigid airships (dirigibles). For a brief interlude in the early decades of the twentieth century, the airship became a rival to the

British Dirigible R-34 Successfully Trans-Navigates Atlantic From Scotland to United States

(ABOVE)
Aerial Age Weekly *announces the successful transatlantic crossing of the British dirigible, the R-34, July 14, 1919.*

(OPPOSITE)
The fiery end to the most famous of all passenger airships, the Hindenburg, *at Lakehurst, New Jersey, on May 6, 1937.*

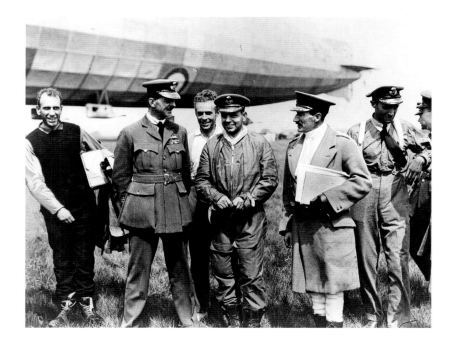

(TOP)

The British airship R-34 emerges from its "shed" in Scotland.

(BOTTOM)

The crew of the R-34 passenger airship. Major George H. Scott of the Royal Air Force commanded the R-34 on its memorable round-trip flight across the Atlantic in 1919.

The R-34 was a lumbering giant of the air that required special operating procedures. When the airship reached Long Island, New York, in 1919, onlookers were *startled when a crew member of the R-34 parachuted to the field below, where he led the effort to secure the huge flying machine to the ground.*

airplane as the optimal mode of commercial air travel. Cigar-shaped dirigibles were awe-inspiring to those who saw them, flying majestically across the skies and casting their enormous shadows over the ground. They were lifted skyward by means of enormous gas bags (often filled with highly flammable hydrogen), which were fitted inside a large rigid framework of light-weight aluminum or aluminum alloy and then covered with fabric for aerodynamic effect.

Often, in the popular shorthand of that era, these craft were called "Zeppelins," in honor of Ferdinand von Zeppelin, who had pioneered the design of dirigibles in the first part of the twentieth century. By the 1930s, Zeppelins routinely flew across the oceans and even made dramatic forays to the North Pole. For the devotees of the airship, the Zeppelin offered a luxurious mode of travel, indeed something that airplanes at that time could not match in terms of range, load capacity, and passenger comfort. As critics noted, however, there was one built-in hazard in most airships, the use of highly flammable hydrogen gas for lift.

Still, at the dawn of the twentieth century many considered the dirigible as the technological marvel of the new air age. Rudyard Kipling's imaginative book, *With the Night Mail, A Story of 2000 AD* (first published in 1905), forecast a future when airships would be a vital part of a global transportation system, routinely delivering the mail across continents on the eve of the twenty-first century. Others speculated on the airship's use in war. H. G. Wells, in his novel *War in the Air,* told of a future where Zeppelins would rain down destruction on cities. During World War I, in fact, Germany deployed its Zeppelins for reconnaissance missions and even the bombing of London.

However, the wartime use of Zeppelins proved limited and largely ineffectual. The airship was too slow and too vulnerable to ground fire or enemy interceptors ever to become a real air menace, despite the widespread fears.

By the end of World War I, many proponents of lighter-than-air technology explored how the Zeppelin might be used in commercial air travel. As early as 1919, this potential became evident with the transatlantic saga of the British airship, the R-34. This large airship made a remarkable round trip flight from Scotland to New York, a feat no airplane at the time could match.

The R-34 belonged to a family of large airships. It came equipped with four engines and boasted a crew of 30 men. For those flying the lumbering R-34, there was the keen sense of disaster, with the airship's vulnerability to shifting wind patterns, storms, and the potential for a fire with the craft's huge gas bags filled with hydrogen. As a Zeppelin clone, the R-34 cast an enormous shadow, being 643 feet long, 79 feet in diameter, and with a 92-foot tail. A special shed or hangar had to be constructed to house this airship and its sister craft. The inner framework of a dirigible consisted of aluminum girders and braces, which contained 19 huge hydrogen-filled gas bags. Linen fabric covered this large structure. The four 250-horsepower Sunbeam engines were mounted on gondolas beneath the hull. As with an airplane, the R-34 possessed control surfaces similar to an airplane—horizontal stabilizers, a rudder, and vertical fins.

(OPPOSITE)

Dirigibles were constructed with lightweight internal skeletal frames fashioned from aluminum, which held huge hydrogen gas bags to provide structural rigidity.

(TOP)

One of the motor gondolas suspended from the Graf Zeppelin.

(BOTTOM)

The multilayered fabric and rubber outer covering of the Graf Zeppelin *required constant attention.*

The forward control gondola (with one of the R-34's engines) housed the captain's cabin, flight controls, compass, altimeter, radio shack, and observation deck. The officer and crew messes were located in the bow of the airship. Along the keel, the longitudinal girder at the bottom, there was a long catwalk, which allowed access to fuel tanks and storage areas, the crew quarters, and the gondolas.

For the transatlantic flight in 1919, Major George H. Scott, an officer in the Royal Air Force, took command of the R-34 airship. As with all airships, the R-34 used the lexicon and organization of the nautical world. For the trip to North America, Major Scott was assisted by second and third officers, who shared the round-the-clock administration of the airship. There was also an engineering officer, engine technicians, telegraphers, coxwains, riggers, and cooks.

The crew worked in two shifts. Everyone on board slept in hammocks suspended from the girders. There was the real fear that any fall from the hammock might result in a crew member breaking through the thin linen fabric covering of the airship; such a fall would be fatal. For safety the airship was stocked with parachutes and flotation devices, just in case there was an emergency or ditching into the Atlantic Ocean. The crew often used the long keel at the base of the hull for exercise. Also, for the 1919 flight, the crew took along a gramophone with horn to provide some music diversion.

Officers and crew moved around the huge airship with ease, using a warren of passages and ladders. It was possible for riggers to move up and down the inner structure of the R-34 to inspect the gas bags for leaks. There were even walks on the very top of the hull, a distance of nearly 200 yards, to inspect the airship or to get a clear view of the flight path ahead. Only a hand rope held the riggers on the perilous passageway.

(TOP)

The Graf Zeppelin *floating in the morning fog, waiting for passengers to board.*

(BOTTOM)

Passengers on the Graf Zeppelin purchased large-sized tickets for their flight, in this case an airship journey from Brazil to Germany in August 1933.

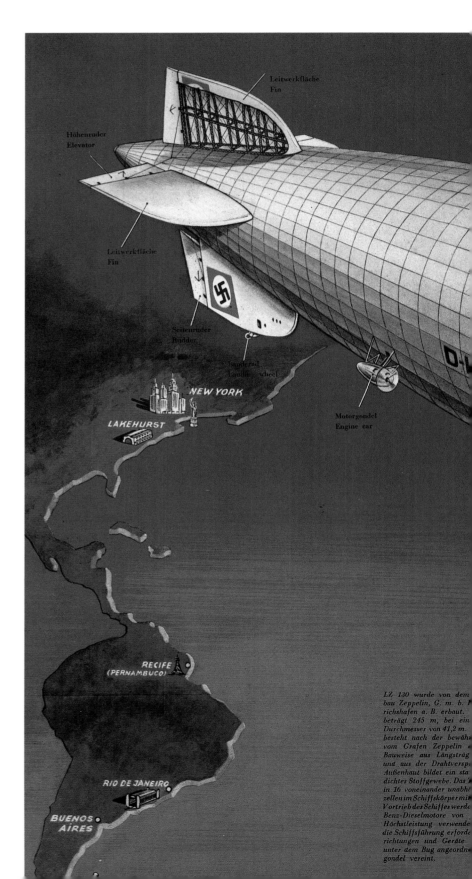

A cutaway drawing from a Zeppelin factory brochure showing the design for the proposed second Graf Zeppelin, the LZ-130. The sketch gives a sense of the enormous size and the accommodations of airships during their heyday in the 1930s.

LZ 130 „Graf Zeppelin"

Längsträger
Longitudinal girders

Hilfsring
Intermediate ring

Hauptring
Main ring

Entlüftungshutzen
Ventilation hoods

Entlüftungsschacht
Ventilating shaft

Gaszelle
Gas cell

Achssteg
Axial corridor

Küche
Kitchen

Speisesaal
Dining room

Rauchzimmer und
Trinking room

Treiböl
Diesel oil

Fracht
Freight

Mannschaftsräume
Crew's quarters

Halle
Lounge

Kabinen
Cabins

Navigationsraum
Navigating room

Führergondel
Control car

Anker-Konus
Bow mooring cone

FRANKFURT a. M
HALLE I

HALLE

RHEIN-MAIN

Count Ferdinand von Zeppelin (at left with a white hat) with the crew of an airship.

Loading mail bags on an airship. Carrying air mail, often with commemorative stamps, did much to popularize airship travel.

There was always the fear that a sudden blast of air or shift in the attitude of the airship could cast a rigger overboard. Being on the R-34 certainly had its intoxicating moments.

For the trip to North America, the R-34 followed the great circle route, leaving near Glasgow on July 2 and then taking a steady path across the North Atlantic to Newfoundland, Nova Scotia, and the United States. The initial hours of the flight were spent on a slow ascent to altitude because the airship was burdened with over 4,000 gallons of fuel for the engines. The R-34 consumed this large reservoir of fuel only gradually. One great fear was that the R-34 would exhaust its fuel reserves against strong headwinds and storms, a situation where the dirigible would find itself drifting aimlessly over the ocean. By the morning of the third day, the crew of the R-34 spotted icebergs for the first time, a grim reminder of the dangers that the North Atlantic held for ocean-going vessels; memories of the *Titanic* disaster of 1912 still persisted in everyone's mind. The R-34 flew well above any dangers from icebergs, but the airship could not escape the severe weather at such northern latitudes.

The R-34 passed Newfoundland and then made steady progress southward along the coast of North America, reaching the gulf of the St. Lawrence, Nova Scotia, New England, and finally New York. There was one anxious moment over the Bay of Fundy, when a storm buffeted the huge R-34 about like a feather in the wind. The crew donned parachutes and lifebelts, fearing the R-34 might break up under the pressures. Yet, the R-34 passed through this gauntlet of bad weather unscathed.

The R-34 crossed over Montauk and continued eastward toward Hazelhurst Field, Mineola, for a landing. For the first time Scott and his crew could observe the traffic streaming

(TOP)

The spacious navigator's station on the Graf Zeppelin.

(BOTTOM)

The "bridge" or control room on the Graf Zeppelin *was fitted with a six-spoke wheel to steer the huge airship.*

out of New York City toward Mineola—crowds on their way to see the landing of the R-34. Upon reaching the landing site, there were only 140 gallons of fuel remaining—the R-34 had reached its goal, but only with the narrowest of margins. The R-34 was secured at Hazelhurst Field at 1:54 p.m. on Sunday, July 6, 1919. The extraordinary flight to the United States from Scotland had taken 108 hours and 12 minutes.

President Woodrow Wilson hosted a gala reception for Major Scott and the crew of the R-34 on the last day of their visit to the United States at the Town Hall in New York City. Popular interest in the R-34 and its crew was intense for the brief period prior to the return flight to Great Britain. Taken on board the R-34 for this return leg were a number of things: a vast quantity of letters, copies of American newspapers such as the *Philadelphia Public Ledger*, and a film of the Jack Dempsey–Jess Williard fight. Even Thomas Edison took a keen interest in the R-34, offering the crew a new gramophone with a fresh stockpile of records.

On the night of July 9, the R-34 took off from Mineola for the return trip to Great Britain. Taking advantage of a strong tail wind from the southwest, the R-34 made a memorable pass over New York City. Once over Manhattan, searchlights caught the R-34, even as the crew took in the nightlights of the city. Crowds gathered in the streets around Broadway to cheer the R-34 as it set a course for the return flight across the North Atlantic. Running now on four engines, the R-34 cleared the American coast by 2:17 a.m. The return trip covered 3,811 miles. The R-34 reached Pulham at 6:57 a.m. on July 13. Favorable winds and decent weather allowed the airship to sustain a faster speed on the homeward journey, averaging around 50 miles per hour, with a total flying time of 75 hours, 3 minutes—roughly three days over the Atlantic.

The Graf Zeppelin, *along with its sister airship, the* Hindenburg, *offered elegant accommodations for its passengers. Only the very wealthy could afford airship travel, which provided unique luxury for those seeking passage across continents and oceans.*

Private cabins matched those on ocean liners in style and appointments. However, the brightly flowered "walls" of the Graf Zeppelin *were lightweight frames covered with floral-decorated fabric.*

The saga of the R-34 became a harbinger for subsequent transoceanic and far-ranging global flights by airships. Hugo Eckener, who assumed leadership of the Zeppelin firm after the death of Ferdinand von Zeppelin in 1917, piloted the LZ-126 across the Atlantic in 1924. This particular dirigible had been built especially for the United States as part of the war reparations agreement of the Treaty of Versailles (1919). This particular airship was renamed the *Los Angeles.* It was ironic that Eckener, who had played no small role in the development of Zeppelins for the German army in World War I, now became one of the most visible leaders in adapting the Zeppelin technology for peaceful civilian uses.

Eckener's greatest moments as an airship commander came at the helm of the giant *Graf Zeppelin.* This fabled airship made 590 flights, carrying a total of 13,100 passengers. In many ways, the *Graf Zeppelin* and its sister airship, the *Hindenburg,* represented the apogee of airship service, linking continents, transporting passengers to far-flung destinations, and establishing the first reliable air mail service between continents.

The crew of the *Graf Zeppelin* were alert to all dangers, taking great care to provide for the security of hydrogen-filled gas bags of the airship. Not all the dangers were internal, as the crew learned on the maiden crossing of the Atlantic in 1928. On the third morning of the voyage, just south of the Azores, Eckener steered the huge airship directly into the black shroud of an advancing ocean storm at full speed. A downdraft dipped the nose suddenly, only to give way to a violent updraft, propelling the unsuspecting passengers at breakfast into an unexpected oscillation that appeared to threaten the survival of the airship. People, along with their tables and chairs, moved forward and then backward in a

Caught in a convergence of searchlights, the Graf Zeppelin *takes on a ghostly aspect in the night sky.*

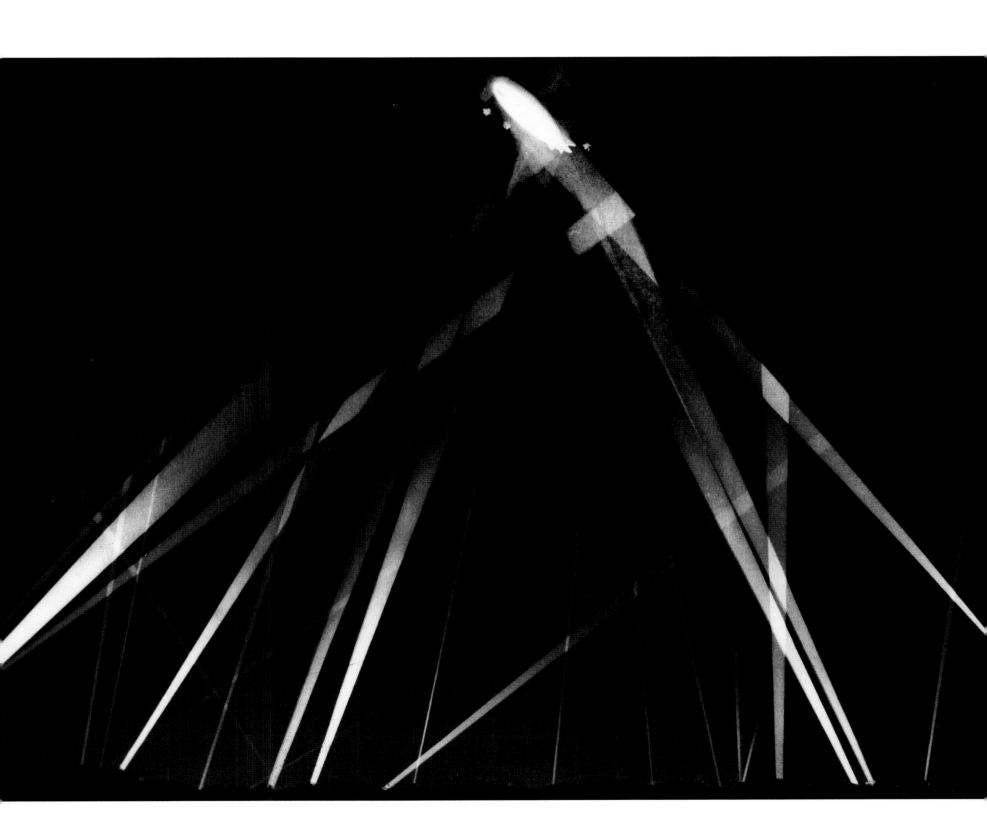

(TOP)

The Graf Zeppelin *casts its huge shadow over the cityscape of Sofia, Bulgaria. The photo was taken from the airship as it passed near the Orthodox Cathedral in the center of the Bulgarian capital.*

(BOTTOM)

When Adolf Hitler took power in 1933, his regime fully exploited the propaganda potential of airships, as evident in this photo of the Graf Zeppelin *in flight above Nazi banners in Germany.*

maelstrom of screams and crashing dishes, food, and tableware. The storm had torn away a portion of the fabric covering of the port stabilizer, with streaming cloth threatening to jam the control surfaces of the rudder and elevators. At great risk, volunteers climbed out on the exposed girders and managed to repair the damaged stabilizer while in flight. Over Bermuda, the airship endured another violent storm, and once again survived the unpredictable weather of the Atlantic. The *Graf Zeppelin* finally reached Lakehurst, New Jersey, in 111 hours and 44 minutes of nonstop flying. The fact that there was no reliable means of weather reporting for airships crossing the Atlantic made each voyage from Europe to America a dangerous undertaking.

The most ambitious voyage of the *Graf Zeppelin* came in 1929, when Eckener made a highly publicized around-the-world flight. Five years before, a team of American army pilots had made an around-the-world flight in two Douglas World Cruiser aircraft (they had started with four aircraft). Such trips were arduous and fraught with mechanical mishaps and delays; the airplanes had departed Seattle and returned home after six months, making a total of 72 stops along the way. Eckener hoped to outclass this earlier circumnavigation of the globe in terms of speed, safety, and comfort to demonstrate that the airship, in fact, was the optimal means of air travel across great distances.

Eckener's around-the-world saga originated at Lakehurst, New Jersey, on August 7, 1929, with an initial leg to the Zeppelin home base at Friedrichschafen, Germany. Then on August 15, Eckener set out with 20 passengers and 43 crewmen. While each passenger was allowed a mere 50 pounds of luggage, the *Graf Zeppelin* offered in its spacious gondola luxurious appointments, not unlike a modern ocean

(TOP)
The Graf Zeppelin *on a transoceanic flight path. Passengers avidly photographed the spectacular views offered by the slow-flying* Graf Zeppelin *and her sister airships.*

(BOTTOM)
The Graf Zeppelin *over Washington, D.C., in 1928, offering a close-up perspective of the Lincoln Memorial and the unfinished Memorial Bridge across the Potomac River.*

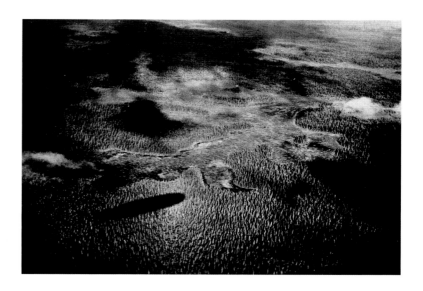

liner. Moving slowly, depending on the availability of a tail wind, the airship might typically cruise at 70–75 miles per hour. This lumbering speed meant a lot of leisure time en route, prompting passengers to attend to their diaries, write letters or postcards, play cards, pull out their cameras to capture images of the unfolding towns and countryside below, or listen to the phonograph. Food was plentiful and of a high quality: salmon, meats, including venison, an assortment of vegetables and fruits, pastries, and wine.

The *Graf Zeppelin* appeared to many as a Jules Verne incarnation, the "clipper of the skies." Eckener controlled the airship from a spacious control room linked to separate chambers for radio and navigation. The spacious airship also boasted a kitchen and dining hall. For the passengers, there were 10 double state rooms. These rooms were not austere, appointed with flower decor wall coverings, vanity tables with sinks, and windows with curtains. A sofa filled one side of the chamber, which could be reconfigured as a bed at night. For dinner and other meals, the *Graf Zeppelin* used special porcelain dishes and tableware. Elegance and comfort dictated the design of the airship.

For the crew, of course, the accommodations were spartan. Typically, two crew were assigned to each cabin, where they slept on hammocks or narrow mattresses. The crew was large, to allow around-the-clock shifts, with three people assigned to each post. Depending on the time of day, crewmen worked two- or three-hour shifts. Given the many special functions of the airship, the *Graf Zeppelin* hired crew with a variety of skills, from electricians to cooks to engine technicians.

The *Graf Zeppelin* took a northeasterly heading out of Friedrichshafen, then a great circle flight path over the

Danube, northern Germany, East Prussia, and finally the vast Soviet Union. The fact that the Zeppelin planned to move across the continental mass of revolutionary Russia, through a total of eleven time zones, to reach Asia gave the voyage a special significance. The arching trajectory of the airship meant sweeping across northern Russia above Moscow, across the cities of Vologda and Perm into Siberia. Being so far north brought a chill to the airship, forcing passengers to wear fur coats in their cabins.

Relentlessly, the *Graf Zeppelin* continued its journey, passing over forest and marshland into the largely uninhabited northern reaches of Siberia. Once Eckener and company reached Yakutsk on the Lena River, there was a sense of triumph. Eckener flew the airship over the remote trading center, dropping bags of mail to be sent home. Ahead were mountains to traverse, many still uncharted, but the *Graf Zeppelin* cleared these formidable natural obstacles without mishap. On the evening of August 19, wildly enthusiastic crowds greeted the *Graf Zeppelin* at Tokyo and Yokohama. Eckener had steered his craft over 7,700 miles.

The passage across the North Pacific to San Francisco proved to be less dramatic, with a total of 67 hours for the ocean crossing. Much of the flight path had been shrouded in fog and mist, so the passengers saw little on this leg of the journey. The *Graf Zeppelin* reached the Golden Gate on the afternoon of August 25, prompting a spirited response by the locals. Hundreds of ships filled San Francisco harbor to welcome the remarkable flying machine. After receiving the plaudits of San Francisco, the *Graf Zeppelin* continued on to Los Angeles, landing at Mines Field, completing a voyage of 79 hours from Tokyo.

The final leg for the *Graf Zeppelin* called for a leisurely transcontinental flight across the United States from California to Lakehurst, New Jersey—a flight that took 52 hours and covered some 3,000 miles. Unlike a modern airliner flying above 35,000 feet today, the *Graf Zeppelin*— typically flying below 12,000 feet—afforded its passengers a unique platform to see the country in a low-level trajectory—a dramatic sequence of vistas that included deserts, mountains, rivers, farms, villages, and major cities. Once the airship reached the east coast, there were a series of celebrations, including a ticker-tape parade in New York City and later a reception at the White House, where President Herbert Hoover compared the aerial feat of the *Graf Zeppelin* to the feats of Columbus and Magellan. For the record, the airship had traveled a stunning 20,500 miles in 12 days.

The impressive voyage of the *Graf Zeppelin* did not necessarily consolidate the airship's apparent hold on transcontinental commercial travel. The airplane, beginning with the DC-3 airliner in the mid-1930s, challenged the airship for dominance in commercial travel. Airplanes were faster and soon would possess the range and load capacity to make them the preferred mode of commercial travel. The whole dirigible era ended abruptly at Lakehurst, New Jersey, in May 1937, when the *Hindenburg*—the largest flying machine ever built—was destroyed in a fiery inferno. This air tragedy exposed the inherent dangers of the airship.

As a footnote, the *Graf Zeppelin* survived into World War II. But in that wartime context few in Germany saw any military utility in the venerable airship. The head of the Luftwaffe, Herman Goering, ordered the famous airship scrapped in 1940, with remnants of its metal structure used to build a radar tower.

*Escorted by a U.S. Coast Guard
Douglas RD-4 Dolphin Flying
Boat, the* Graf Zeppelin *flies over
the huge airship shed, or hangar, at
Lakehurst, New Jersey.*

JOHNSON
PATHFINDER TO AUSTRALIA

THE WORLD took notice of Amy Johnson in May 1930. A newcomer to long-distance flying, she had flown alone in her single-engine Gipsy Moth biplane, *Jason*, from London to Darwin, Australia. Her 19 ¹/₂-day aerial trek across the Middle East, India, Burma, Singapore, and the Dutch East Indies (present-day Indonesia) had not established a new air record, but for women aviators this flight represented an important milestone. Many of her contemporaries were stunned when they learned that the young woman from Yorkshire, England, had undertaken this high-risk flight across the Asian subcontinent with a mere 85 hours recorded in her flight log.

Johnson's origins were distinctly nonaristocratic. She was the daughter of a fish merchant from Hull, England. Born on July 1, 1903, just months before the Wright brothers flew, she grew up to be a strong-willed woman, keen on finding her place in the world—even if it required entry into competitive realms typically run by men. For a brief period in the 1920s, she attended Sheffield University. Her incompatibility with academic life, however, quickly became apparent, and she struck out on her own. For a period of time, Johnson worked with her father, followed by a stint as a clerical worker with an advertising agency in London. Such jobs offered a means of survival, but little more. Amy Johnson aspired to live a more adventurous life.

When she joined the London Aeroplane Club in 1928, Johnson quickly developed a passion for flying. Seeing the airplane as a vehicle to a new life, she earned her pilot's license and then a second license as a ground engineer (powerplant mechanic). No one questioned her high seriousness when it came to aviation as her new chosen profession. Her natural bent for flying became evident to her peers when she soloed after only 16 hours of flight instruction. Once licensed, she displayed a shrewd instinct for self-promotion, seeking out patrons in the male-dominated world of aviation.

While still green as a pilot, Johnson decided to promote herself as a long-distance flyer. She told a reporter that she aimed to break Bert Hinkler's 1928 record of flying from England to Australia in 15¹/₂ days. Being a neophyte in every respect and lacking any sort of position of influence in the British aeronautical community, she must have realized that her chances were, at best, a long shot.

Flying from England to Australia offered unique challenges even for the most skilled long-distance pilot. Two Australian lieutenants, Ray Parer and John McIntosh,

(ABOVE)

Amy Johnson made her debut as a woman aviator in 1930, flying from London to Australia. At the time of her extraordinary long-distance aerial trek, she had only limited experience as a pilot. However, her background included training in aircraft propulsion, where she held a license as an aircraft engine mechanic or "ground engineer."

(OPPOSITE)

Enthusiastic crowds greet Amy Johnson's motorcade in Australia in 1930.

Amy Johnson's de Havilland DH. 60G Gipsy Moth, Jason, *which she flew from London to Darwin, now on display at the Science Museum, London.*

made the pioneering aerial jaunt to Australia in 1920. While awaiting repatriation home at the conclusion of World War I, the two men heard of a prize of £10,000 for the first aviator(s) to link England and Australia by air.

Their remarkable odyssey in a war surplus DH. 9 biplane mirrored all the perils, human and mechanical, that one could imagine on a long-distance flight. Fuel pump problems, a defective magneto, and bolts popping from the propeller proved to be only minor mishaps. While over the Adriatic Sea, the engine caught fire, which was extinguished by putting the DH. 9 into a steep dive. Because of repeated mechanical breakdowns they took 44 days to reach Cairo, with only 40 hours of actual flying. Over the Saudi Arabian desert, they were forced to make an emergency landing for repairs, only to be met by marauding tribesmen intent on robbing them: while Parer hurriedly made repairs, McIntosh held off the attackers by tossing grenades and firing a revolver.

Parer and McIntosh managed to extricate themselves from one crisis after another as they continued their arduous journey across India, the Dutch East Indies, and the Timor Sea to Australia. Parer aptly remarked, "We'll fly this bloody crate till it falls to bits at our feet." They managed to reach Baghdad, endure two major crashes, spent six weeks in a jungle field making repairs, and landed triumphantly in Darwin with only a single pint of fuel remaining in the DH. 9's tank.

Johnson encountered many of the same obstacles and dangers faced by Parer and McIntosh, but she took pains to approach her long-distance flight to Australia with greater attention to planning. To set a new air record, Johnson realized the importance of proper backing. Financial

Amy Johnson with her flying gear strides next to her de Havilland DH. 60 Cirrus Moth. As a prominent aviator in the decade of the 1930s, Johnson flew a variety of aircraft, including aircraft equipped for long-distance flying.

support for her project became the first hurdle. Johnson's father provided a base line of support in the form of cash.

This timely parental stipend allowed her to abandon her labors as an office worker and to purchase an airplane. She then canvassed a number of prominent figures to seek out their financial support, an initiative that won her the enthusiastic support of Lord Wakefield, the Castrol oil company magnate. As her patron, Lord Wakefield played a key role in placing adequate stores of fuel along the projected flight path to Australia.

Johnson selected a de Havilland DH. 60G Gipsy Moth biplane, dubbed *Jason*, for her epic flight to Australia. The *Jason* was a small, single-seat, open cockpit design, equipped with additional fuel tank capacity for the long journey. While the Gipsy Moth cruised at only 85 miles per hour, it was a sturdy and reliable flying machine, powered by a four-cylinder air-cooled engine of 100 horsepower. While the small biplane certainly lacked power and speed, it possessed great range, the most critical factor for any flight across continents and oceans.

The flight itself began with little fanfare at dawn on May 5, 1930. A small crowd of friends and family gathered at Croyden Airport to see Johnson off. The first day called for a crossing of the English Channel and a more-or-less direct flight through French air space to Asperne airport in Vienna, Austria. This initial leg ended at 5:50 p.m. and recorded over 800 miles. Johnson encountered no problems, only the fatigue of such a long journey.

The second leg, from Vienna to Istanbul, began the next day, although the departure actually took place at mid-morning, not at dawn as planned. This jaunt called for another 800 miles and Johnson faced the challenge of

Refueling Amy Johnson's biplane,
Jason, *while en route from London*
to Australia.

Amy Johnson in the open cockpit of her biplane, Jason. *Her route across deserts, mountains, and oceans offered few airfields with ample* supplies of spare parts. *Consequently, Johnson took certain critical spares with her, as evident in the propeller tied to the side of the* Jason.

(TOP)

Amy Johnson taxis the Jason *to a stop after reaching Australia.*

(MIDDLE)

Local dignitaries and an enthusiastic crowd greet Amy Johnson upon her arrival in Australia.

(BOTTOM)

After returning to London from Australia, Amy Johnson speaks to a crowd at Croydon airport.

reaching her destination before sunset. She spent a total of 12 hours aloft that day, landing at Istanbul's San Stefano Aerodrome in the evening. Again there was no mishap or difficulty, except for rain storms encountered while crossing the Balkans.

On May 7, the third day out, Johnson once again found herself flying over some rugged terrain—the Taurus Mountains of Turkey, with peaks as high as 12,000 feet. Her goal that day was the airfield at Aleppo, in Syria, 550 miles from Istanbul. Flying through turbulent air at 8,000 feet, she encountered dense clouds, forcing her to fly over a long stretch of mountainous terrain with minimal visibility. At times in the narrow passage through the mountains, the wings of her airplane came within feet of the steep rocky edge of mountains. Once she made it through the treacherous passage, she elected to follow a railway line into Aleppo. Being alone over such a hostile environment in an austerely equipped airplane that lacked a radio offered a daunting challenge to the young woman from Hull.

The fourth day brought violent storms along the flight path from Aleppo to Baghdad. The new challenge was untimely because, at this juncture, Johnson was still ahead of Bert Hinkler's record pace. This particular leg called for a flight of 470 miles, mostly across desert. The first few hours over this austere stretch of territory went well. Then, unexpectedly, she encountered a strong gale, which forced her downward relentlessly from 7,000 feet to nearly ground level, despite all her efforts to retain altitude. Dense clouds of sand obscured the flight path, so she decided to land in the desert.

Once down on the ground and with fierce winds buffeting the *Jason*, Johnson hurriedly positioned luggage

The de Havilland DH. 80A Puss Moth Jason II, *flown by Johnson from England to Toyko, Japan, in July 1931. The following year she made another memorable flight from London to Cape Town, earning the young English aviator additional fame as a long-distance flier.*

Amy Johnson's DH. 80A arrives at Croydon airport after her return from Tokyo in 1931.

Amy Johnson and her Jason II *airplane at the conclusion of her historic flight to Tokyo.*

and tool boxes at the wheels to prevent the airplane from being flipped over. There was little she could do, except to wait out the storm. Two hours passed and the storm abated enough to allow another takeoff. Once airborne, she managed to locate the Tigris River, a sure benchmark to plot the final course into Baghdad. She landed at the British-run Imperial Airways airport at Baghdad on May 8, prompting a great outpouring of relief among those who had watched the skies anxiously for her arrival.

Baghdad offered more of an emotional respite than a physical one. Amy Johnson realized that her sojourn in this welcome place could only be momentary if she planned to break Hinkler's record. So, on May 9, she was aloft again—on her way to Bander Abbas, some 840 miles to the southeast on the Persian Gulf. Upon landing, she suffered a setback when one of the wing struts broke, but this was quickly repaired and she was off to Karachi the next day, May 10, covering another 730 miles.

Reaching Karachi—then a city in British India—in a mere six days set an absolute record for a solo flight from London. At this juncture Johnson was two days ahead of Bert Hinkler's record flight. She was greeted in Karachi as a new heroine of the air. It was remarkable indeed that this young and inexperienced flyer had done so well against such formidable odds. The momentum for breaking the Hinkler mark and setting a new record appeared strong. Yet, fate would soon bring a sequence of challenges that would destroy Amy Johnson's fond hope of setting a new record; ahead was the most difficult stretch of the aerial trek to Australia.

Departing for Allahabad in British India on May 11, Johnson discovered that her fuel capacity dictated that she

(TOP)

*Amy Johnson at her home in
London, preparing for her 1936
solo flight from London to Cape
Town, South Africa.*

(MIDDLE)

*The Percival Gull Six aircraft
flown by Amy Johnson in 1936.*

(BOTTOM)

*Johnson makes a radio broadcast
after her return to England from
Australia on December 18, 1932.*

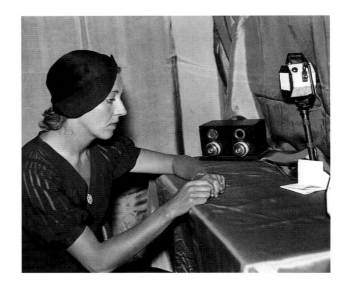

plan a shorter trip, one that required her to land at a parade
ground at Jhansi. This unanticipated stop—some 200
miles short of Allahabad—brought near disaster: when she
landed she crashed the *Jason* into a post, damaging one
wing. While inspecting the damage, she realized the
problem was not as serious as she had thought. Everything
worked out well; a local carpenter and tailor quickly
repaired the smashed wing. The local British army garrison
provided the essential fuel to resume the journey. By the
next morning she was airborne and on her way to
Allahabad, where she refueled quickly and headed for
Calcutta. Despite strong head winds, she landed
successfully at the Dumdum airfield at Calcutta on the
evening of May 12.

As the flight unfolded, Johnson became increasingly
fatigued from the rigors of flying 10 to 12 hours a day with
little more than three to four hours of sleep each night.
The pressure to break Hinkler's record often meant risky
flights into bad weather conditions. This was the case on
May 13, when Johnson began the arduous passage from
Calcutta to Rangoon, Burma—approximately 650 miles.
Despite the grim weather projections, she departed Calcutta
at 7:00 a.m. She encountered rain storms and strong head
winds. The *Jason* passed successfully over the Yomas range,
but then the visibility only worsened, forcing Johnson
to descend to about 200 feet. Finally, she decided to fly
to the Burmese coast and then hug the coast until she
reached Rangoon.

The intended landing spot was the Rangoon race track.
However, Amy Johnson could not locate the track in the
rain and overcast. Seeing a large soccer field, she descended
for what became a perfect landing. But her success quickly

In 1933, Amy Johnson and her pilot-husband, Jim Mollison, flew a de Havilland DH. 84 Dragon, the Seafarer, *from Pendine Sands, Wales, to New York. The long-* distance flight to New York was designed to set the stage for another flight, a long-distance trek from New York to Baghdad.

gave way to an unexpected accident: while taxiing across the wet playing field, she ran the *Jason* into a ditch. resulting damage to the wings, undercarriage, and propeller—if not fatal to the ultimate goal of reaching Australia—meant a costly delay, one that ended any chance of breaking Hinker's record.

Again, Johnson found herself aided by strangers who were more than willing to repair the damage to the Gipsy Moth. The soccer field, as it turned out, belonged to an engineering school. Both faculty and students looked upon the *Jason* with great fascination and made elaborate plans to repair it. Johnson had brought a spare propeller with her, which she had strapped to the side of the fuselage during the long passage from London to Rangoon.

Repair of the wing went well, although there was a momentary crisis on how the new fabric patch could be glued in place. The locals devised a clever way to resolve this problem: a druggist came up with a special improvised dope to make the fabric adhere to the wing. Soon the *Jason* was airworthy again.

The necessary repairs at Rangoon consumed three precious days. After a few test flights at the Rangoon aerodrome, Amy Johnson felt confident that she could resume her flight to Australia. The next leg was relatively short, a 340-mile flight from Rangoon to Bangkok. But the weather again posed a problem, with constant rain and minimal visibility. Rather than wait for the uncertain arrival of good weather, Johnson decided to press on to Bangkok. The most difficult challenge came when she had to pass through a narrow mountain pass in low clouds and rain. Once Johnson had cleared this natural barrier, she discovered that she was lost with no clear landmarks to

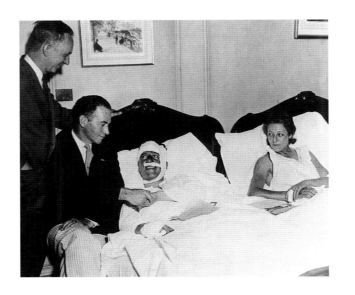

guide her. Finally, after some confusion, she discovered a railroad leading toward Bangkok. Her arrival there was timely—the *Jason* was nearly out of fuel when it landed.

Flying southeastward on May 17–18, Johnson covered the Malay Peninsula to Singapore. This leg proved largely carefree, except for some strong head winds along the way and the fact that the substitute propeller operated in a less-than-optimal way. On the approach to Singapore, Johnson found herself escorted to the local aerodrome by two Royal Air Force aircraft. Upon landing, she dined at the RAF officers' club. Singapore also offered a welcome rest and a chance to make further repairs to her Gipsy Moth.

The next obstacle facing Johnson was the long journey over the Dutch East Indies (today Indonesia). Her flight plan called for an initial leg of 1,000 miles to Surabaya on the island of Java. But these plans were soon altered by a series of emergencies, forcing a landing at Tjomal, in central Java. The malfunctioning propeller caused her great alarm and compelled her to cruise at less than full speed. Worst of all, she discovered her airplane was very low on fuel—some 200 miles short of Surabaya. Looking for an emergency field, Johnson could only find an open area on a sugar plantation. To her credit, she placed the *Jason* down on this postage stamp area with great skill. However, the landing path took her across a field where some bamboo stakes had been laid to mark a future construction site. The bamboo poles scraped the underside of one wing, causing significant damage.

The local plantation owner was hospitable and he offered his unexpected guest a place to rest while the *Jason* was repaired once again. The only means available to repair the wing was adhesive tape—a crude, if effective, way to patch the torn fabric. Finding fuel for the airplane proved to be easier. On the morning of May 20, Johnson took to the air for the Surabaya airfield. For this critical leg, a Dutch mail plane served as an escort.

Further perils awaited Johnson in the Dutch East Indies. Departing Surabaya on May 22, she aimed to reach Atambua, some 900 miles away, at the end of the day. For those at Atambua, alerted to Johnson's flight plans, there was considerable concern that evening when the *Jason* did not appear; they feared she had crashed. On the following morning news reached Atambua that Johnson had made an emergency landing at Haliluik, only 12 miles away. There was no telephone in the small village, so news of her whereabouts could not be forwarded. Her landing at Haliluik, in a remote tropical area, had aroused the keen interest of the locals, who took her to the local Catholic priest. A night at the mission provided welcome shelter. By May 23, Johnson finally reached Atambua, the launch point for the final phase of her aerial trek to Australia.

To make the hop from Atumbua to Port Darwin on the northern coast of Australia, Johnson had to cross the Timor Sea—a total of 500 miles of open water characterized by strong head winds. The slow-moving *Jason*—cruising at 85 miles per hour—would have to perform well on this last phase of the journey. Any ditching in the vast and isolated Timor Sea would surely mean death; Johnson realized that there was little chance of rescue if she failed to make it across this vast stretch of water.

She departed on May 24, Empire Day. Nearly three weeks had passed since her takeoff from Croyden Airport in London. Having crossed some 9,900 miles of territory in Europe, the Middle East, the Indian subcontinent, and the

Amy Johnson outfitted in her full flying suit, including parachute.

Dutch East Indies, the elusive goal of Australia was now in sight. The weather over the Timor Sea was excellent. Midway across the watery barrier, the *Jason* passed over a Shell Oil tanker, the *Phorus*, which signaled Port Darwin that Amy Johnson was en route. This news prompted several pilots at the Port Darwin airport to fly out to greet the *Jason*. But they failed to find the elusive British aviator. Alone and quietly, Amy Johnson arrived over Australia at 3:30 p.m.

Following her successful landing, Johnson became the object of popular acclaim in Australia and throughout the world as a result of radio and press coverage. The press heralded the young woman pilot as one of the heroines of the air age. The passage to Australia had been remarkable, especially for such an inexperienced pilot. There were messages from the king and queen; Ramsey MacDonald, the British prime minister; and various dignitaries across the globe.

Amy Johnson had flown 11,000 miles, the first woman to fly alone to Australia from England. Her subsequent career in aviation lasted little more than a decade. In 1932 and 1936, she set two world records for flights from London to Cape Town. She married famed pilot Jim Mollison, only to divorce him in 1938. The shortlived marriage included several record-breaking flights as the "Mollisons."

With the advent of World War II, Johnson joined the Air Transport Auxiliary, ferrying aircraft from British factories to operational RAF air bases. On one ferrying mission, on January 5, 1941, she crashed into the Thames Estuary and drowned under mysterious circumstances. As with Amelia Earhart, Johnson's death has sparked no small amount of debate and speculation.

BANNING AND ALLEN
FLYING AGAINST PREJUDICE

DEPRESSION-ERA America was a time when Jim Crow laws still dominated the South and widespread racial discrimination existed in other parts of the country. African-Americans faced daunting challenges. There were segregated seats on buses and trains, racial exclusion at many hotels and restaurants, and widespread barriers to prevent blacks from obtaining training in technical fields. James Herman Banning belonged to a small company of black pilots who had overcome the racism of the era by qualifying for a pilot's license. His achievement was a splendid display of will and flair for flying, but for Banning his career in aviation became one of isolation and obscurity.

This was an era of aerial spectaculars, a time when pilots vied with one another to set new air records. Banning personally dreamed of setting a new air record for himself and his race: a transcontinental flight from Dycer Field in Los Angeles to Valley Stream airport in Long Island, New York. Banning hoped such a flight, if successful, would demonstrate that the new air age was open to all races.

He obtained his flight training in Iowa in 1927, shortly after Charles Lindbergh made his flight across the Atlantic to Paris. Banning had sought out an individual flight instructor, a veteran fighter pilot of World War I, who agreed to give him flight lessons. For many blacks aspiring to become pilots, this was often the only realistic possibility to enter the field of aviation. In the case of one black pilot, C. Alfred Anderson, he had to purchase his own plane in advance before a white instructor agreed to offer him flight training.

Most aeronautical schools routinely barred blacks from admission. There was a widespread notion that blacks were not to be included into the new air age or, for that matter, any technical career. Echoing the bias of the time, the United States Army Air Corps, in a 1925 formal study, determined that blacks lacked the physical aptitude and mental acuity to become pilots. This convenient "scientific" document gave the Air Corps license to continue a policy of strict racial discrimination. This restrictive policy would be enshrined in the Air Corps until the eve of World War II, when a small group of black cadets were trained in Alabama and later became the Tuskegee Airmen. Most whites shared the popular attitude that blacks lacked any capacity for technical jobs, particularly aviation, and that all blacks should be relegated to menial jobs.

Richard Wright captured the grim reality of racism in Depression America in his celebrated novel, *Native Son*, where he imaginatively tells a story of two black youths

(ABOVE)

James Herman Banning belonged to a small group of licensed black pilots in the late 1920s.

(OPPOSITE)

Banning in the cockpit of his "Miss Ames" during his brief career as a barnstormer.

(TOP)

Bessie Coleman won her pilot's license from FAI (Federation Aeronautique Internationale) on June 15, 1921.

(BOTTOM)

William J. Powell, Jr., a successful Chicago businessman, moved to Los Angeles in 1928 to train as a pilot. He is pictured here in World War I, when he served as an infantry officer in an all-black unit in the American Expeditionary Force.

watching a pilot perform intricate aerobatics. "I could fly a plane if I had a chance," the one youngster says. But his companion responds, "If you wasn't black and if you had some money and if they'd let you go to that aviation school, you could fly that plane." The message was clear: blacks were not part of the air age.

Wright wrote his novel at a time when aviators enjoyed immense popular esteem. This was the so-called Golden Age of Flight, roughly the two decades after World War I (1919–1939). Certain names from that era have lingered in our historical memory—Charles Lindbergh and Amelia Earhart, to name just two. Both men and women aviators pushed the envelope in these years, flying "faster, farther, and higher." It was a time for air heroes and dreams of aviation transforming the world. Blacks suffered under the unique circumstance of being the only group excluded on racial grounds from participation in this new realm of technology.

Despite the barriers, a few blacks had managed to break into the elite world of aviation. One in particular stood out: Bessie Coleman. Growing up in poverty, Coleman displayed a fierce determination to break into the aeronautical world. She became one of the first women to obtain a pilot's license, having traveled to France to study at an aeronautical school in 1920. She returned to the United States and made a brief career for herself as a barnstormer before her untimely death in 1926. For Banning and other black youth, Coleman occupied a special niche in the pantheon of great aviators, being a sort of shooting star and a source of inspiration for those who aspired to become pilots even in the face of the entrenched racism of the era.

Banning's prospects for entering the world of aviation mirrored the dismal reality of Wright's novel, but his passion for flying equalled Bessie Coleman's. As with his generation, regardless of race, Banning expressed great admiration for Charles Lindbergh and his epic transatlantic flight of 1927. Moreover, Banning's own sense of adventure prompted an admiration for the barnstormers, those stunt pilots who thrilled large crowds with death-defying aerial maneuvers. At county fairs or on an isolated farm field, the barnstormers would arrive to perform and take awe-struck onlookers for their first airplane ride. They performed intricate aerial maneuvers, loops, spins, wing walking, and parachute jumping.

Among the small coterie of licensed black pilots, there was one genuine visionary—William J. Powell, Jr. He stood out in those times for his spirited appeal to black youth. Powell realized that blacks were largely spectators in the new air age, but he did not accept this condition as natural or permanent. His optimism stemmed from his own assessment of the air age. He saw the airplane as an invention with universal meaning, not just the plaything of one race or nation. Powell dreamed of a time when black pilots would be commonplace, when a black-owned airline would compete with other air carriers, and when blacks would be admitted into military aviation. Most important for Banning, Powell was an enthusiastic supporter of his proposed transcontinental flight. He was able to be a patron for black involvement in aviation, since he had liquidated a small chain of gas stations in Chicago prior to his move to California.

Powell convinced Banning to join him in Los Angeles in 1931, to become a lead pilot for the newly organized Bessie

One Million Jobs for Negroes

★

READ BLACK WINGS
Are Negroes planning to quit riding the segregated railroads and busses in the South?

READ BLACK WINGS
Are Negroes afraid to fly?

READ BLACK WINGS
Why are so few Negroes in Business and Industry?

READ BLACK WINGS

Romance	. . . . Mistrust	Race Prejudice
Adventure	. . . Perseverance	Patriotism
History	Science	Superstition
Sacrifice	Fiction	Intrigue
Skepticism		Tragedy

The Negro in Aviation

ALL THESE ARE COMBINED IN BLACK WINGS
by LIEUT. WILLIAM J. POWELL

★

EVERY AMERICAN SHOULD READ THIS BOOK

Send money order for $2.00 and book will be mailed you—Postage Prepaid.

CRAFTSMEN OF BLACK WINGS,
3408 Budlong Avenue,
Los Angeles, California

(TOP)

The Bessie Colman Flying Club in Los Angeles became an important center for blacks to learn to fly. The club offered classes, sponsored air shows, and established contact with black youth across the country who aspired to become pilots.

(BOTTOM)

A montage with photos of James Herman Banning and Thomas Allen and their Alexander Eaglerock biplane, which made the historic 1932 transcontinental flight.

Coleman Flying Club. Few black pilots of the time could match Banning in experience, with over 700 hours of flying recorded in his flight log. Banning had attended Iowa State College, in Ames, where he first became interested in flying. For a period of time, Banning worked the barnstorming circuit in the Midwest. This line of work offered few rewards, and even less money. But Powell's invitation offered a new arena for Banning to pursue his passion for aviation—southern California in the 1930s was a major center for aviation in the United States.

After reaching Los Angeles, Banning became a powerful force in the city's small segregated black aviation community. Powell had sponsored the first all-black air show at Los Angeles' Eastside Airport in December 1931. This event drew thousands, and by 1932 Banning had emerged as one of Powell's leading pilots. Banning and Powell endured one harrowing experience that same year when they were forced down in the desert of Mexico's Baja California on a long-distance flight. While Powell actively encouraged Banning in his quest to fly across the United States, he alone lacked the deep pockets to supply financial support. Also, the flying club lacked the financial resources to sponsor the proposed transcontinental flight.

Thomas C. Allen, a skilled mechanic with some flight instruction, had moved to Los Angeles from Oklahoma. He approached Banning with the proposal that he join the project. He also had a small amount of personal cash that he was willing to donate to the cause—not enough to subsidize the trip, for certain, but enough seed money to assure him a place in the cockpit.

There would still be an immense shortfall in money for fuel, hangar fees, and living expenses. Allen complained that

A surviving and fully restored Alexander Eaglerock biplane in flight. Banning and Allen flew a similar type from Los Angeles to New York in 1932.

First Lady Eleanor Roosevelt visited the Tuskegee Army Air Base in 1941, where she took a ride in one of the trainers.

(MIDDLE)

In Chicago, Cornelius Coffey organized aeronautics classes for blacks in the late 1920s.

(BOTTOM)

The Chicago-based Challenger Aero Club, organized by Cornelius Coffey and John C. Robinson, shown at their hangar in 1933.

they would be begging all the way across the country, "just like hobos." Banning retorted, that's fine, we will call ourselves the "Flying Hobos!" The historic flight across America would depend, literally, on the kindness of strangers.

For the 3,300-mile trek across the United States, Banning and Allen obtained a used Alexander Eaglerock biplane. Arthur Dennis, a local black businessman, made his Eaglerock available to the team, but told the duo that he could not provide any cash to sustain them. Dennis was keen on donating the Eaglerock for what he saw as an "honest effort to aid Negro progress" with a transcontinental flight.

Dennis himself had taken some flying lessons, and even soloed, but he did not wish to participate in such a high-risk demonstration flight. However, Dennis was confident that Banning possessed the skills and determination to make the flight a success. Banning and Allen were subsequently able to raise sufficient funds needed to cover the initial engine repairs on the Eaglerock, a new steel propeller, and money for fuel.

As it turned out, Banning and Allen had $25 between them as they began their transcontinental flight. Banning was supremely confident that the "Flying Hobos" could raise money along the way. He planned visits to black churches, where he would have a bully pulpit to preach his own "gospel of aviation" and the importance of blacks establishing a foothold in this new technology. The widely scattered black communities, he also correctly reasoned, were potential havens of support for the purchase of fuel and food. Fate might deal them an unfriendly hand, but they felt the transcontinental trek would garner

Images from a color documentary film produced by William J. Powell, Jr., in 1935. These film clips provide rare glimpses of the Bessie Coleman Flying Club in Los Angeles.

enthusiasm along the long flight path, perhaps even from whites.

The black press offered another crucial avenue of support. If the black newspapers covered the flight in progress, there was a strong possibility that enthusiasm would build within black communities across the nation. These same newspapers were attentive to the fact that the first transcontinental flight by blacks would also depend on the largess of whites. The *Chicago Defender*, one of the key black newspapers, reported that the team "had to depend on their ability to win and convince hostile whites with their sincerity and their personal worth in order to get the necessities of life, and for their plane's fuel."

For the flight across the United States, Banning selected a route that traversed Arizona, New Mexico, Texas—the American Southwest—and then took a northeasterly heading across the Midwest to New York. Reaching Yuma, Arizona, on the second day marked the flight's first milestone. The team of Banning and Allen, flying their used Alexander Eaglerock, had flown through the San Gorgonio Pass, successfully passing through one of the mountainous regions that stood in their way.

While in New Mexico, Allen sold his watch and spare suit to raise money for fuel. This proved to be only the first occasion where they had to improvise to sustain their journey.

En route over west Texas, they were forced to fly blind through heavy clouds and rain. There was the high risk of becoming disoriented and putting the Eaglerock into a potentially fatal spin. Banning later remarked that they were foolish to fly through this cloud formation without proper instruments: "Plenty of nerve—no sense!"

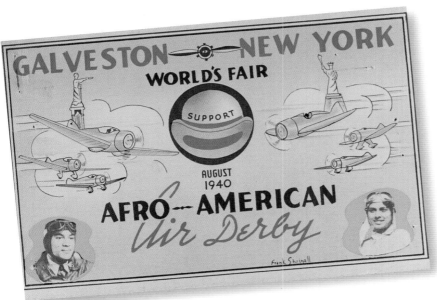

Each day, the flyers flew over a new geographical landmark— the Salton Sea, Tucson, El Paso, the Pecos River, and Oklahoma City. Allen typically sat in the front seat, with Banning in the pilot's position behind him. A church meeting raised a total of $11, just enough to keep them airborne. As each benefactor made a contribution, Banning inscribed the name of the person on the Eaglerock's left wingtip. One major supporter appeared in Tulsa in the person of businessman William Skelly, who provided enough funds for the trip as far as St. Louis.

On the leg to St. Louis, Banning made an emergency stop to repair the engine. The whole enterprise was salvaged when some white students at a trade school helped the team rebuild the tired Eaglerock engine with parts obtained from a 1928 Nash automobile in a junkyard.

The Banning and Allen duo slowly edged their way across the country: the Illinois farm country, followed by a sequence of stops at Terre Haute, Indiana, and the Ohio cities of Springfield and Columbus along historic U.S. Route 40. Farther along on their eastward heading, the Eaglerock developed engine problems over the hill country near the small town of Cambridge, Ohio. They were forced to make another emergency landing. Here, Banning made an extraordinary descent across fences and around trees to an open field. Banning remarked in the aftermath of his white-knuckle landing that "you don't die every time your motor does. Sure we are going to sleep under the wings tonight. Won't be the first time." The sojourn in Cambridge proved to be short and soon the intrepid aviators were on their way.

The next stop was Pittsburgh. Here they were welcomed enthusiastically by the black community. Also at the

After decades of exclusion, blacks were offered limited access to military aviation training at the Tuskegee Army Air Base in 1941. The pilots who trained at this segregated facility later became *known as the Tuskegee Airmen. The group photo (top) shows one class of cadets at Tuskegee. The poster (bottom) appealed to racial solidarity in World War II.*

Pittsburgh stopover, Banning and Allen met with a group of black dignitaries led by R. L. Vann, the editor of the black-owned *Pittsburgh Courier.* Vann proved to be an air enthusiast and did much to promote the transcontinental flight. He arranged for Banning and Allen to drop campaign literature for the Democratic candidate for president, Franklin Delano Roosevelt. They dropped over 15,000 leaflets as they moved across the wide expanse of Pennsylvania, passing the cities of Johnstown, Harrisburg, and Philadelphia.

The transcontinental flyers finally reached Valley Stream airport on Long Island, New York, on October 9, 1932. They had taken 22 days to complete their crossing of the United States. Their actual time in the air, however, was a mere 41 hours. While the mainstream press largely ignored Banning and Allen, they received a spirited welcome in New York City, where they visited the night clubs and met Cab Calloway and Duke Ellington. Learning of their transcontinental flight, New York City mayor Jimmie Walker gave the two black aviators the key to the city.

The script for the return trip called for Banning to fly the Eaglerock home to Los Angeles. This was never to occur. The Eaglerock crashed in Pennsylvania westbound. The two airmen were then forced to ride buses on the long trip back to California.

Thomas Allen lived on into the 1980s. He later opened his own flying school in Los Angeles and worked for many years at Douglas Aircraft. James Herman Banning's fate was tragic; he was killed in a plane crash in 1933, not as a pilot but as a passenger. "The dead aviator was a trail blazer," the *Pittsburgh Courier* stated at the time, "fearless, laughing at the odds, flirting with death, and the type of pioneer America could be proud of."

(ABOVE)

Benjamin O. Davis, Jr., led the Tuskegee Airmen in World War II, where they flew in the all-black 332nd Fighter Group in the 15th Air Force, serving in North Africa and Italy. In the postwar years, Davis became a general in the U.S. Air Force.

(RIGHT)

A painting by William Phillips depicting the air victory of Clarence "Lucky" Lester of the 332nd Fighter Group in his North American P-51D against a German fighter, in 1944.

CHKALOV
STALIN'S FALCONS OVER THE POLE

DURING THE GOLDEN AGE of Flight, many aviation enthusiasts considered Valery Chkalov to be "Russia's Lindbergh." The parallels are striking, if superficial: Chkalov—like Charles Lindbergh—was a national hero, a record-breaking pilot, and the subject of widespread public adoration in his native land. Soviet propaganda, in fact, took great pains in those days to cast Chkalov as the Russian counterpart to Lindbergh, if not his successor.

It should be noted that Chkalov's wild and impulsive persona stood in stark contrast to his taciturn American counterpart. The two men met only once, at an air show in the Soviet Union, in the summer of 1938. This dramatic encounter, as it turned out, came just a few months before Chkalov's untimely death while testing a new prototype fighter. The brief meeting of Lindbergh with Chkalov set the stage for a rather unseemly incident. Soviet newspapers accused Lindbergh of making some disparaging remarks about Soviet aviation, portraying it as a sort of cardboard reality—more propaganda than actual achievement. These purported remarks deeply offended Chkalov, who then openly and with the active encouragement of the Soviet propaganda agencies criticized Lindbergh for his praise of German aviation. Consequently, a huge chasm developed between the two national air heroes on the eve of Chkalov's death. Lindbergh, in fact, held rather negative views of Soviet aviation, but he had not openly attacked the Soviet aeronautical community.

The Soviet leader, Joseph Stalin, took great pains to promote aviation in the decade of the 1930s, at a time when he presided over a vast program of industrialization and social change. "Stalin's Falcons," as the Soviet's record-breaking pilots were called, performed aerial spectaculars in a studied effort to showcase and legitimize the Bolshevik regime. The airplane was an exemplar of modernity, in the same fashion as new factories, the construction of the Moscow Subway, and the building of hydroelectric dams.

This was an era of state-sponsored exploits to usher in a new world, one that would pave the way for communism. Herculean efforts were commonplace, such as the legendary travail of a miner named Aleksei Stakhanov, who mined 102 tons of coal on a single shift, giving birth to the "Stakhanovite movement" to rally workers to new levels of productivity. There was a studious praise of the grandiose. Everything was on a massive scale, even in the sphere of aviation: Stalin ordered his talented aircraft designer Andrei Tupolev to build the eight-engine *Maxim Gorky*, a giant red-winged aircraft. The *Maxim*

(TOP)

An English poster promoting the 1929 flight of the Land of the Soviets, *from Moscow across the North Pacific to Alaska and the United States.*

(MIDDLE)

Soviet airmen pose with their airplane, the Land of the Soviets, *in 1929.*

(BOTTOM)

Soviet airmen flying the Land of the Soviets *are welcomed to Seattle, Washington, in 1929. This early flight set the stage for Soviet transpolar flights in 1937.*

Gorky toured the country, landing at collective farms to showcase the Soviet Union's latest technological triumphs. The lumbering propaganda airplane met an unexpected fate after a fly-over of Red Square on May Day in 1935: it crashed after a mid-air collision with an escort fighter.

Valery Chkalov found himself at the epicenter of the Stalinist aviation world. Joined by navigator Alexander Belyakov and copilot Georgiy Baidukov, he led the Soviet team that made the first transpolar flight in 1937. This particular flight, if largely forgotten today, sparked universal praise at the time and, briefly, gave substance to the Soviet claim that the Communist regime had developed one of the most advanced aeronautical communities in the world.

Since Stalin's approval of the transpolar flight depended on a favorable weather forecast, Soviet meteorologists monitored arctic weather patterns in June 1937, looking for a favorable window of opportunity to attempt the flight. In the Golden Age of Flight, at a time when nations competed fiercely for air records, a country's prestige was often perceived as riding on the success of recording-breaking flights. The Soviet regime, in particular, surrounded the feats of Stalin's Falcons with great propaganda and public acclaim. Care was taken in advance to assure success, and weather was always a key factor in planning. Chkalov himself expressed great impatience with slow-moving meteorologists. "The view of weather," Chkalov joked, "is like that of beauty: some people like it and others do not." Finally, his persistence won out and the meteorology team approved a departure date of June 18.

Valery Chkalov fit well the Bolshevik mold of a "heroic aviator." His background was proletarian. In many respects he represented the new elite, coming from the lower social

(TOP)

Alaskan children greet Soviet airmen of the Land of the Soviets. *The Soviet long-distance flight pioneered an air bridge from Moscow, across Siberia, through the Aleutians, to Seattle, Washington.*

(BOTTOM)

Soviet airmen pioneered cold-weather flying, making flights to the Arctic Circle in the early 1930s. These Tupolev-designed ANT-6 airplanes were equipped with skis and landed on ice floes to assist Soviet polar scientists.

order and identified with the official Communist ideology. Born in a small village along the Volga River, he was a "man of the people," not an aristocrat who had made peace with the revolutionary regime and now sought to pursue his career under a new banner. No less important, Chkalov—with Baidukov and Belyakov at his side— headed a team of aviators who reflected the regime's ideological stress on collective action.

Yet, Chkalov's own persona ran counter to the discipline normally expected from those who served and represented the Soviet state. He was impulsive and fearless, not given to patience or accepting the lead of men he perceived to possess less talent than himself. His natural aptitude for flying often prompted him to stretch the rules, becoming on occasion his own version of a "Lone Eagle." As a young pilot in the Soviet Air Force, he had recklessly flown his fighter under a bridge in Leningrad, a wild display of flying skill that nearly ended his career in the military. Chkalov preferred the open cockpit and daredevil antics of the barnstormers familiar to Americans. Always on the cutting edge, he earned a wide reputation among his air force peers as one of the Soviet Union's premier pilots. In 1933, he resigned from the military to take his place in the elite ranks of Stalin's Falcons, quickly becoming a record-breaking pilot—the exemplar of Soviet aviation. His selection to lead the first transpolar flight in 1937 reflected his standing as a national hero.

For the transpolar flight from Moscow to the United States, Chkalov and his crew took care to prepare for any eventuality. Food and survival gear, sleeping bags, maps, medicine, special clothing, and navigation instruments were assembled for the trip. The cache also included

The ANT-25 Stalinskiy marshrut *(Stalin Route), flown by Valery Chkalov, Georgiy Baidukov, and Alexander Belyakov from Moscow to Vancouver, Washington, in June 1937.*

Valery Chkalov's ANT-25 on takeoff prior to the 1937 transpolar flight.

parachutes, three balloons, and a rubber raft. One critical device, as the crew eventually discovered, would be the oxygen containers included among the supplies.

The aircraft selected for the transpolar flight was the ANT-25, a long-range single monoplane already tested in a series of flights across the Soviet Union. Andrei Tupolev, the leading Soviet aircraft designer, had built the ANT-25 as a powered glider in many respects—a short narrow fuselage (112 feet) with huge wings (372 feet) attached. Much of the wing and fuselage area had been designed to hold internal fuel tanks in order to give the lumbering aircraft maximum range. The aircraft was an all-metal, cantilever type powered by a 750-horsepower engine designed by Alexander Mikulin. Designated the AM-34R, and fitted with a three-bladed propeller, the engine performed well in the critical categories of speed, fuel consumption, and range. Chkalov and his crew found the ANT-25 an ideal and trustworthy aircraft, allowing them to cruise at 150 miles per hour and to fly just under 7,000 miles nonstop. Valery Chkalov dubbed his ANT-25 *Stalinskiy marshrut* or "*Stalin Route*."

Departure came at 4:05 a.m., Moscow time, June 18, 1937. The overloaded ANT-25, with its red wings and dark blue fuselage, climbed into the morning sky after a long and bouncy takeoff run. For the initial leg of the trip, Chkalov took the controls. Baidukov served as his copilot, alternating with Chkalov in the cockpit. Belyakov served as navigator. The discipline for the crew dictated six hours on duty, then three hours of rest. A sleeping bag made of dog skin was placed behind the pilot's seat for a crew member to sleep when off duty. To reach America, they anticipated at least 60 hours of nonstop flying, nearly three

An early variant of the ANT-25 in flight over Russia. The sturdy, dependable ANT-25 was chosen for Chkalov's epic transpolar flight.

Date **20** month **June** year **1937** Watch

Pilot **BAIDUKOV**
Navigator **BELYAKOV**

from 6.30 to 16.20 Baidukov"

Coordinates or name	Greenwich mean time	Flying time	Compass course	Deviation	Magnetic course	Variation	True course	Drift	Actual track	Air speed k/hr	Ground speed k/hr	Altitude meters	True course by the sun compass	Temperature at an altitude	True wind direction (where to)	Velocity k/hr.	r.p.m.	Altitude control reading	Readings of the petrol consumption gauge	NOTES EN ROUTE
	13.30	By the radio-compass are 200° from the Seattle radio range beacon																		
	14.00																			
	14.12	130° to the Portland radio range beacon in zone A																		
		Between two heavy layers of clouds.																		
	14.33	Arguing as to position.										3000		Call signs ----- — --- true.						
		Descending under the clouds near the city of Portland (in circles).										2800							11.239	but judging from the petrol level gauge 1½ ton of petrol remains in the central tank
	14.46	Baidukov has put on his head-telephones. The lower layer of the cloud is awful. The wings are already wet, but from above we can see that the layers are not so thick everywhere. Descent very slow—in spirals. Took us 13 min. to descend. That's too bad, below torn clouds almost reaching the ground. Sighted Portland H=300 m. ahead mountainous land, therefore decided to climb. Things are bad with water. The pointer [1] is falling. Emptied everything we had into the reserve tank, but we can't pump it out of there. Very little petrol left in the working tank.																		
	15.41	Turning back to Portland.															1800			
	16.20	Landed at Vancouver										2500		Petrol hand-pump won't work.					11.437	after switching off the engine.
		Total time in the air 63 hrs. 16 min.												Petrol consumed 7933 lit. =5658 kg.						Amount carried 5735 kg. −5658 Should remain ..... 77 kg.

A. BELYAKOV.

(OPPOSITE)

Copies of the original flight log maintained by Valery Chkalov and his crew, with English translation. This particular segment covers their dramatic landing at Pearson Airfield at Vancouver, Washington, after a 62-hour flight from Moscow.

(RIGHT)

Three photos of the crew of the ANT-25 while en route to North America over the North Pole.

days in the air, over some of the most hostile terrain on the planet.

The itinerary for the transpolar flight called for a circular route from Moscow across the forests of north Russia to the Arctic Ocean, over Franz-Josef Land above Norway, to the North Pole. Once the team reached the polar ice cap, they were to direct the ANT-25 southward across Canada and the Bear Lake region. There was a planned dogleg before entering American air space—Chkalov and his crew would temporarily fly westward to the North Pacific and then down the coast to the United States. For the Soviets, the flight would end in the San Francisco area, giving Chkalov and the crew the opportunity to break the world's existing long-distance record. Moscow anticipated that the flight of the *Stalinskiy marshrut* would achieve an unparalleled aerial feat for the Soviet Union—the first transpolar flight and possibly a new distance record.

Navigation over the North Pole required special equipment because at these latitudes the magnetic compass becomes inoperable. Belyakov used a sextant and sun compass to chart the course of the ANT-25 over the pole. He also carefully charted out every stage of the journey, collecting accurate maps, identifying radio stations with notes on their frequencies and call signs, and jotting down a sequence of airfields and landing spots in case of an emergency. Neither Belyakov nor anyone else took the time to learn rudimentary English or even bring along an English dictionary. This was an odd omission in an otherwise systematic process of preparation for the flight: once over Canada and the United States they would be in an all-English realm.

During the first hours of the transpolar flight, Chkalov maintained a constant cruising altitude of around 6,000 feet.

(BELOW)

A rare color photo of Valery Chkalov's ANT-25 shortly after its landing at Pearson airfield.

(RIGHT)

Crowds gather at Pearson airfield, then an Army Air Corps base, to view the Russian ANT-25 airplane after its historic flight over the North Pole.

(RIGHT)

Scenes at Pearson airfield shortly after landing the ANT-25 Stalinskiy marshrut. The local press took a keen interest in the Soviet crew as they removed gear from the plane. At bottom,

Alexander Belyakov (left), the navigator, talks with Valery Chkalov (right), the renowned Soviet pilot who led the team effort to be the first to make a nonstop flight across the North Pole.

The outside temperature read minus 25 degrees Fahrenheit, but the cockpit heater sustained a comfort zone for the crew. With the passing of several hours of flying, Chkalov faced his first crisis when the windshield frosted over and there were clear indications of icing on the propeller tips and the forward edge of the wings. Deicing equipment quickly restored normality, but the situation provided a grim warning of the dangers of flying over the Arctic region.

There were constant threats of shifting weather, in particular weather fronts moving, in the words of Baidukov, as "high, feathery clouds, which were yellow under the effects of the sun's rays." For Baidukov, these fast-moving cloud formations "wandered like apparitions along an enormous aerial ocean." They frightened the Soviet crew because they could enhance the dangers of icing and offer stiff headwinds to slow their progress. Chkalov flew around these nomadic islets of weather whenever he encountered them.

The passage north brought the ANT-25 across Cape Barents, the Franz-Josef Land archipelago, and Rudolph Island. From the cockpit Chkalov and his crew viewed a world below of snow, ice fields lined with deep crevices, and blinding storms. On the edge of the polar basin, as the second day of the flight began, there was an opportunity to communicate with the Soviet Arctic station. In the early 1930s, the Soviets had established a series of scientific stations on ice floes, where they made the first Arctic landings of multiengine aircraft specially equipped with skis.

The ANT-25 crossed the North Pole at 4:00 a.m. on the second day, June 19. Belyakov determined that they had

Winner in Pole Vault Event

(TOP)

Portland's Oregonian *newspaper published this cartoon on June 22, 1937, to celebrate the Soviet transpolar flight as a major milestone in aviation.*

(BOTTOM)

Aviation periodicals in the United States were impressed with Soviet air spectaculars in the 1930s, as evident on the cover of Bill Barnes Air Trails, *which was widely read by American youth.*

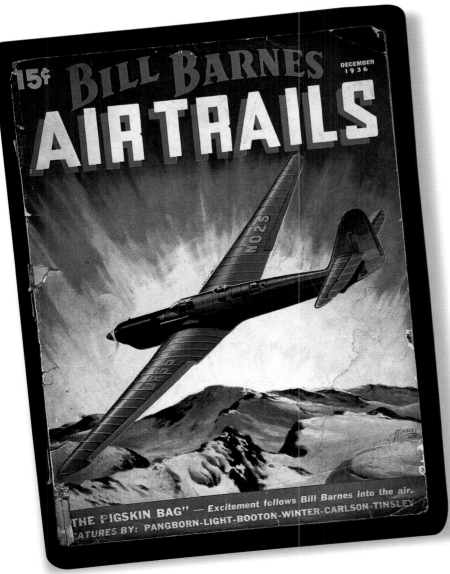

swept by the pole at 90 degrees north latitude, at the point of the axis of the earth's rotation. Flying at around 16,000 feet, Baidukov recorded that they looked out on a "gigantic frozen wasteland that was pocked by small and large crevices and patches of ice-free water." At this elevation over the top of the world, they watched with fascination as their compasses "became more and more sensitive and would crazily spin around with the slightest pitch or yaw." This was a remarkable and unforgettable moment for the transpolar flyers.

Saying bon voyage to the polar ice cap, Baidukov steered the ANT-25 southward toward Canada. Belyakov shot the angle of the sun at 4:43 a.m. and determined the new heading. The time was reset to match the 123rd meridian. At 5:10, Belyakov sent out a telegram to alert Moscow that the ANT-25 had completed the first phase of the aerial trek: "We have crossed the pole—a tail wind—white ice fields with crevices and expanses of open water—our mood cheerful." Back home in Moscow, Stalin himself followed the progress of the flight with great interest, knowing that the prestige of the Soviet Union rested with the three transpolar flyers.

At 9:40 a.m., Baidukov would remember, the crew found themselves afflicted with fatigue and oxygen deprivation. For hours they had flown above 15,000 feet, and in this thin atmosphere had made use of the oxygen tanks on board. Chkalov complained that his left leg pained him so much that he found it difficult to sit in the pilot's seat for any period of time. Sleep became difficult for all. Any exertion of energy led to rapid heartbeats and acute discomfort. This diminished capacity became a problem at this juncture when they were called upon to

(TOP)

General George Marshall (center), then commander at the nearby Vancouver Barracks, joins (left to right) Belyakov, Soviet ambassador Oleg Troyanovsky, Chkalov, and Baidukov.

(MIDDLE)

Chkalov received a tumultuous welcome upon his return to Soviet Russia in the summer of 1937.

(BOTTOM)

Chkalov embraces Soviet leader Joseph Stalin, who promoted the advance of Soviet aviation in the decade before World War II.

manually pump oil to the engine or turn the valve to switch fuel tanks. Even the robust Chkalov appeared weak and very pale in the manipulation of the hand pumps.

On the approach to Canada the ANT-25 cruised at 17,000 feet, but turbulent and shifting air masses offered a new challenge. There was a continual need to make course corrections and adjust altitude. Outside the temperature was 22 degrees Fahrenheit. Chkalov and Baidukov alternated at the controls and with the use of the oxygen mask. There was great apprehension of another episode of icing. All eyes were on the leading edge of the wings to detect any telltale signs of ice. The buffeting air cast the aircraft around like a straw in the wind. Control became increasingly difficult, especially as the windshield began to ice over. When downdrafts lowered the altitude to around 9,000 feet, there was a palpable fear that the ANT-25 might break up under the extreme pressures. At this juncture, they realized that they were between two cloud layers.

Suddenly a stream of liquid spurted from the cowling of the engine. There was the distinct smell of alcohol and Baidukov quickly determined that there was some sort of rupture or blockage in the cooling system pipes. The worse case scenario, Baidukov feared, would be a rupture in the "little line," which was situated above the cooling system tank and fed water to cool the engine cylinders; any loss of this vital coolant meant the overheated engine would seize up—in six minutes. He then lowered the engine throttle and began "to work the hand water pump madly."

Shouting that "the pump isn't drawing any water," Baidukov warned of the imminent danger of engine failure. The crew began to think of a crash landing in the icy

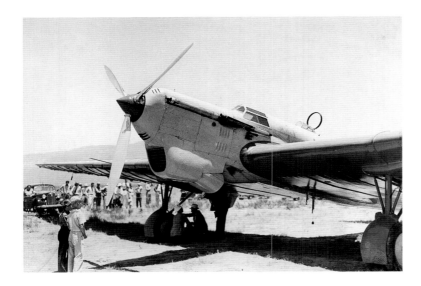

Mikhail Gromov led another flight by an ANT-25 from Moscow over the North Pole in July 1937, just weeks after the Chkalov milestone. Gromov flew farther, reaching San Diego and setting a new world record for long-distance flying.

A third flight over the North Pole was launched in August 1937, but met with disaster. Sigismund Levanevsky, flying a four-engine ANT-6, disappeared over northern Canada without a trace.

wasteland above Canada. At this juncture, Chkalov leaped for an extra water tank, only to discover that it was empty. Where now to find water? Hurriedly Chkalov and Belyakov began cutting open the rubber bags holding emergency rations of water. But this source of water proved disappointing: much of the water had frozen. Breaking the crust of the ice, they managed to obtain a small quantity of water, which they quickly poured into the tank. Baidukov then resumed his pumping, but to no avail; the engine remained starved of water.

The ever-resourceful Baidukov then shouted: "The balloons!" At the rear of the fuselage there were three balloons that were used to collect and store urine waste during the flight. Chkalov rushed to retrieve these balloons and promptly poured the contents into the tank, even as Baidukov resumed his work on the hand pump. The odd mixture of water and urine brought immediate results. The water float pin clearly showed the system back to normal. Baidukov then throttled the engine revs back to cruising speed. The crew relaxed, feeling that they had passed through their most perilous moment. The Mikulin engine, the sole source of power for the ANT-25, once again had responded faithfully to all commands, even on the threshold of overheating. Any engine failure meant certain disaster.

The course southward called for the *Stalinskiy marshrut* to pass over Banks Island in Canada. The chosen altitude for this leg was around 10,000 feet, and the skies were clear of storms. The brown image of Banks Island came into view at 4:40 p.m. For the first time in many hours of flying, the crew felt the anticipation of leaving the seemingly limitless expanse of the Arctic ice and ocean.

Stalin also showcased his women aviators in the 1930s, here the crew of the Rodina *(Motherland), which made a record-breaking flight across* the Soviet Union, September 24 to 25, 1938. Left to right: Valentina S. Grizodubova, Polina D. Osipenko, and Marina M. Raskova.

Another milestone came at 6:00 p.m., when the crew could see Bear Lake in the distance, a clear indicator of having penetrated well into Canadian air space. The ANT-25 was at 9,000 feet, in smooth air, and on course. Baidukov then sent a radio message to Moscow via Canadian radio stations to relay the news that all was well and the *Stalinskiy marshrut* was on course. The message was addressed first to Joseph Stalin, with greetings to various Communist party officials and important figures in the aviation industry. The Soviet public—having been alerted to the flight—was keenly interested in the fate of Chkalov and his crew.

The desolation of northern Canada struck Baidukov as a land best described as "lifeless, having a naked brown color." He was impressed with the enormity of the landscape, a largely uninhabited territory appearing to him as a "scorched desert." As with the northern stretches of his native land, which shared the same climate, Baidukov was struck with the serenity and striking beauty of the landscape.

As the Soviet flyers made slow progress across Canada to the Pacific Northwest of the United States, popular interest grew in the flight. A total of 12 hours of silence passed without Chkalov and his crew establishing contact with anyone. Since no one on the *Stalinskiy marshrut* spoke English, any sort of communication with the Canadians or Americans was difficult at best. Finally, the Soviets crossed to the Pacific Ocean, near Sitka, Alaska, on Saturday, June 19. This fact was established by an American radio station, which had successfully monitored the sporadic radio messages in Russian from the *Stalinskiy marshrut*.

That same evening the Soviet consulate in San Francisco began to make preparations for a landing of Chkalov and his crew at Oakland, the preset landing spot for the transpolar flight. At that time they did not realize that shifting weather patterns would dictate a different outcome.

When Chkalov reached the mouth of the Columbia River, the border between the states of Oregon and Washington, on Sunday morning, June 20, he encountered thick fog. This inclement weather prompted him to abandon distant Oakland, California, for a landing at Portland's Swan Island airport. The weather there was marginal at best, with low clouds, fog, and drizzle. As the *Stalinskiy marshrut* followed the radio beacon into Portland and the local radio station announced the imminent arrival of the Russians, a huge crowd gathered at Swan Island to see the "mystery plane" from the Soviet Union.

Once Chkalov circled Swan Island and saw the crowd, he feared a chaotic landing scene reminiscent of Lindbergh's landing at Le Bourget a decade before, so he opted to land across the river at Pearson Airfield, an Army Air Corps facility at nearby Vancouver, Washington. This military airfield, Chkalov thought, offered a greater measure of protection to him, his crew, and the aircraft.

With Baidukov at the controls, the ANT-25 landed on the wet grass strip at Pearson at 8:00 a.m. Only a guard at the edge of the field greeted the Soviet pilots on the successful end to their transpolar flight. They were still some 580 miles from the intended landing spot in Oakland, so they did not establish a new distance record that day. But Chkalov and his crew had flown over the North Pole—a singular achievement that would catapult Chkalov to world renown in 1937.

RIEDEL
SOARING TO WASHINGTON

THE CITY of Elmira, located in the Finger Lake district of upstate New York, hosted a soaring competition in 1938. The competition included Peter Riedel, a young soaring enthusiast from Germany. A friend of Richard DuPont and numerous American glider pilots, Riedel had come to test his skills against some of the most talented American glider pilots. A German participating in any international event in the late 1930s faced many obstacles, including boycotts and even open hostility from the public. The Nazis had assumed power in 1933, and as Adolf Hitler quickly consolidated his power, he neutralized all political opposition and fostered racial theories, especially the policy of official anti-Semitism. These racial ideas became manifest at the 1936 Olympics in Berlin, when German athletes were showcased as exemplars of German racial superiority. By 1938, at the time of the Elmira soaring contest, Riedel faced a growing opposition in America to Nazi Germany. Nonetheless, winning a major competition that year was highly desired by Riedel as a way to consolidate his position in the international soaring community.

Riedel came to Elmira as a representative of the German Aero Club, which meant that the Nazi swastika insignia, then an official insignia of the state and broadly used as a symbol of Germany, was carried on the rudder of Riedel's Kranich glider in the form of a black swastika on a red field. His ground crew consisted mostly of Germans, although he was assisted by members of the German-American Aviation Club in New York. Riedel himself was unabashedly German in his personality and identity, but expressed a studied indifference to politics. Throughout his sojourn in America as a glider pilot he consistently felt embarrassed about the Nazi movement, even as he sought out avenues to serve his country. This ambivalence would eventually lead Riedel down a path to personal peril in Hitler's Germany.

The day selected for the flight was July 3, 1938, the eve of America's Independence Day. Twenty aircraft were in this competition sponsored by the Soaring Society of America. Riedel decided to make a bold move and attempt to fly his Kranich to Washington, D.C., nonstop. His confidence was based on the ideal weather situation on the day of the race: northerly winds moving across central New York promised to catapult the Kranich all the way to Washington. The flight path consisted of a 225-mile flight path across the Allegheny mountains, the city of Baltimore, and the District of

(ABOVE)

Peter Riedel kneels next to his glider at Elmira on the eve of his historic flight to Washington, D.C., in July 1938.

(OPPOSITE)

A ground crew member signals the launch of a sailplane at Harris Hill, Elmira, New York.

Crowds gather at Harris Hill for the launching of gliders.

Peter Riedel's Kranich sailplane awaits its turn for a tow launch at Harris Hill, July 1938.

Peter Riedel stands next to his friend, noted German woman test pilot Hannah Reitsch, at the National Championship Air Races, Cleveland, Ohio.

Columbia. The landing site would be Hoover airfield, which at that time was on the Virginia side of the Potomac where the Pentagon now stands.

In distance flights, each pilot competed for points. The scoring regulations required each competitor to record a prerace goal. This critical aspect of the competition possessed a certain formality, with each pilot stating in writing the destination, typically an airfield. Distance flown and precision landings meant high points. There was always an element of uncertainty in calculating one's route and target destination. Trying to reach a distant spot and failing could put the entrant at a disadvantage in competition with someone who set a lesser goal and successfully landed there. By the same token, a pilot who displayed little boldness in setting a goal could easily be outclassed by someone blessed with favorable winds en route to a distant airfield. To add another incentive, there was a prize of one thousand dollars for the first pilot to make a nonstop flight from Elmira to Washington.

Riedel did not decide to attempt the flight to Washington, D.C., impulsively; he was cautious and attentive to detail. Waking on the morning of July 3, Riedel carefully examined the weather conditions. To his delight, the skies suggested optimal weather, with towering cumulus clouds with blue-hued undersides taking shape and drifting in a northwesterly corridor toward the Appalachian mountains outside Elmira.

Using the wings of his glider as a desk, he quickly filled out the required official declaration of his goal—Hoover Airport, Washington, D.C. The Kranich glider, a two-seater, was a tested flying machine, one that gave Riedel supreme confidence that he could reach the runway at Hoover

(TOP)

A glider approaches a landing area at Harris Hill, Elmira, New York.

(MIDDLE)

An aerial view of Harris Hill at Elmira and the surrounding countryside.

(BOTTOM)

Cover of the program for the 1939 National Soaring Contest at Elmira. In the late 1930s, at the time of Peter Riedel's flight, soaring was a truly international sport, attracting a wide audience.

Airport by evening. One lingering question persisted—whether the powerful thermals over Elmira would appear all along the intended flight path to Washington.

Riedel pulled on his parachute and fastened himself into the cockpit for a 10:30 a.m. departure. His crew had hurriedly placed in the crammed cockpit some provisions for the day-long flight: a bottle of water, some bananas, and several slices of cake. More important, the soaring authorities oversaw the installation of two barographs, which were sealed and then turned on. The barographs, placed beyond the grasp of the pilot, provided a tamperproof means to record height; any touchdown short of the targeted goal would be evident to the officials. The ticking barographs were a constant and familiar background noise for any competitive glider pilot.

Using a winch, an aircraft pulled Riedel's Kranich skyward to 500 feet so he could capture the strong upcurrents. Once airborne and in motion, Riedel flew parallel to a long ridge in anticipation of leaping into a powerful thermal. Within minutes one of the passing cumulus clouds overtook the glider, allowing Riedel to push the Kranich into the rising air currents. His ascent became rapid; he reached 3,000 feet; then 4,000; finally topping out at 6,000 feet. Riedel then maneuvered into the thermals offered by the first huge cloud heading southward away from Elmira.

For Riedel, or any experienced glider pilot, there was a keen desire to achieve maximum altitude in the initial ascent, especially in hilly or mountainous terrain. Such a maneuver often meant riding a favorable upcurrent into a large moving cumulus cloud. Once Riedel entered the dark and turbulent interior of the cloud, he was flying blind, cut

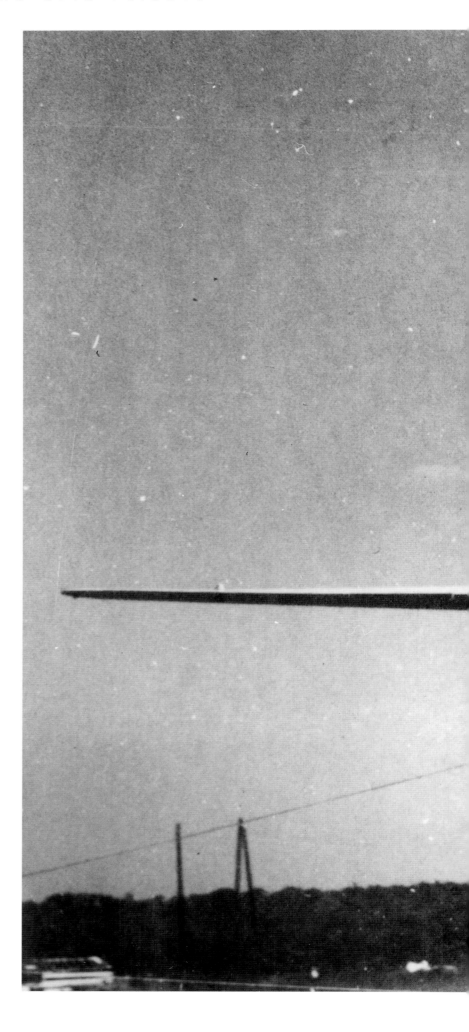

Peter Riedel's Kranich under tow as it prepares for release. As a member of the German national soaring group, Riedel's glider bore the swastika, then the national insignia of Germany.

off from familiar reference points on the ground and in the sky. Visibility was nil, with the outer tips of the wings obscured by the enveloping fog. The Kranich, like most gliders of the 1930s, offered the pilot a minimal ensemble of instruments. An altimeter and a compass, to measure height and direction, were essential, but other vital instruments such as an artificial horizon were not routinely placed in gliders. Moreover, a typical glider lacked a radio since most gliders had no electrical system. One important instrument was the so-called variometer, which indicated rates of ascent and descent. Riedel's aircraft also had an air speed indicator and a turn and slip indicator. The latter instrument, with two needles to measure any turn or slip, allowed Riedel to detect and avoid any spin or overstressing of the aircraft. Riedel was experienced in riding a powerful thermal in an upward spiral through a sequence of circles. The plywood construction of the Kranich made it appear fragile, but in the hands of a skilled aviator the aircraft was equal to the challenge. For extreme emergencies, the parachute offered an escape, if the veteran glider opted to use it.

With some 3,000 feet separating him from the ridges below Elmira, Riedel set his course for Washington. He possessed considerable forward speed, being at the top of a spiraling thunderhead cloud. Above him was a vast sunlit expanse; below a sea of white cumulus clouds. Breaks in the ocean of clouds revealed the meandering Susquehanna River pointing to the south and the distant Hoover Airport beyond the horizon. To reach Harrisburg, Pennsylvania, the first major geographical benchmark, Riedel would have to cross the Appalachian Mountain Range. For this initial leg of the journey, the weather was most cooperative, with each thermal allowing Riedel to climb and catapult himself forward.

(TOP)

Peter Riedel climbs into the cockpit of his sailplane. Riedel was assisted by a team of German-American soaring enthusiasts in 1938.

(BOTTOM)

A glider under tow passes the control tower and spectators at Elmira.

The passage toward Washington was steady and sure: Riedel pushed his Kranich glider through a series of ascents and descents, climbing turns and leaps forward—all done with an attentiveness to sustaining altitude. By late afternoon, Riedel saw in the distance a huge urban area— he knew this could only be Baltimore and he knew also that he was roughly on course, requiring only a slight correction.

Upon reaching the air space above Baltimore at 5:00 p.m., Riedel sensed the change in weather and atmospheric conditions. The sun was now on its inevitable path toward setting, denying Riedel the warm thermals encountered earlier in the day. The air was cooling; the clouds no longer churned with bellowing upcurrents. The sun now cast its bright rays at an oblique angle. Shadows deepened. Riedel knew that time was his adversary. He realized there was only a brief window of time to make the final descent in to Washington.

Still flying at a comfortable 7,000 feet, Riedel calculated that he was around 40 miles from his goal. He made concerted efforts to sustain his altitude with repeated circling in the desperate hope of riding the late afternoon thermals. The Kranich responded with small gains in altitude, but the thermals were weak at best. Slowly and inevitably, Riedel found himself descending. The Kranich possessed a glide ratio of roughly 20 to 1, which meant theoretically that he could glide 20 feet for every foot aloft. The math suggested that he might make it to Hoover Airport by a narrow margin. But there were other climatic factors to consider, such as a sudden downdraft that could deny him precious altitude, with few chances of a strong upcurrent to compensate.

Enjoying a beautiful summer day, soaring enthusiasts gather around the specially equipped truck, which used a winch to launch gliders at Elmira, then a major center for soaring in the United States.

Riedel now entered the most frenetic phase of his extraordinary aerial trek, the final passage to Washington in an air space of diminishing thermals. For the entire journey he had used an automobile road map to help identify towns and highways. Now he could see in the distance the Washington Monument, with its distinctive pointed crown breaking through the haze. Riedel steered his Kranich toward this historic landmark by following the north-south highway connecting Baltimore to the District of Columbia. Riedel's descending flight toward Washington revealed the clear outline of city, even the Capitol. His sense of exhilaration mixed with another pressing emotion—he was losing altitude at a rapid rate. Riedel prayed for just one more favorable thermal.

At 2,500 feet, a sudden thermal provided a momentary reprieve, halting the rapid descent and pushing the Kranich upward again. The change in altitude was welcome, but it did not produce a dramatic change in Riedel's overall plight. Now 10 miles separated him from Hoover Airport. He was over the northern suburbs of the capital with few open areas to make an emergency landing—if one were required in this context of diminishing thermals. Even as Riedel's options narrowed, there was the tempting alternative of landing at historic College Park airfield, which was located in Maryland, on the northern edge of the District of Columbia. A landing there, if feasible, would mean the abandonment of his official goal, a grim disappointment after this spirited effort to set a new record in soaring. Riedel decided to resist this siren call and continued his descent toward Hoover Airport.

No sooner had Riedel made his fateful decision to press on than he faced the most feared shift in the atmospheric

conditions—a sudden swath of sinking air. The altimeter indicated the inevitable drop in altitude. Now over house tops and suburban streets filled with automobiles, Riedel struggled to sustain a steady course even as he looked for an open space to land the Kranich. No open field, ball park, or golf course appeared to offer a safe avenue to conclude the long flight.

Riedel reasoned that he might still encounter an upcurrent, since the summer sun had heated the streets and rooftops of the many buildings below. This urban environment no doubt had cooled more slowly than the countryside surrounding the District of Columbia. Reason suggested hope, but the tension only mounted. Riedel persisted in his glide and soon encountered a mild thermal, allowing him to stabilize his low descent over the city at an estimated altitude of 750 feet. Could this altitude be sustained for the remainder of the flight?

As the Kranich began to attract the attention of startled onlookers in the city streets below, Riedel banked toward the

(TOP)

Peter Riedel landed his Kranich at Washington-Hoover Airport, located on the Virginia side of the Potomac River, where the Pentagon now stands.

(BOTTOM)

A telegram from Germany's Secretary of State for Air Erhard Milch, congratulating Riedel on his historic flight from Elmira to Washington D.C.

Mall. This large expanse of park land extended from the Capitol to the Washington Monument to the Lincoln Memorial. The Mall was filled with tourists on the eve of the July 4th holiday. Riedel now experienced the intoxicating thrill of gliding silently across the Mall. This brief moment allowed him to glance downward to see the historic Smithsonian Castle and museums hugging the perimeter of this famed public space.

Arrival over the Mall signaled to Riedel that he could make it—if he skillfully flew the short passage from the Mall to Hoover Airport on the northern Virginia side of the Potomac. The nearby airport was now in his sight. As Riedel circled and banked toward his target, he experienced a sudden and powerful upcurrent, allowing the Kranich to level off at 3,000 feet. Blessed with this unexpected upward surge over the Potomac, Riedel thought momentarily that he now ironically possessed enough altitude to perform some aerobatics, perhaps some loops or sharp banks as he approached the runway at Hoover. But this temptation gave way to a determined effort to land safely. Riedel made a successful landing at 6:20 p.m., completing his long journey of over 200 miles from Elmira in upstate New York to Washington, D.C.

Peter Riedel emerged from the successful flight as the leader in points among all competitors. An American, Emil Lehecka, came in second. Being a German national, Riedel could not assume the U.S. National Championship; Lehecka therefore accepted the mantel of champion. Though denied the championship, Riedel found himself regaled by numerous aviation notables in the United States who marveled at his manifest skills as a glider pilot.

~153~

(TOP)

In 1939, Peter Riedel became the assistant military attaché at the German Embassy in Washington, a post he held until the outbreak of war between the United States and Nazi Germany in December 1941.

As an alien diplomat, Riedel was repatriated home in April 1942, on the Swedish ocean liner, the Drottingholm. *He was taken to Lisbon, Portugal.*

(BOTTOM)

Peter Riedel (second from right) arrives in Lisbon with his American-born wife, Helen (left). Both spent the war in Germany. Riedel returned to the United States in the postwar years and became an American citizen.

E. J. Noble, head of the Civil Aeronautics Board, met with Riedel and took a flight in the Kranich glider. One special moment for Riedel came when Igor Sikorsky, the famed Russian American aircraft designer, decided to fly with Riedel in the Kranich. The year 1938 marked Riedel's apogee in international soaring competition.

Riedel's subsequent life brought many challenges and adventures. In 1939, he accepted a position at the German Embassy in Washington as assistant military attaché for air, a post he held until the time of Pearl Harbor and the declaration of war by Germany on the United States. Along with other Axis diplomats, he was interned at the Greenbrier Hotel in White Sulphur Springs, West Virginia. He and his American wife Helen (they had been married in the summer of 1941) were shipped back to Germany in April 1942. Always an admirer of American aviation, Riedel found himself in some difficulty back in his native Germany.

The German Air Ministry in Berlin displayed little confidence in Riedel's prediction that the United States would soon be producing vast quantities of military aircraft. After a short stint with Heinkel aircraft, Riedel was posted to Stockholm to serve as air attaché. With the attempt on Hitler's life in July 1944, Riedel fell under suspicion, although he had played no part in the plot. Riedel then defected rather than return home and risk arrest. Ultimately, in a series of adventures, Riedel made it to South America and then to the United States, to be reunited with his wife. Finally, in 1958, Peter Riedel became an American citizen, which opened a context for a continuing career in aviation in his adopted land. Riedel died in 1998.

ARCHBOLD
LOST WORLD IN THE SKIES

WRITING in the 1930s, explorer W. S. Shackleton described New Guinea as "a cruel land of liquid mud and steam, furnace-like heat, crocodiles, snakes, and mosquitoes." Located just south of the equator above Australia, this vast island—the second largest on earth—possessed an impenetrable primeval landscape of jungle, mangrove swamps, limestone and lava crags, and meandering rivers. Snow-capped mountains towered over the jungle lowlands. Some of New Guinea's tallest peaks, it was estimated at the time, reached an elevation of 15,000 feet.

For centuries, the rugged terrain of New Guinea had stubbornly resisted the efforts of outsiders to penetrate its remote interior. From the days of Don Jorge de Meneses, the first explorer to reach the shores of the island in 1526, Europeans found themselves restricted to small enclaves on the coast. Even as late as the nineteenth century, during the era of high imperialism when the Dutch, British, and Germans laid out claims to this exotic island, the imposing central highlands remained beyond the reach of everyone—empire builders, missionaries, gold seekers, traders, and scientists.

In 1938, Richard Archbold of the American Museum of Natural History decided the moment had arrived to explore the cloud-shrouded central highlands. His plan was simple and made use of the latest in aviation technology. Rather than attempt an arduous trek overland, Archbold argued for the use of a seaplane to reach a lake in the hidden interior of New Guinea. There was a precedent for Archbold's bold plan: in 1929, Elmer W. Brandes had made effective use of a Fairchild FC-2 seaplane to explore the northern coast of New Guinea for the United States Department of Agriculture. The seaplane allowed Brandes, who was in search of exotic strains of sugar cane, to move his scientific team and supplies over miles of coastline and up mighty river systems.

Archbold's high-risk endeavor, coming nearly a decade after Brandes, aimed to circumvent the jungle by flying a modern seaplane into the remote interior. He planned to seek out uncharted rivers and lakes as base camps for an ambitious exploration of New Guinea's last frontier. A seaplane, Archbold believed, was the only quick, reliable, and safe means to reach the highlands. This air bridge scheme

(ABOVE)

Richard Archbold pioneered exploration of the highlands of New Guinea in association with the American Museum of Natural History.

(OPPOSITE)

Richard Archbold (far left) and his crew with the Guba *aircraft prior to their exploratory journey to the highlands of New Guinea.*

A Fairchild FC-2 floatplane being refueled off New Guinea in 1929. Aviation offered a quick and efficient means to reach remote parts of the island, in this case the coastline along the north shore. This particular floatplane had a range of 800 miles, often extended by placing stores of fuel at strategic locations along the coast.

offered unique opportunities for Archbold's team of scientists and naturalists to conduct their work without risking the hazards of an overland journey into the mountains.

Archbold purchased a Consolidated PBY Catalina, which he dubbed *Guba II.* The PBY Catalina was Archbold's second seaplane; as a civilian he purchased his first Catalina in 1937. When the Soviet long-distance pilot Sigismund Levanevsky and his six-man crew disappeared that same year over the Arctic in an ill-fated transpolar flight, Archbold made his PBY available to the Russians in the vain hope of finding Levanevsky. Both the Russians and Archbold discovered that the twin-engine Catalina was a highly maneuverable seaplane, an ideal vehicle in which to reach remote areas.

The selection of the Catalina for the aerial trek into the uncharted interior of New Guinea turned out to be a shrewd choice, providing Archbold with a state-of-the art seaplane. The *Guba II* was an all-weather Model 28-3, fitted with four reinforced platforms inside the hull to hold over five tons of cargo. Seating capacity on the *Guba II* was only 10 passengers, which meant the seaplane would be called upon to make numerous flights to transport a team of over

200 people to the highlands. Archbold also fitted the *Guba II* with a 9-horsepower outboard motor in the rear hatch—to allow slow and deliberate movement once the seaplane landed on a river or lake. The durability of the *Guba II* is reflected in its service record: Archbold used the seaplane to transport 568,000 pounds of food and supplies into the central highlands between June 1938 and May 1939.

The Catalina later won fame in the Pacific War against Japan in World War II, flying countless reconnaissance and liaison missions for the U.S. Navy. While versatile and ideal for the Archbold saga in New Guinea, the Catalina nonetheless had certain faults. Pilots often complained that it was rather slow and always a challenge to fly for the inexperienced pilot. It was known for its tendency to vibrate, it was noisy, and it was legendary for its "heavy controls." Still, the two Pratt & Whitney engines were excellent, and the Catalina's sturdy construction allowed for confident use in heavy seas and inclement weather.

Archbold's 1938 airborne expedition into New Guinea promised some firsts. For the scientific team, there was the prospect of studying the island's most inaccessible flora and fauna. Geographers yearned to learn more about the topographical details of the largely uncharted interior. Finally, all members of the Archbold team were intrigued with the prospect of meeting the region's isolated inhabitants and to discover what human communities existed beyond the mountain barrier.

What was known of New Guinea to outsiders in the 1930s was superficial, at best. European political control of the island was more formal than real, being relegated to an isolated administrative cadre in coastal towns: the Dutch in the Western half of the island (today Irian Jaya, a province of

The interior of the Fairchild floatplane. Throughout the exploration of the northern coast of New Guinea, the pilot routinely slept on the mattress laid out on the floor of the cockpit, a cautionary move to protect the airplane from curious locals.

Indonesia), the British and Australians in the East (today's Papua New Guinea).

Europeans exerted only minimal influence over New Guinea's inhabitants. The island's heterogeneous population lived, as they had for countless centuries, in widely scattered communities. Separated by the rugged geography, they spoke literally hundreds of mutually incomprehensible languages. The island had acquired a reputation for head-hunting and cannibalism. While these images were highly exaggerated in press accounts, New Guinea presented palpable dangers to outsiders who ventured into the interior.

Except for small coastal towns such as Milne Bay, Finschafen, Wewak, Hollandia, and Port Moresby, the vast island's population lived in the rugged forests in the interior, where evergreen oaks dropped acorns the size of baseballs and spiders grew to the size of dinner plates. No tigers, rhinos, or elephants moved across the land of New Guinea, but the island provided a welcome habitat for no less than four species of kangaroo that lived in trees. When Archbold first surveyed the island, most of the flora and fauna had never been examined or catalogued. New Guinea, in fact, remained one of the planet's last unexplored regions.

The targeted central highlands were at that time largely uncharted. What Archbold and his team called the "Grand Valley" is known today as the Baliem River Valley. The towering Puncak Trikora Mountain (called Wilhelmina Peak under the Dutch colonial administration) overlooked the Baliem Valley. This particular mountain peak stood as a formidable barrier with an elevation of some 15,580 feet above sea level. The Baliem Valley, then and now, was densely populated by the Dani tribe, who, as Archbold discovered, lived in thatched huts called *honais,* practicing a highly developed form of agriculture, with the sweet potato as the primary crop.

Flying the *Guba II* to New Guinea in the summer of 1938, Archbold quickly assembled his scientific team on the coast for the exploration of the highlands. He worked closely with the Dutch authorities at Hollandia, who exercised nominal sovereignty over the highlands. The American Museum of Natural History was the official sponsor of the expedition, but Archbold—a wealthy mammalogist and patron of science—supplied the key financial backing.

Setting up a series of base camps and moving vast stores of supplies into the interior required a large support team. For this critical work, Archbold recruited Dyak workers from Borneo; they provided the demanding physical labor required for the expedition. The *Guba II* was the sole means of transport in and out of the highlands for Archbold and

The Consolidated Model 28 Catalina, dubbed Guba II *by Archbold. Archbold used this modern seaplane for his exploration into the highlands of New Guinea.*

This same type of seaplane was used by the U.S. Navy and given the designation PBY. The PBY became legendary for its many uses during the Pacific War against Japan.

his team. Any mishap with the seaplane would mean isolation in the interior, with only meager prospects for rescue or walking out.

To fly to this distant target, Archbold recruited Russell R. Rogers, a skilled Consolidated test pilot. He served as Archbold's copilot and performed many of the demanding maneuvers with the *Guba II*, landing on wide stretches of rivers and ultimately on a remote lake in the highlands. Before any initial landing, Rogers and his crew took special care to ascertain the depth of the water. Measuring the depths for any landing required dropping ropes tethered to a weight, with a float attached to the other end. The length of the rope was precisely five feet, the minimum depth for landing and taking off the Catalina. This simple method of measuring water depth proved effective throughout the expedition.

With Archbold and Rogers at the controls, the *Guba II* made its first successful pass through the mountain barrier in June 1938. For Archbold and his team, there was great exhilaration at the discovery of an unexplored world. As they swept down a valley—their "Grand Valley"—they were stunned to discover that this hidden green trough in the mountain range was a patchwork of small villages, cultivated fields, and terraced gardens. The Grand Valley inhabitants had cleared much of the area of forest to make way for this permanent and highly complex agricultural system. Archbold marveled at the contrast of this agrarian world with the "helter-skelter" agricultural practices he had encountered elsewhere in New Guinea. In the highlands, the farmers had learned the principles of drainage and erosion control. On the ground, the Archbold team examined the elaborate fencing and ditches associated

Archbold's Guba II *after landing on a lake in New Guinea. The PBY could land on both rivers and lakes, which allowed the Archbold expedition extraordinary range and a quick means of resupply.*

Wherever Archbold's seaplane landed—along the coast, on rivers, or lakes in the interior—it invariably attracted the attention of the locals, many of whom were seeing an airplane for the first time.

with each cultivated area. "From the neat stone fences surrounding their carefully weeded fields," Archbold observed, "it was easy to imagine that we were in New England rather than in an isolated valley of the last Stone Age man."

This elaborate man-made environment, they discovered later, was home for some 60,000 people. The indigenous population of the hidden valley lived in round and rectangular-shaped structures, clustered near gardens and cultivated plots. The populace appeared to live in their own Garden of Eden. The locals grew sweet potatoes, taro, spinach, cucumbers, and beans. In the many hamlets there were also bananas and tobacco. Archbold and his team would spend considerable time in the months ahead studying the Baliem Valley communities with their "stone age" tools and sophisticated agriculture techniques. Archbold was astounded by the fact that these communities had been sealed off for thousands of years from any contact with the outside world.

For the initial landing, Archbold and Rogers selected a large body of water located at the western end of the Grand Valley, to be known to outsiders as Lake Habbema. The hidden crystal clear lake was at an elevation of 11,000 feet. There was no small amount of excitement as the *Guba II* landed successfully and taxied to a safe mooring on the lake, surrounded by steep hills.

Archbold quickly made his first move: he ordered a small landing party of two men to row ashore in a collapsible boat. They took a radio and some emergency equipment. With the landing party remaining on shore, Rogers gave the *Guba II* full throttle and the Catalina slowly gained speed, lifted into the thin air, and made a

wide circle around the lake. With the first test takeoff a success, Rogers set the seaplane down again on the lake. The reunited Archbold advance party enjoyed their first hours in the Baliem Valley by making a brief survey of the lakeshore. There was great elation at the success of the *Guba II* in bringing them to remote Lake Habbema.

Archbold captured the emotion of the moment: "An awesome stillness settled upon us as we shut off the engines. I opened the after hatch and looked about. Thin, fir-like trees dotted the hillsides, which frowned down on this strange bird of ours. We were on top of little known New Guinea and entirely dependent for safety upon the two motors of our ship. Were they to fail us, we should be lucky to get back to the coast alive."

To appreciate how inaccessible the Grand Valley was to all travelers in those days, one must recount the

The Guba II *near an improvised mooring dock during Archbold's expedition to New Guinea.*

off-loading of supplies from the *Guba II*, which began on July 31. A total of 105 men and more than 60,000 pounds of supplies eventually found their way to the Archbold expedition site by this air connection.

Eventually the roar of the *Guba II*'s engines echoing in forested hills and ridges above the lake caught the attention of the local population, who looked upon these strange visitors with awe and suspicion. While cutting wood in the nearby forests, the Dyak workers were the first to catch fleeting images of the local population. The Dyaks were aware that their movements were being monitored. For days, this was the only fleeting contact with the inhabitants of the Grand Valley.

Finally, two observers from the local population decided to make tentative contact with their uninvited guests. They approached the Archbold team with bravado, impressing everyone with their dignified bearing and confidence. They were painted with charcoal and dressed scantily in gourd "aprons," bracelets, and mesh head coverings. Both men, if self-assured in their posturing, were still wary of the Archbold team. They squatted on the ground with their backs to the forest, with their bows and arrows ready, just in case the strangers turned hostile. This encounter set the stage for the Archbold team to establish a cordial relationship with the locals.

Archbold and his men offered the two men gifts, consisting of shells, cigarettes, sugar, and dried fish. The two locals first accepted the gifts and then handed them back, in Archbold's mind a gesture of independence. One of the visitors to the Archbold camp followed this exchange by pulling an axe from his shoulder bag for the expedition team to examine. When offered a new axe as a gift, the

experiences of mountain climber J. H. G. Kremer. In 1921, on a trek to Mount Wilhelmina, Kremer had crossed the headwaters of the nearby Idenburg River (also a landing spot for the Archbold team). This earlier overland trek, passing one range of mountains after another, had brought Kremer to a place just west of the hidden Grand Valley. Still, despite being so close, Kremer and his party missed entirely the lush green Grand Valley of cultivated farms and hamlets.

The exploration of the Grand Valley began in earnest on July 19, when six men made the long flight to Lake Habemma and set up a working camp. The reliable *Guba II* also transported the first payload of supplies, a cargo of lumber, tents, radio equipment, and a month's supply of food. This first contingent of visitors quickly built a pier on the northwest side of the lake to allow for the easy

Two members of the Archbold team stand on the mooring dock. The historic landings of Archbold's Guba II *on Lake Habbema in the highlands of New Guinea provided* an air bridge from the coast to the remote interior, a means to transport Archbold's team, and a way to sustain them with essential supplies.

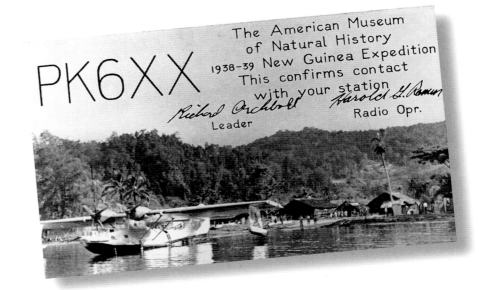

Maintenance, especially engine repairs, were difficult in the primitive context of New Guinea. The Archbold expedition was required to bring all essential spare parts and supplies with them.

The Archbold team unloads supplies at night. The expedition, in collaboration with the Dutch colonial government, hired Dyak tribesmen to serve as carriers of supplies.

visitor refused it. The 15-minute session possessed a palpable sense of excitement and uncertainty, but the meeting ended happily with smiles and handshakes all around. In the course of 9,000 years this was the first such encounter between the locals of the Baliem Valley and the outside world.

Forays by Archbold's team into the surrounding hills and forests allowed for additional contact with the indigenous population. They, in turn, made frequent visits to the Lake Habbema camp. The hospitality shown to the expedition members soon became a nuisance, as friendly locals took more than a keen interest in the visitors and their strange bird, the *Guba II.* Eventually, a lively trade developed as the team of scientists and workers traded shells and various items for botanical and bird specimens. The expedition party also made a systematic survey of the valley and surrounding mountains, even as they studied the culture and language of the local inhabitants.

One extraordinary aspect of the Grand Valley was the cold climate—despite the fact that the latitude of this part of New Guinea was four degrees south of the equator. Water in wash basins froze overnight. Those who had grown accustomed to the tropical heat of the lowlands found the central highlands to be frigid, and they required extra clothing and blankets to keep warm.

For the scientific team, the sojourn at Lake Habbema proved to be a bountiful one. Rats three feet long were

(OPPOSITE)

*A postcard from the Archbold
expedition's radio operator, with
the expedition's radio call sign—
PK6XX.*

(BELOW)

The Guba II, *dwarfed by the
mountains and low-lying clouds,
begins its takeoff from Lake
Habbema in the highlands.*

(TOP)

The seaplane dropped supplies to the widely separated members of the Archbold team.

(BOTTOM)

Members of the expedition trek through the high grass in the highlands of New Guinea.

discovered, along with opossums and muskrats unique to the region. The collection of plants offered even greater variety: over 25 different species of rhododendrons; orchids growing wild in moss on the ground and trees; and buttercups, daisies, and a multitude of flowers unique to the highlands. There were manifold species of butterflies, moths, and flies thriving in the mountains above the vegetation line. The team even found a snail at 14,000 feet elevation. The *Guba II* provided a convenient vehicle to transport these treasured specimens to the base camp on the coast.

The Archbold expedition finally abandoned the highlands of New Guinea in May 1939, completing one of the great scientific undertakings of the twentieth century. Despite all the rigors of the expedition, the team collected a unique body of data and specimens from the hitherto unexplored interior of the Earth's second largest island. Among all the discoveries, the observation of a large number of bird species stood out as one of the expedition's singular achievements. This confirmed that many migratory birds from Asia nested in the highlands for a season each year. Also, the resident bird of paradise—the object of much fascination—was monitored closely, especially its elaborate courtship pattern.

Archbold and a small crew flew the *Guba II* home, while the remaining members returned home by ship. The Archbold team had explored one of the last uncharted frontiers of the planet. For those who had participated in the Archbold expedition, there was an enduring sense of accomplishment and pride in adapting modern aeronautical technology for scientific ends.

(FAR LEFT)

Dyak carriers move supplies across the rapids of the Wamena River, downing a tree to provide an improvised hand rail for the treacherous crossing.

(LEFT)

One of the locals who greeted the Archbold team in the highlands.

(BELOW)

The striking and rugged beauty of the New Guinea interior.

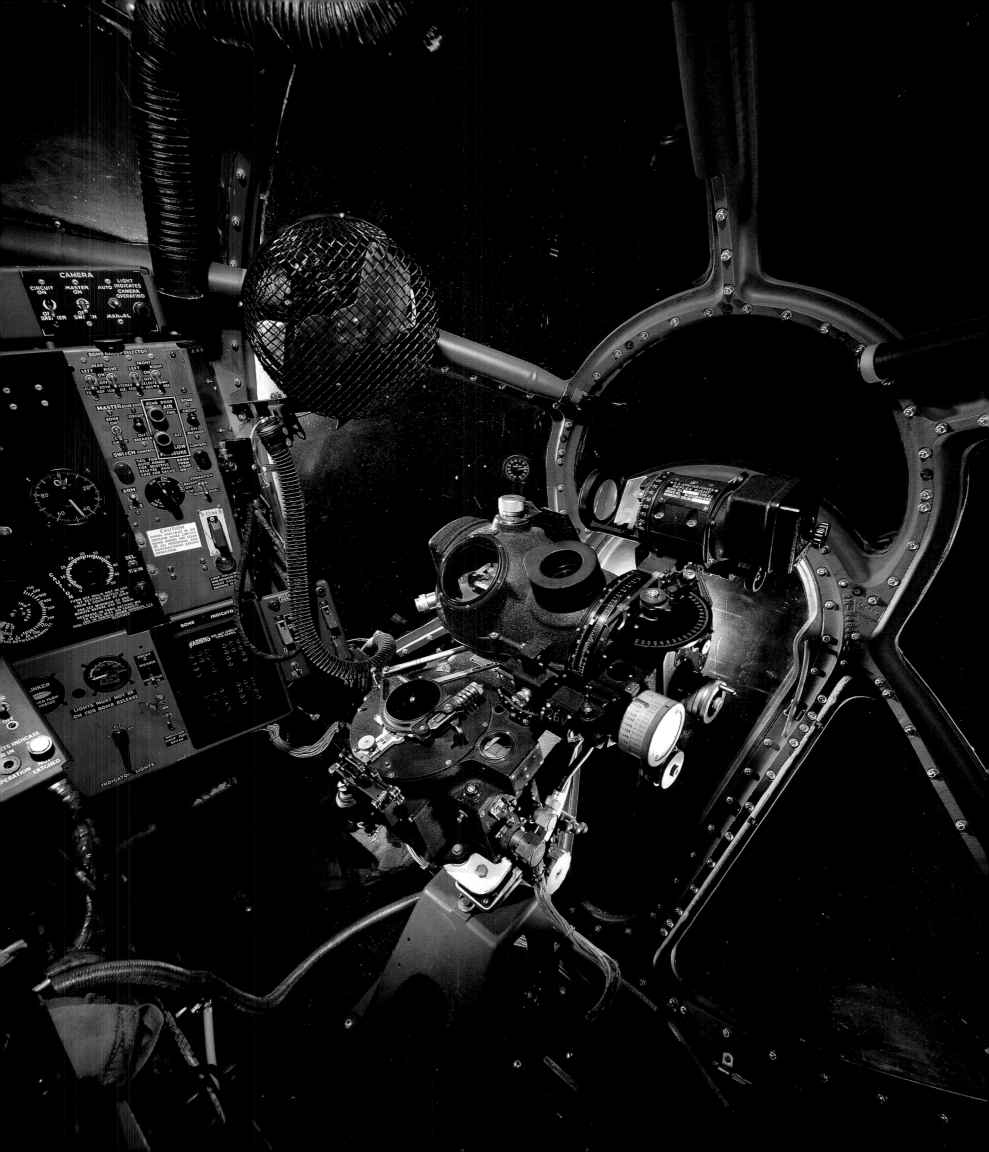

BOCKSCAR
CARRIER OF NUCLEAR FIRE

HIROSHIMA: The word evokes in our mind images of nuclear devastation—blinding light and fire, an ascending mushroom cloud of dust and debris, a city reduced to rubble in an instant, one bomb and one airplane, the dawn of a new epoch in human experience. The atomic bombing of Hiroshima on August 6, 1945 (and Nagasaki three days later), lingers in our collective historical memory and is an event that gave birth to both positive and negative consequences. Hiroshima and Nagasaki, for certain, recast how World War II ended in the Pacific. The original script, then playing out in an escalating spiral of violence and death, had called for an American invasion of Japan as the final act. Such a massive undertaking became unnecessary in the wake of the atomic bombings, no doubt saving innumerable lives on both sides.

The advent of atomic weapons—a quantum leap in destructive power—ushered into existence a new era in which the lethal potential of nuclear energy haunted the post-1945 world and shaped the character of international relations. The ensuing Cold War between the United States and the Soviet Union only heightened fears that nuclear weapons might threaten civilization itself.

The atomic bombing missions to Hiroshima and Nagasaki, it should be remembered, were part of America's strategic bombing campaign against Japan. The Manhattan Project, concealed in secrecy and fueled by a war-induced clamor to be the first to build a nuclear bomb, bequeathed to the United States in the summer of 1945 a decisive instrument to force militaristic Japan to accept unconditional surrender. For the American leadership, ending the war was the highest priority; no weapon—in particular a weapon with the magnitude of an atomic bomb—could be overlooked as a strategic option to end hostilities and bring the American armed forces home.

We remember Colonel Paul W. Tibbets, Jr., and the crew of the B-29 Superfortress *Enola Gay* for dropping the first atomic bomb, "Little Boy," on Hiroshima. By contrast, the second atomic bombing mission to Nagasaki, led by Major Charles W. Sweeney at the controls of another Superfortress named *Bockscar*, has slipped into the fog of history. Few today remember *Bockscar* or understand even vaguely its historic role in the Pacific War. History's shorthand has placed the *Enola Gay* at center stage, and for many people it is the single controversial symbol of the nuclear age.

(ABOVE)

A rare photo of bombardier Charles Love on Bockscar *during the atomic mission to Nagasaki.*

(OPPOSITE)

The cockpit of the B-29 Enola Gay, showing the bombardier's station in the forward compartment.

(OPPOSITE)

The flight line of B-29s on Tinian, where Boeing B-29s of the 444th Bombardment Group await servicing in preparation for their next mission.

(TOP)

Rows of B-29s with the 20th Air Force on Tinian at the close of World War II. The massive strategic bombing campaign launched from Tinian and bases in China brought the war home to Japan at the end of the Pacific War.

(BOTTOM)

A war production poster displays the design of the B-29 Superfortress.

One could nonetheless argue that *Bockscar* played the more decisive role: the devastation of Nagasaki, following so quickly in the aftermath of Hiroshima, raised in the minds of Japan's rulers the prospect that the United States possessed a vast inventory of atomic weaponry. *Bockscar*'s fateful mission on August 9, 1945, prompted Emperor Hirohito to urge his reluctant nation to accept surrender, knowing that the United States now possessed a weapon that could destroy Japan.

The Japanese did not know at the time that *Bockscar*, in fact, had dropped America's second and sole remaining atomic bomb in the Pacific theater. Moreover, for the Americans there was the realization that *Bockscar* had achieved success by the narrowest of margins: unlike the *Enola Gay*, *Bockscar* had flown a mission punctuated with mishaps, bad weather, and, fatefully, shifting targets. The last-minute decision to bomb Nagasaki, the designated secondary target, came only after the failed and time-consuming effort to reach the industrial center of the city of Kokura. *Bockscar* was a singular demonstration of an old truism that epic moments in military conflict are often shaped more by chance than design.

The story of *Bockscar* began with the 509th Composite Group, the special United States Army Air Forces (USAAF) air unit organized to deliver the atomic bomb. Flying B-29 Superfortresses, the 509th had been mobilized at Wendover Field, Utah, in September 1944, "for an undetermined period of time to accomplish a special War Department Project." This opaque mission statement deliberately concealed— even to those airmen mobilized for the 509th—the fact that they had been selected to perform a unique mission in the history of air power.

(TOP)

Bomber crews receive their final briefing before embarking on a mission to Japan.

(BOTTOM)

Missions from Tinian in the Marianas were long and arduous, typically launched at dawn to allow crews to return to base before dusk.

(OPPOSITE)

Two B-29s on the way home to Tinian. The Superfortress in the distance has lost one of its engines on the port side. In emergencies, some B-29s landed at Iwo Jima, while still others were required to ditch at sea.

Training for the elite 509th took a special path of its own. While scientists attached to the Manhattan Project rushed in 1943 and 1944 to perfect the atomic bomb, members of the 509th Composite Group began learning how to equip their B-29s to drop the super weapon. A nuclear device would be heavy, would require special procedures for arming and release, and would compel crews of the 509th to execute a special escape maneuver to avoid the blast of the bomb. Colonel Tibbets fashioned the new air unit to meet these new technical and tactical requirements.

As it took shape in 1944 and 1945, the 509th became a rather peculiar entity within the USAAF, organizationally set apart, shrouded in secrecy, and offered all the human and technical resources deemed necessary to complete its mysterious mission. Many who had been mobilized to serve in the 509th knew little—until the final moments—about its special mission. Attached to the 509th at Wendover were several support entities to provide either technical or security functions: intelligence, armament, air transport, communications, photo interpretation, meteorology, and military police. The aim was to constitute the 509th as a highly autonomous and self-sufficient air unit. Air personnel of the 509th lived under severe security rules, compelled to conceal from families and friends the nature of their work. Even on passenger trains, members of the squadron ate alone under guard; only when they finished were other personnel allowed into the dining car. Other USAAF air units were given information on the high-priority work of the 509th only on a need-to-know basis.

Tibbets personally led the crucial effort to train his bomber crews for the planned atomic missions to Japan in

B-29s of the 20th Air Force drop incendiary bombs over Japanese cities.

A striking photograph of a night raid showing the effects of the firebombing of Japan's cities.

1945. At one juncture, to remove the 509th from the stateside air force context, Tibbets led a training mission to Cuba, where 10 B-29s flew out of Batista Field near Havana. In ideal weather, the crews performed various bombing and navigation training sorties to Bermuda, Puerto Rico, and the Virgin Islands. Proficiency in all the demanding aspects of heavy bomber aviation was achieved, including armament, radar, and communications.

While many in the 509th did not know the ultimate purpose of their atypical training, some were gradually allowed access to the top secret character of their mission. Often, in the period after January 1945, one or more crews "disappeared" for a week or more, flying to a destination cryptically called "I," "A," or "Y." These small contingents of the 509th were granted access to the most secret dimension of the training regimen, their first orientation on the atomic bomb and the process of dropping this new and formidable weapon.

By April 1945, the 509th began the slow process of transferring its command and assets to Tinian, the huge Pacific base for B-29 bombing missions in the Marianas islands. Once the aircraft arrived at Tinian, they were positioned on coral hard stands on a secluded portion of the air base, the former headquarters of the 18th Seabee unit. The personnel of the 509th had to adapt quickly to the hot and humid environs of Tinian. They occupied a rough-hewed open space filled with tents and canvas cots. While the 509th received special priority on supplies, the secured world at Tinian, at best, was primitive and functional. In time, the 509th, operating in high secrecy and outside the normal routine, prompted suspicion and resentment among other air units in the 20th Air Force stationed at Tinian.

(TOP)

Numerous B-29s were lost in accidents, often on takeoff or landings. Any mishap on takeoff was especially hazardous, with the bomber carrying a maximum payload of bombs and fuel.

(BOTTOM)

Despite the losses, the missions continued relentlessly.

Although the 509th carried out its first operational mission against the Japanese on July 20—an attack on the Niigata area using 10,000-pound "pumpkin" bombs (test bombs used for training)—Colonel Tibbets continued to put the crews through special training sequences in anticipation of dropping an atomic bomb. These included a high-altitude bombing run and the release of a bomb followed by a descending turn of 155 degrees to reverse direction away from the blast. Such a maneuver was deemed critical, to give the B-29 carrying an atomic bomb a minimum of 10 miles separation from the blast. Aircraft of the 509th flew four of these practice bombing runs in July 1945 over Japan.

That same month, the core of the first atomic bomb arrived at Tinian, carried across the Pacific by the U.S. Navy cruiser *Indianapolis,* an ill-fated warship later sunk by a Japanese submarine off the Philippines. The survivors of the *Indianapolis* then endured one of the more harrowing experiences of the Pacific War cast adrift for days in shark-infested waters. No one on Tinian knew of this unfolding tragedy. The 509th now received its clear mandate: the new atomic bomb would be dropped on Japan on the first clear day after August 3. No less important, the United States prepared to send additional bombs to Tinian "as soon as made ready."

In the early morning of August 6, 1945, the *Enola Gay,* commanded by Colonel Paul Tibbets, undertook the fateful first mission to Hiroshima. A total of six B-29s participated in the mission: three weather aircraft in advance of the *Enola Gay* and two additional Superfortresses to provide observation and photography. Fifteen minutes into the flight, the atomic bomb was armed. Once over the target, the *Enola Gay* encountered excellent weather, allowing for nearly unlimited visibility.

Bockscar *with its crew on Tinian in the Marianas, from where the aircraft and crew flew to drop the atomic bomb on Nagasaki.*

The crew of Bockscar *added the distinctive nose art to their historic Superfortress shortly after the Nagasaki mission of August 9, 1945.*

The bomb was released at 8:15 a.m. from an altitude of 31,600 feet. Only 43 seconds passed before the atomic bomb ignited over the city at a height of 1,900 feet and only 700 feet from the intended aiming point. The immense power of the Hiroshima bomb could be measured in the 70,000 deaths and the destruction of over 80 percent of the city's buildings.

During the *Enola Gay* mission, Major Charles Sweeney flew an observation aircraft B-29 named the *Great Artiste*. In the aftermath of the *Enola Gay's* successful sortie to Hiroshima, Sweeney was given the nod to lead the second atomic mission to Japan. The proposed date for that mission was August 11, but with worsening weather it was decided to launch the bombing run on August 9, just three days after Hiroshima. For the nuclear mission, Sweeney took command of the B-29 Superfortress *Bockscar*, named after fellow pilot Fred Bock. Unlike the smoothly executed *Enola Gay* sortie, the flight of *Bockscar* would be remembered for its troubled passage to and from Japan on America's second atomic bombing mission.

The huge four-engine B-29 bomber, at the time the state-of-the-art strategic bomber, possessed extraordinary range and payload capabilities. As one of 15 late-model B-29s assigned to the 509th, *Bockscar* possessed many structural modifications for carrying an atomic weapon. The forward bomb bay structure had been reinforced and a large shackle with a single lug had been installed to handle a 10,000-pound bomb. Special sway bracing was also installed to prevent any lateral or longitudinal movement of the bomb. In addition, *Bockscar*—like other B-29s assigned to the 509th—came with highly sophisticated electronic equipment: fuel-injection for the Wright R-3350 engines (2,200 horsepower); electric reversible pitch propellers, a state-of-the-art system that even allowed for the B-29 to be backed into the bomb loading pit at Tinian; and pneumatic actuators for the rapid opening and closing of the bomb bay doors. Finally, and at some calculated risk, *Bockscar* was stripped of most of its defensive armament, which reduced drag and allowed for a larger payload. The B-29s, in the parlance of the time, were "silverplate" versions of the Boeing Superfortress design.

The bomb *Bockscar* carried to Japan was dubbed "Fat Man," aptly named to reflect its round and blunt silhouette. Covered with graffiti and adorned with a pinup of Rita Hayworth, this second nuclear device differed markedly from Little Boy, the bomb dropped by the *Enola Gay*. Where Little Boy possessed a U-235 projectile in a gun-type design, Fat Man came equipped with a plutonium Pu-239 core in a spherical assembly that was compressed to a super-critical mass by an implosion to ignite. One question haunted the crew: Could the Fat Man bomb be accidentally detonated?

Thirteen men were on *Bockscar* for its historic flight to Japan on August 9: Major Charles W. Sweeney, pilot, and

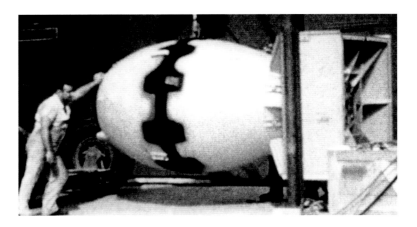

The Fat Man atomic device—the bomb dropped on Nagasaki by the crew of Bockscar—*arrives at Tinian.*

Captain Fred J. Olivi, copilot, were at the controls. Other crew included Lieutenant Philip M. Barnes, bomb electronics officer; Lieutenant Jacob Beser, radar operator; Captain Kermit K. Beahan, bombardier; and Captain James F. Van Pelt, navigator. For this critical mission, Navy commander Frederick L. Ashworth held the pivotal position of operations officer and bomb commander. Many on board *Bockscar* and the escort planes had participated, in various ways, in the first mission to Hiroshima. Each member of *Bockscar*'s crew received cyanide pills, an option to avoid capture.

This second mission was called "Special Mission No. 16." The designated target was Kokura, an industrial city largely unscathed at this juncture by America's strategic bombing campaign against Japan. The secondary target was Nagasaki, the old port city and leading ship building center for the Japanese navy. Briefings for the flight called for a bombing run at 31,000 feet. Two weather planes were assigned to fly over the target area and report on visibility. Radio silence was to be maintained with no exceptions.

Bockscar flew independently to Japan, with plans to rendezvous over Yokoshima with two other B-29s—*The Great Artiste* and *Full House*—equipped with scientific instrumentation and cameras. The script called for Sweeney to linger at the rendezvous point for no more than 15 minutes. Because the other aircraft failed to rendezvous on time, Sweeney found himself circling the designated area for some 45 minutes. Another problem arose to make the mission problematical: while en route to Yokoshima, Sweeney learned that the fuel pump for *Bockscar*'s reserve tank—containing some 600 gallons of precious fuel—was inoperative.

Frustrated by the failed rendezvous with the escort

bombers and now faced with a growing fuel crisis, Sweeney decided to press on to Kokura. This decision raised the risk that there would be no photographic record of the mission—the cameras for recording the bombing were in the bomber *Full House*, which had failed to rendezvous with *Bockscar*.

Sweeney found himself wrestling with other problems. The black box housing the electrical switches for arming the Fat Man bomb had a red light, which normally blinked at regular intervals. Barnes was the first to notice a sudden and jarring malfunction, one with great portent for disaster: the red light was now blinking in a random and wild fashion, suggesting that something was seriously wrong with the bomb. Joined by Commander Ashworth, Barnes attempted to locate the problem. He quickly discovered that the wiring for two rotary switches had been reversed.

If these had been the timing fuses, the crisis would have proved fatal—the crew would have had only a minute or even less to discover the problem before the bomb would have gone off, atomizing the plane.

On the approach to Kokura, the weather worsened. Forecasts had indicated that the weather around the city would be favorable, allowing for a visual bombing. Instead, the cloud cover above Kokura had obscured the target. Moreover, lingering smoke from an air raid the previous day on nearby Yawata had moved across Kokura. Sweeney was alarmed to discover that his primary target was shielded by haze and clouds.

After hurriedly conferring with Ashworth, Sweeney directed *Bockscar* to head for Nagasaki, the alternate target. "I was now an hour and a half behind schedule," Sweeney recalled. "The 'Fat Man' was still resting in the bomb bay. I would have one shot to get this done when we arrived at

A photograph of the "mushroom" cloud rising over Nagasaki, seen from Bockscar *as it maneuvered to head home.*

Nagasaki. God only knew what awaited us there. Can any other goddammed thing go wrong?"

Upon reaching Nagasaki, Sweeney's worst fears materialized: the city was 90 percent cloud-covered with only small breaks allowing the crew to see fleeting images of the cityscape below. Further discussions followed between Ashworth and Sweeney, the two men in control of the bomb and airplane, respectively. Should they drop the bomb by radar, in contradiction to explicit orders to make a visual bombing run? Niigata, the third target option, was too far away, given the desperate fuel situation and with the Fat Man bomb armed. Sweeney did not relish the idea of returning to base with this extraordinary cargo on board. To add to the anxious mood, there was fear that *Bockscar* could not make it back to Okinawa, and that any ditching maneuver in the East China Sea would be a disaster.

Just as *Bockscar* made its sweep over the Nagasaki area, using radar to seek out the target area, Beahan, the bombardier, shouted, "I've got a hole! I can see it! I can see the target!"

Beahan then shouted, "Bombs Away," and then quickly corrected himself, "Bomb Away!" It was 11:01 a.m. The chance discovery of a few holes in the clouds that day over Nagasaki sealed the city's fate.

Sweeney later described the tension-filled scene following the release of Fat Man: "At the moment of release the airplane lurched upward, suddenly ten thousand pounds lighter.... The bomb bay doors slammed shut. I took us into a steep, diving, 155-degree turn to the left, in a northeasterly direct, to get away from the blast. Time seemed suspended. As the seconds ticked by, I began to wonder if we had dropped a dud. Then suddenly the entire horizon burst into a superbrilliant white with intense heat—more intense than Hiroshima. The light was blinding. A moment later, the first wave of super heated air began hitting us with unexpected force. . . . As I completed my turn, I could see a brownish horizontal cloud enveloping the city below. The bomb had detonated at 1,890 feet. . . . From the center of the brownish bile sprung a vertical column, boiling and bubbling up in those rainbow hues—purple, oranges, reds—colors whose brilliance I had seen only once before and would never see again."

Robert Laurence, a reporter for *The New York Times*, observed the extraordinary and historical moment from *The Great Artiste*, the observation Superfortress escorting *Bockscar*. Laurence, who later wrote the book *Dawn Over Zero*, was one of the few civilians allowed access to the atomic missions. "We watched," he later wrote, "a giant pillar of purple fire, 10,000 feet high, shoot upward like a meteor coming from earth rather than outer space. . . . It was no longer smoke, or dust, or even a cloud of fire. It was a living thing, a new species of being, born right before our incredulous eyes. . . . It kept struggling in an elemental fury, like a creature in the act of breaking the bonds that held it down."

Nagasaki was a port city nestled between hills, a bowl-like terrain that enhanced the destructive blast of the bomb. Nearly one and one-half square miles of territory was destroyed, much less than the incendiary raids conducted over Japanese cities like Tokyo using conventional bombing, but highly destructive of Nagasaki's industrial complexes. As with Hiroshima, the loss of life could never be calculated accurately, but the United States Strategic Bombing Survey estimated that over 35,000 were killed, over 5,000 missing, and another 60,000 injured.

For the crew of *Bockscar*, there were mixed feelings—a sense of awe over the event they had just observed and a growing anxiety over the fuel crisis that had been momentarily forgotten with the dropping of Fat Man.

Bockscar then transmitted a simple message back to Tinian: "Bombed Nagasaki 090158Z visually. No opposition. Visible effects about equal to Hiroshima. Proceeding to Okinawa. Fuel problem."

The flight to Okinawa proved to be a white-knuckle affair, with *Bockscar* finally reaching the airfield with its usable fuel tanks nearly empty. For landing, Sweeney made a direct approach to the field, coming in high and fast, knowing he had only one chance to make it. From the cockpit Sweeney and his copilot Fred Olivi could see emergency trucks and equipment speeding to the runway. The plane touched down in the middle of the airstrip at 150 miles per hour, a speed well in excess of safety standards. As *Bockscar* touched down, it swerved to the left, almost hitting a line of parked B-24s. Just as Sweeney gained control and taxied off the runway, the number two engine quit. Only drops of fuel remained. *Bockscar* had made it back, but just barely. Thus ended one of the most remarkable and historic missions of World War II.

On August 15, less than a week after the bombing of Nagasaki, the Japanese sued for peace. World War II had ended. The nuclear age had begun. Air power had launched the Pacific War at Pearl Harbor on December 7, 1941. Now, after the passage of four years and a brutal struggle, air power had brought a sudden and dramatic end to the conflict. *Bockscar*—soon to slip into historical obscurity—had played no small role in these events.

The devastation of Nagasaki as a consequence of the atomic bombing on August 9, 1945.

MACH 1 AND MACH 2
BREAKING THE SOUND BARRIER

SHOCK WAVES reverberated across the desert floor at California's Muroc (later Edwards) Air Force Base on October 14, 1947. The loud chap signaled the advent of the supersonic age. At that moment, Captain Charles E. "Chuck" Yeager pushed his rocket-powered Bell X-1 into a new dimension of flying. The experimental X-1, painted a distinctive yellow-orange hue and dubbed the *Glamorous Glennis* after Yeager's wife, had broken through the sonic wall, achieving the speed of sound or Mach 1.

Yeager's extraordinary flight set into motion a spirited competition to establish new supersonic milestones, a competition that often pitted the Air Force's X-planes against the Navy's supersonic research aircraft. Breaking sound barriers defined test flying in the years before Sputnik and the advent of the space age.

High-speed flight had long posed many challenges to aviators. During World War II, for example, pilots in power dives in the P-38 *Lightnings* and RAF *Spitfires* experienced control problems as they edged toward the threshold of the speed of sound, at around 0.7 Mach: there was extreme buffeting, increased drag, and the loss or reversal of controls. The transonic zone offered many mysteries and dangers at a time when the nature of high-speed flight was imperfectly understood.

At this fast speed, the airplane encountered the phenomenon of "compressibility," when the air flowing over the top of the wing reached the speed of sound even as the aircraft remained at subsonic speed. Shock waves interrupted the smooth flow of air over the tail surfaces, making control marginal or nonexistent. Some aeronautical engineers theorized that the shock waves could trigger the disintegration of an airplane at the speed of Mach 1. This prophecy came true for Geoffrey de Havilland, Jr., when his DH-108 *Swallow* experimental plane broke up in an ill-fated attempt to break the sound barrier in 1946. De Havilland's death haunted all those who dared to venture to the sonic wall and attempted to fly beyond it at supersonic speeds.

Chuck Yeager defied the widespread notion that there was a physical sound barrier. It was the advent of jet and rocket engines that set the stage for pilots such as Yeager to cross the hitherto sonic barrier. The X-1 emerged from the Bell factory at Niagara Falls, New York, in December 27, 1945, in the immediate aftermath of World War II. In every aspect of its design, the X-1 pointed to the future. It was 30 feet and 11 inches in length, and nearly 11 feet high. It was a semimonocoque design with stressed aluminum alloy

(ABOVE)

U.S. Air Force Captain Charles E. "Chuck" Yeager stands next to the Bell X-1 Glamorous Glennis, *named after his wife.*

(OPPOSITE)

The U.S. Air Force Bell X-1, as a rocket-powered airplane, represented a new generation of test aircraft capable of reaching the speed of sound (740 miles per hour at sea level).

(ABOVE)

The lanky Chuck Yeager found the cockpit of the Bell X-1 to be a tight fit.

(RIGHT)

Designed for speed and research, the X-1's cockpit offered little in the way of space or comfort.

~186~

(TOP)

The X-1 was powered by an XLR-11 rocket motor, fitted with four chambers that could be fired individually or in combination for varying amounts of thrust.

(BOTTOM)

Rocket motor technology required careful maintenance and systematic ground-testing of the XLR-11 engine.

skin, fashioned in the shape of .50-caliber bullet, and was fitted with short and thin wings (low aspect ratio wings). Lacking conventional wings, the X-1 required forward movement to stay aloft—if the air speed dropped below 240 miles per hour, the X-1 fell into a stall. One critical factor for an air launch was to save weight with the landing gear design and to eliminate the need for additional fuel for a takeoff from the ground.

Once airborne, the X-1 was highly maneuverable. The Bell airplane was fitted with a four-chamber rocket engine, the RM1 XLR-11, burning LOX or liquid oxygen and ethyl alcohol. Great care had to be taken in loading the fuel, always at night when the temperatures were cooler, in order to minimize the chance of an explosion of the highly volatile fuels. Given the weight of the fuel, the actual burn time on the fuel was a mere 2 and one-half minutes. The cockpit for the X-1 was small and visibility was not optimal, but the aircraft was fully capable of achieving its purpose—to fly supersonic.

As an Air Force test pilot, Yeager embodied a powerful mix of technical skill and personal bravado. Tom Wolfe captured Yeager's persona in his book, *The Right Stuff,* seeing in the wartime ace and legendary test pilot a "special bravery, beyond courage." He was at the top of the so-called Ziggurat in the world of test pilots; he was, as Wolfe noted, "the greatest test pilot" and "the fastest man on earth."

Yeager's opportunity to make his "Mach 1 Ride" in the X-1 nearly fell victim to a personal act of recklessness on the eve of the flight scheduled for Tuesday, October 14, 1947. Two days before, he and his wife, Glennis, decided to saddle up some horses for a ride across the desert. Upon their return, Yeager rode his horse into a gate and then plummeted to the ground. He landed hard on his right side. The next day, in extreme

(TOP)

Loading the X-1 into the belly of the B-29 mothership became a time-consuming task. The first step in the complicated procedure was to place the X-1 in a pit so the test aircraft with its vertical tail assembly could be attached to the B-29.

(MIDDLE)

The Bell X-1 was raised by a winch and sling to be secured to the shackles in the B-29 mothership.

(BOTTOM)

The B-29/X-1 combination ready for takeoff. After climbing to altitude, the X-1 pilot entered the open bomb bay and lowered himself into the cockpit of the test plane just prior to air launch.

pain, he learned from the doctor in a nearby town that he had broken two ribs. Rather than alert anyone to his injury, Yeager decided to make the historic flight notwithstanding the pain. How he managed to conceal this injury and make the historic flight is part of the Yeager legend.

The actual flight of the X-1 began at 26,000 feet, when the B-29 mother ship made a shallow dive to release the X-1 with Yeager seated tightly in the cockpit. Dropping like a bomb from the Superfortress, Yeager's cockpit filled with sunlight once the shadow of the B-29 pulled away. He then ignited the four rocket chambers of his engine in sequence, surging the X-1 upward, almost in a vertical climb. He pushed the plane forward in small increments, edging toward the transonic zone. Once he reached a speed of 0.87 Mach, the X-1 began to buffet violently. Yeager considered this turbulence normal, if fraught with certain perils. He also was convinced that once he reached supersonic speed the violent buffeting would give way to stable flight.

As Yeager predicted, the passage to supersonic speed did see the X-1 smooth out in its trajectory. At 0.92 Mach, the X-1 had reached 42,000 feet altitude; then at 0.98 Mach, Yeager experienced a sudden acceleration, prompting the Machometer on his instrument panel to vibrate momentarily—Yeager was now flying at Mach 1, moving over the California desert at a speed no other human had ever achieved. He was also in control of his intact aircraft, alive, and even gaining speed! As the shock waves rippled over the X-1, the needle on the Machometer sustained the reading of Mach 1.06. On the ground below, Air Force personnel monitored the progress of the *Glamorous Glennis* with radar. There was a sudden clap of thunder overhead, the telltale sign that Yeager indeed had broken the sound barrier.

The X-1 test team consisted of a number of talented pilots and specialists, including test pilots Chuck Yeager, Bob Hoover, and Robert Cardenas. Pictured below is flight-test project engineer Captain Jack Ridley, who played a vital role in the program.

High-speed flight experiments continued in the aftermath of the Yeager flight. For example, Yeager persisted in his test flights, pushing the envelope to a record Mach 1.45 on March 26, 1948. NACA (National Advisory Committee for Aeronautics, the forerunner of NASA) and even the Navy entered the competition, all aiming for the elusive Mach 2 milestone. The rapid pace of the competition rested on two factors, the coming of jet and rocket engines and new streamlined aerodynamic designs. As the 50th anniversary of the Wright brothers flight at Kitty Hawk approached on December 17, 1953, the Air Force planned for Yeager to attempt Mach 2 flying the Bell X-1A.

With minimal fanfare, the Navy decided to fly its Douglas D-558-2 *Skyrocket* in November of that year in a bid to leap ahead of the Air Force to achieve the coveted Mach 2 record. To fly the *Skyrocket*, the Navy enlisted Scott Crossfield, a former Navy aviator and NACA test pilot. He also possessed a master's degree in aeronautical engineering from the University of Washington. His initial work for NACA had been completed at the High Speed Flight Research Station at Edwards (formerly Muroc), the locale for the Yeager flights. Crossfield flew a series of research planes, including the X-1, X-4, X-5, and the Navy's D-558 *Skyrocket* series.

By November 20, the Navy was ready to make a single attempt to fly at Mach 2. If successful, the Navy would best the Air Force in the competition for high-speed records. A B-29 mother ship took the D-558-2 to its launch altitude of 32,000. Crossfield entered the cockpit of the *Skyrocket* from inside the B-29. The Navy research plane dropped away without difficulty, falling momentarily into the void. Crossfield then ignited the *Skyrocket*'s LR-8 rocket engines

With its fuel tanks filled with alcohol and liquid oxygen, frost envelops the Bell X-1 as the B-29 carries it to altitude for launch.

and nosed the aircraft toward the stratosphere; for those below, there was only a white contrail visible in the sky as Crossfield climbed to an altitude of 72,000 feet.

He then pushed over his research plane in a shallow dive toward the earth. The *Skyrocket* quickly topped Mach 1. The Machometer shook as Crossfield moved relentlessly toward his goal—1.7, 1.8, 1.9, and then 2.0 at 62,000 feet altitude. Crossfield later remarked, "I knew we had made it. But I didn't say a damn word until I got back." Crossfield's achievement that day placed him in the pantheon of test pilots. He would be remembered with Yeager as one of the aviation pioneers of the twentieth century. As a footnote, Yeager soon matched the milestone of Mach 2, demonstrating the continuing role of the Air Force in high-speed flight.

Crossfield emerged in the 1950s as America's top civilian test pilot, moving on to fly the North American X-15, a rocket-powered aircraft with 60,000 pounds thrust. Crossfield demonstrated the enormous potential of the X-15—an aircraft with a potential to soar to 67 miles altitude, where one could look out on a black sky filled with stars and see the curvature of the earth. This meant that the X-15 had reached the edge of space. Accordingly, the X-15 became a link between aircraft and spacecraft. The highest flying plane ever built, it ultimately flew to a record altitude of 354,200 feet.

The X-15 was a revolutionary design, with a mission to engage in some of the most demanding high-speed and high-altitude research on thermal heating and control/stability. The X-15 was constructed of alloys that were new and exotic for the time, but primarily of titanium and steel. The airframe was encased with Inconel X nickel, an outer skin capable of withstanding temperatures up to 1,200 degrees Fahrenheit. Late in its flying career, the X-15 was covered

The rocket-assisted Douglas D-558-II Skyrocket *roars aloft.*

with an ablative material (MA-25S) that could burn away with the intense heat above 1,200 degrees. Power for the X-15 came from two Reaction Motors (Thiokol) XLR99-RM—two rocket engines that burned a liquid fuel composed of liquid hydrogen and anhydrous ammonia capable of 57,000 pounds of thrust—and, for the initial flights, by two XLR-11s with 8,000 pounds thrust each. All flights were conducted at Edwards AFB, and the X-15 was dropped from a B-52 bomber at an altitude of 45,000 feet.

Scott Crossfield made his first flight of the X-15 on September 17, 1959. He made 13 crucial demonstration flights at the dawn of the X-15 program, a test program that extended into 1960. His tenure as a test pilot keynoted the saga of the X-15, setting the stage for a total of 199 test flights made by some 12 test pilots. Crossfield described the X-15 as a "fine mount," an apt metaphor indeed for a research plane with a unique performance envelope, a flight trajectory that eventually took controlled manned flight to the threshold of space at unbelievable speeds of nearly Mach 7, or 4,520 miles per hour. The flight log of the X-15 thus mirrors the unquenchable urge to test the outer limits of human technology in the air age. Scott Crossfield contributed to this endeavor in a dramatic way through his tenure as a test pilot for the X-15.

One harrowing experience for Crossfield in high-speed flight involved a rocket engine explosion during a ground check, a blast that catapulted Crossfield, seated in the cocoon of the cockpit, down the runway in a massive cloud of orange flames. A fire truck approached from the front, pouring waves of water on the fiery scene. With the assistance of a brave technician, Art Simone, Crossfield was able to push the cockpit canopy open and leap to safety.

(TOP)

The North American X-15 ignites its rocket motors after release from the NASA B-52B mothership.

(BOTTOM)

The rocket-powered research plane X-15 in flight.

(OPPOSITE)

Climbing to the edge of space, an X-15 leaves a gigantic contrail in its wake.

Another time, his X-15 broke its back during an emergency landing necessitated by an in-flight explosion and fire. When Crossfield successfully put the X-15 down on Rosamond Dry Lake near Edwards AFB, he decided to remain in the safe environs of his cockpit, not knowing if the fire still threatened him and his research plane. Among his rescuers that day was a physician who feared that Crossfield was injured, misunderstanding the radio chatter to mean that Crossfield, not the X-15, had a "broken back." When Crossfield saw the physician approaching his plane, he assumed that the fire was out, so he slowly began to open the X-15's cockpit canopy to deplane.

Still believing that Crossfield was severely injured, the doctor and accompanying rescuers attempted to open the canopy fully, as a preliminary to extricating the "injured pilot." Crossfield unsuccessfully attempted to wave them off. He then found himself in a wresting match with his rescuers to prevent the canopy from being opened fully; pushing the canopy to full open position would have triggered the ejection seat! Such were the dangers associated with test flying.

Scott Crossfield's flights also included some narrow escapes. Arguably, one of Crossfield's most important flights came on November 15, 1960, when he made his first flight in the X-15-2, powered by XLR99 engine. This particular demonstration flight went extremely well, with no mishaps. Crossfield demonstrated the efficiency of the XLR99 engine at 50 percent thrust (28,000 pounds). Crossfield dropped from the B-52 carrier at 46,000 feet, falling into the sunlit expanse. From this elevation, Crossfield—even with minimal power—soared to 81,200 feet at a speed of Mach 2.97. A second flight allowed Crossfield to test the engine's

With its high landing speeds, the X-15 did not have wheeled main landing gear, relying instead on skids placed under the tail section of the aircraft.

Landing the high-speed X-15 was complicated with many control problems at touch down. On one difficult landing, Crossfield encountered serious damage to his X-15.

Flying at the edge of space, the X-15 pilot required a special flying suit. Scott Crossfield is shown suited up for a near-space flight.

restart and throttle controls. By December 1960, Crossfield had made a third and final flight with the XLR99 engine, confirming the X-15-2's operational efficiency. At this juncture, Crossfield left the X-15 program to work for North American Aviation, and testing of the X-15 became the sole responsibility of government test pilots.

Scott Crossfield was the first to fly the X-15. That distinction alone placed him at the forefront of one of the most important flight research programs in the era of the Cold War. His demonstration flights set the X-15 program on a confident trajectory that would yield many key results for those attentive to the requirements for high-speed and high-altitude flying machines on the eve of the space age.

While Crossfield's departure for North American Aviation in 1960 precluded further work with the X-15 test program, his critical role in the program's success is undeniable. Certain aspects of the X-15 program were essential to the manned space program that would follow in the 1960s. Pilots of the X-15 experimented with the techniques of high-altitude trajectories and reentry into the lower atmosphere. Associated with these experiments was a stream of data related to the biomedical impact of weightlessness and high-g maneuvers. Interestingly, the data from the X-15 flights would prove more useful for NASA's space program than the atmospheric flights.

The Yeager-Crossfield supersonic flights moved aviation into a new sphere. America's high performance research planes, from Yeager's X-1 to Crossfield's D-558-2 and X-15, challenged the test pilots' technical skills, discipline, and courage. Scott Crossfield described the U.S. Air Force's Bell X-1, the first of these remarkable planes, as a stable and forgiving aircraft, even in the transonic regime of flying.

The U.S. Navy's Douglas D-558-2 *Skyrocket*, in which Crossfield later flew at Mach 2, required, in his words, a "delicate touch to bring out all the aircraft's best characteristics and to avoid its idiosyncrasies." With the X-15, Crossfield observed, the test pilot had to fly "attentively and intelligently," for this "eager ready stallion" could be unforgiving to anyone with a heavy hand or reckless manner. Crossfield would find the X-15—always responsive to the touch of an experienced test pilot— nonetheless a flying machine with unique dangers. Crossfield himself survived rocket engine failures and a narrow brush with death in a crash landing. Still, he eventually took the X-15 to the edge of Mach 3.

By the late 1950s, the space age offered a new arena of research for test pilots. A small number of them made their way into the highly competitive Mercury program. Given

his renown as a test pilot, Crossfield appeared as a natural for the Mercury astronaut program. Yet, he declined to participate.

Crossfield never expressed Yeager's open disdain for the manned space program, the belief that riding in a space capsule and splashing down in the ocean was not really flying, after all—as Yeager said, "A monkey's gonna make the first flight." But for Crossfield, it was the unreasonable and demanding medical tests that, in the final analysis, prompted him to reject Project Mercury. The advent of the astronauts signaled a new era in research flying. Both Yeager and Crossfield belonged to the world of the X-planes, which in many ways had been the harbinger for the space age.

Both men set a high standard for technical skill and personal bravery, essential attributes for those who would be selected as the first astronauts.

SAIGON
HELICOPTERS TO THE RESCUE

Color photography by Dirck Halstead

Black and white photography by Major John F. Guilmartin, Jr.

TO SIGNAL the start of the final phase of *Operation Frequent Wind*, the helicopter evacuation of Saigon, planners in the American Embassy arranged for a secret message to be aired on Armed Forces Radio in the early morning hours of the day chosen: "The temperature in Saigon is 105 degrees and rising" followed by a recording of Bing Crosby singing "I'm Dreaming of a White Christmas." Once Americans and Vietnamese earmarked for evacuation heard this clandestine alert, they were to move immediately to the DAO (Defense Attaché Office) compound on Tan Son Nhut airport, where helipads had been prepared in parking lots, tennis courts, and the softball diamond. A few would proceed to the embassy for evacuation. Awaiting them would be a flotilla of helicopters for transport to the ships of the U.S. Navy's 7th Fleet stationed some 30 miles offshore.

The stage was set for *Operation Frequent Wind* by the sudden collapse of South Vietnam in the spring of 1975. Following up on their successes north of Saigon in January, the North Vietnamese Army (NVA) launched a massive offensive in early March with an army of 150,000 soldiers lavishly equipped with tanks, motor transport, and artillery, attacking under a protective umbrella of antiaircraft artillery and surface-to-air missiles. By mid-month, South Vietnamese defenses in the pivotal Central Highlands had collapsed, while in the north, Communist forces were driving on Hue. On March 25, President Nguyen Van Thieu ordered Hue abandoned, a sharp contrast to the staunch defense of the old imperial capital by U.S. Marines and the Army of South Vietnam (ARVN) during the 1968 Tết offensive.

At this apocalyptic moment, American ambassador Graham Martin unwittingly added to the panic, declaring on Saigon television that any Vietnamese seeking refuge in the United States would be welcomed. For those Vietnamese who had fought the Communists or assisted the Americans, Martin's statement offered hope; a wild clamor ensued to join the American rescue effort. Martin's promise proved to be an empty and cruel gesture for all too many Vietnamese: in the days that followed, American officials were hard pressed to find safe passage for their own countrymen and were able to accommodate only a limited number of endangered Vietnamese, who were flown out first on commercial airliners and then aboard U.S. Air Force transports.

Building momentum, the NVA forces pressed on through Hue toward the vital port city of Da Nang, triggering panic among its defenders. On April 29, South Vietnamese

(ABOVE)

Major John F. "Joe" Guilmartin, Jr. (second from right), stands with his crew next to their Sikorsky HH-53C "Super Jolly" from the 40th Aerospace Rescue and Recovery Squadron aboard the USS Midway, *June 1975.*

(OPPOSITE)

An American soldier stands alert as a Marine Sikorsky "Swift" CH-53A Sea Stallion heavy-lift helicopter touches down in a parking lot landing zone during the April 1975 evacuation.

(LEFT)

With Saigon under assault by the North Vietnamese Army, frantic efforts were made to evacuate American and South Vietnamese personnel. A South Vietnamese CH-47A Chinook lands in the midst of the evacuation process on April 27, 1975, at Xuan Loc, north of Saigon.

(TOP)

South Vietnamese soldiers load wounded onto the Chinook helicopter.

(BOTTOM)

As the Chinook leaves, the remaining soldiers are on their own.

(TOP)

Saigon under siege in April 1975.
The historic Cathedral of Notre
Dame in the foreground is visible,
with clouds of dark smoke rising on
the horizon.

(BOTTOM)

South Vietnamese civilians in the
aftermath of a rocket assault on
Saigon, April 27, 1975. Only a few
refugees found their way to safety in
the evacuation process.

forces in Da Nang dissolved in utter confusion, with some soldiers trampling women and children to gain the few seats open on the last departing 727 airliner. Unable to force themselves aboard, panic-stricken men clung to the landing gear as the plane took off, only to fall off in the South China Sea or be crushed by the retracting undercarriage. Such scenes evoked despair in Saigon and Washington.

Moving relentlessly forward, the North Vietnamese Army had reached the gates of Saigon by April, to be halted at Xuan Loc by a desperate ARVN defense. Outnumbered by more than three to one and pounded by heavy artillery fire, the ARVN held out for nearly two weeks in one of the epic struggles of the war, but by April 23 it was over. The remaining demoralized ARVN forces were clearly incapable of serious resistance. A declaration of martial law and the resignation of President Thieu in favor of a new government did nothing to reverse the downward spiral into chaos.

Meanwhile, American military commanders, shocked by the speed of the ARVN collapse, were scrambling to assemble a helicopter evacuation force, guarding against the day when Communist artillery would close Saigon's Tan Son Nhut airport to fixed-wing aircraft. The core of the evacuation force consisted of two carrier-based Marine CH-53 squadrons, HMH-462 and 463, with 16 of the big helicopters each, supplemented by 24 smaller CH-46s, all under the command of Marine brigadier general Richard Carey. Even this force seemed inadequate for the number of potential evacuees, and it was supplemented by 10 Thailand-based Air Force HH-53s (Jolly Green Giants) of the 56th Special Operations Wing (SOW) and 40th Aerospace Rescue and Recovery Squadron (ARRS), flown aboard the carrier USS *Midway*. This was a bold expedient, for the Air Force flyers

(TOP)

An Air America Bell UH-1 sits atop the embassy building during the Saigon rescue operations.

(BOTTOM)

An aerial photo of Tan Son Nhut airport and the surrounding area, with evacuation landing zones outlined with colored tape. Captain Guilmartin used this map during his flights to the landing zones at Ton Son Nhut airport.

had no experience in shipboard operations and their helicopters' rotor blades did not fold, placing deck space at a premium. They arrived on April 20, just as the Battle of Xuan Loc reached its tragic climax.

The United States had brokered a peace treaty with the North Vietnamese in February 1973; though no one in authority would say so openly, it was in reality a cease-fire to allow the Americans to complete their withdrawal from the war after, in Secretary of State Henry Kissinger's words, "a decent interval." But the North Vietnamese were intent on victory once the Americans had been eliminated as a effective force. No sooner had the Americans departed than the NVA pressure on South Vietnam renewed.

Efforts by the Nixon and the Ford administrations to sustain economic and military aid for the Saigon government proved uneven and largely ineffectual. As late as April 1975, as the vise closed on Saigon, President Ford attempted to gain Congressional support for $722 million in emergency aid, but he failed. A sense of defeat pervaded Washington. With the anticipated collapse of the South Vietnam government now measured in weeks, or even days, the only concern was to extract from Saigon as many Americans and endangered Vietnamese as possible.

Decisive action by Washington proved difficult, given the narrow time frame to react. Ambassador Martin displayed a certain inertia in the midst of the crisis, mixed with a false sense of hope that the situation was not beyond redemption or, for that matter, that Americans would have to leave. Martin feared that even the utterance of the word *evacuation* would ignite a panic on the scale of Da Nang just weeks before. Despite all the signs of impending doom, America's chief diplomat in Saigon was slow to move, even

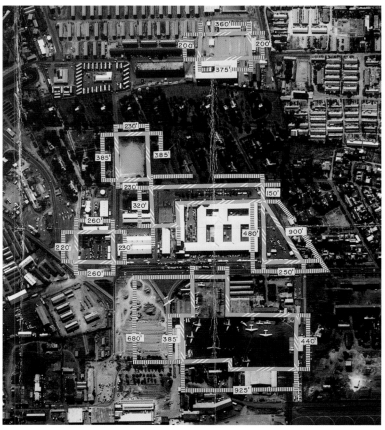

With rotors of a Marine CH-53 Sea Stallion still turning, a ground security force of Marines rush to secure a narrow landing zone.

DAO
THEATER

BOX OFFICE OPENS –

FEATURE (DAILY) – 1900

after the resignation of President Thieu on April 12, which signaled the end of a viable South Vietnamese government.

As the crisis worsened, an effort was made to accelerate the evacuation program at Tan Son Nhut airport, a move spearheaded by Army major general Homer Smith, the head of the DAO. As it turned out, his DAO building at Tan Son Nhut—code named Alamo—was destined to play a major role in the climatic hours of *Operation Frequent Wind.*

In early April, General Smith and his small military staff had managed to evacuate only about 500 people daily. The process was slowed by the embassy's insistence that Vietnamese evacuees establish their eligibility and fill out the proper paperwork. Long lines of desperate people filed into the huge gym at Tan Son Nhut seeking clearance to board waiting C-130s and C-141s. Given the urgency, the process quickly turned into an around-the-clock affair. Rules required an American to vouch for many Vietnamese, leading to impromptu marriages of Vietnamese with American servicemen to gain passage out.

On April 26, former president Thieu flew into exile on a C-118 transport furnished by the U.S. Air Force, an event that only heightened tensions. Still, senior military commanders persuaded Ambassador Martin to ease most of the bureaucratic red tape, and between April 26 and 27, some 12,000 evacuees made it out on 74 flights in fixed-wing aircraft.

This successful effort proved short lived. On April 28, a Communist air raid on Tan Son Nhut, mounted by former South Vietnamese pilots flying A-37 jets captured when Da Nang fell, created havoc at the airfield. Sporadic shelling by NVA artillery and rockets soon made operations at Tan Son Nhut problematical at best. During the NVA assault four

(TOP)

Marine Colonel Alfred Grey coordinated evacuation flights at Saigon on April 29, 1975.

(BOTTOM)

Graham Martin, the United States ambassador to South Vietnam, shows the strain of the evacuation process. Martin would be one of the last American officials evacuated from the embassy.

U.S. Marines were killed, the last combat American casualties of the Vietnam War. Waking belatedly to the possibility of looming disaster, Ambassador Martin requested a maximum effort airlift for the next day, thus unwittingly setting the stage for the implementation of *Operation Frequent Wind's* helicopter option.

Night found dozens of C-130s inbound to Tan Son Nhut, the first three landing shortly before midnight. Just as they were loading, they came under rocket fire that destroyed one of the three. The crew and passengers fled the stricken transport and scrambled aboard the two remaining C-130s and other surviving aircraft to escape from war-ravaged Tan Son Nhut airport. The fixed-wing evacuation was effectively over.

Helicopter rescue was now the sole means of evacuation, but even at this extreme moment the ambassador vacillated, visiting Tan Son Nhut at mid-morning at General Smith's insistence to view the situation firsthand. Martin looked out on a chaotic scene. The airport runways and taxiways were blocked by munitions and external fuel tanks jettisoned by fleeing South Vietnamese aircraft. At 10:30 a.m., Smith, despairing of securing a decision from Martin, decided to make preparations for the helicopter evacuation to begin. Shortly thereafter, Martin yielded to pressure from Washington—reportedly a direct telephone order from President Ford relayed by satellite—and ordered *Operation Frequent Wind* in motion. The taped alert message then went out from Armed Forces Radio.

The word reached General Carey's helicopter crews at about 11:30 a.m. They had wakened hours before dawn to run up their helicopters and stand by in their cockpits for a launch that would put them over Saigon at first light. When the launch order did not come, they were released to stand

*Civilians and military evacuees
scramble to get aboard a Marine
CH-53 helicopter at the DAO,
Tan Son Nhut airport, Saigon.*

Two Marine Sea Stallions *head out over open water for the aircraft carrier* Midway, *which was positioned 30 miles offshore during the evacuation operations.*

down. Martin's belated decision caught them dispersed aboard their ships, in the ready rooms, or on the way to lunch.

In Saigon, all was chaos. The plan was for the bus convoys to roll in the early morning hours when traffic was light. Instead, they confronted a fully aroused populace. One convoy was mobbed and another diverted from Tan Son Nhut to the embassy. The small force of CIA-operated Air America UH-1 helicopters, based at Tan Son Nhut, shuttled across the city, taking evacuees from rooftop helipads to the Tan Son Nhut compound or the embassy. Inside the compound—Alamo—a handful of Marines and Air Force officers assigned to the DAO struggled to maintain control as frantic ARVN troopers tried to force their way in. Outgunned and outnumbered, they finally agreed to let the Vietnamese in if they would leave their weapons behind. It was an uneasy compromise, but it worked. ARVN troops posed a continual and unpredictable threat to the hard-pressed Marines and helicopter crews.

Offshore, the Marine CH-53s began to shuttle back and forth from ship to ship, assembling the Marine ground force to secure the embassy and compound. Constrained by limited fuel reserves, they had to top off their fuel before going in and this took time. It was nearly 3:00 p.m. before the first Marine CH-53 landed inside the DAO compound to discharge its cargo of Marines, load up with evacuees, and head back to the fleet.

Last in line were nine Air Force HH-53s, led in by a three-ship element of Marine CH-53s. Leading the last element of three H-53s, two Rescue and one Special Operations, was Major John F. Guilmartin, Jr. of the 40th ARRS. Shortly after reaching landfall, Guilmartin and his

crew heard radio chatter indicating that an enemy 57mm antiaircraft battery was active to the south of the helicopter ingress route. That posed a serious threat to the helicopters, flying at 6,500 feet, in the heart of the antiaircraft battery's engagement envelope. The chatter was followed by an excited voice on Guard Channel, the common military emergency frequency, calling "Protective reaction! Protective reaction!" Guilmartin later learned that the voice was that of an Air Force pilot flying an air defense suppression "Iron Hand" F-4. The pilot had invoked the protective reaction clause of the highly restrictive rules of engagement in order to destroy the enemy battery with a pod of cluster bombs delivered by his wingman. His timely intervention no doubt saved many lives.

As Guilmartin and his element passed over the Keystone Bridge across the Saigon River and turned west to descend into the DAO compound, they encountered a desperate scene. The Rescue HH-53s or Jolly Green Giants were equipped with radar-warning receivers, and on descent Guilmartin's picked up three active SA-2 antiaircraft missile batteries, all well within range. Inexplicably, they never fired.

At the DAO, fuel oil had been spread on the softball diamond landing zones to keep helicopter rotor wash from kicking up dense clouds of dust, but tracer rounds had set the oil on fire, depriving the evacuation force of three landing zones. That left 15 HH-53s circling over Tan Son Nhut at low altitude trying to get into 12 landing zones. Guilmartin's scanners called out artillery fire impacting on the airfield and he saw a taxiing Vietnamese C-54 transport hit and destroyed. At least one Marine CH-53 exhausted its fuel reserves and had to return to the fleet empty.

*Confused and desperate South
Vietnamese reach the safety of the
carrier* Midway. *Only a small
number of South Vietnamese
seeking evacuation were able to
reach the carriers.*

In Saigon, the scene became even more chaotic. Roaming mobs and alienated government troops provided no small amount of interference for those evacuees seeking to reach the embassy or the DAO. Bus operations had ceased, and it was difficult for cars or taxis to steer through the crowded and panic-stricken streets. Some isolated groups were rescued by Air America helicopter crews, who spent most of the day boldly extracting evacuees from rooftops. Eventually, the Air America crews had to slow their operations when enemy shelling at Tan Son Nhut destroyed their one reliable fuel source.

When news of the final evacuation spread, large crowds gathered at the American Embassy, seeking a way out. Those Americans who made it to the embassy compound had to press forward through the milling crowd at the gate. Marine guards periodically opened the gate to allow approved evacuees to enter. This angered the crowd, forcing the Marines to beat back enraged and desperate would-be evacuees. Inside the embassy grounds, Americans and Vietnamese targeted for evacuation milled about with their suitcases, anxiously watching the sky.

In the distance fires could be seen as the North Vietnamese slowly advanced into the city. For the NVA, the major goal was to reach the Presidential Palace, not the American Embassy; the objective was to unequivocally discredit the rump government that had taken office with President Thieu's resignation by physically occupying the palace. This fact allowed a window of time for continued evacuation efforts at the embassy building.

Helicopter operations actually began around 11:00 a.m. on April 29 and lasted into the morning hours of the next day. During that period of time, some Marine and Air Force crews flew as many as 15 hours without rest. If all went well—and it often did not—the trip from the carriers to the landing zones took 30 to 45 minutes. Once a helicopter reached the landing zone, another 10 to 15 minutes were needed to load the craft with evacuees. All luggage was checked for weapons or contraband. The evacuation dragged on into the hours of darkness. Official figures indicate that over 7,800 evacuees and 989 security force Marines were extracted by military helicopters in the course of the operation. This figure is surely low. Word in the 7th fleet was that the Marine record for a single CH-53 lift was 117 evacuees—impressive for an aircraft rated to carry 38 fully equipped Marines—yet the official accounts refer to loads of 50 evacuees.

The landing zones were small and improvised, hardly ideal for daylight operations, let alone at night. As the evacuation picked up momentum, helicopters were vectored to their landing zones, loaded up, and dispatched with increasing haste. Loads got bigger as time got shorter. The problem was particularly acute at the DAO compound, where traffic densities were greatest. Marine major David Cox and his air traffic control team, perched atop one of the DAO buildings and working with a malfunctioning FM radio, did a magnificent job of sorting out incoming helicopters and matching them up with vacant, or soon-to-be vacant, landing zones throughout the long day.

NVA opposition intensified as the day wore on. On their final run-in, Guilmartin and his wingman took out a pair of 12.7mm machine gun sites firing just east of the compound, using a 7.62mm minigun, at about 9:30 p.m. Liftoff in an overladen helicopter in total darkness posed a real challenge for the rescue pilots: Guilmartin remembered that he peered forward into the inky blackness, hoping to see other helicopters in time to avoid them. On departure, he pulled in full torque and held it until the helicopter cleared a nine-foot cyclone fence circling the landing zone; he then gently pushed the nose down to gain airspeed and climbed out to a safe altitude.

Flights into the embassy grounds—monitored and approved by President Ford—continued into the small hours of the morning of April 30. That morning, at 3:30 a.m., the signal was given to fly out Ambassador Martin. He departed with his pet dog. Now the final steps had to be taken to extract the remaining evacuees and their Marine guards. Some 400 people remained to be removed from the embassy roof. With each helicopter run, the numbers slowly dwindled, finally leaving only a small contingent of Marines to face the anxious and increasingly angry crowds at the embassy walls.

News film coverage caught the climatic moments at the embassy, giving Americans unforgettable TV images of America's final hours in Vietnam. The escape proved to be a narrow one. When the Marines abandoned their positions on the walls, they retreated to the embassy building, closing the mahogany doors behind them. Immediately, the crowd outside sensed they were being abandoned. They rushed forward. The last Americans in the embassy, some 60 Marines, then rode the elevators to the top floor and locked the controls, sealing themselves from the rushing mob. Below, the angry crowd had gained entrance to the building by crashing a fire truck through the embassy doors. As they ran up the stairs, Marines dropped tear gas grenades to slow their progress. At the top, there were heavy fireproof doors at the entrance to the roof, which offered a final and secure barrier to allow the speedy evacuation of the remaining Marines. The rescue team flew a precise and dangerous

mission, one that could easily have failed given the forces at play and the narrow time segment to execute the rescue. This episode, in many ways, became a signature image of the war.

On his climatic run to the USS *Midway*, Guilmartin and his crew faced yet another danger: the enemy, shrouded in the darkness below, directed a shoulder-fired heat-seeking SA-7 missile at their helicopter. Alerted to the presence of enemy fire, the ramp gunners decoyed the approaching missile with hand-fired Mk 50 flares. The missile missed Guilmartin's helicopter by 20 feet dead astern. Landing aboard the *Midway* at 11:00 p.m. brought down the curtain on Guilmartin's rescue work. His work and that of his fellow pilots and crews were emblematic of the remarkable bravery and initiative shown by all who flew sorties into Saigon on April 29–30.

During the long day, the deck crews on *Midway* and other Navy vessels stationed offshore soon discovered that they had become a magnet for ARVN helicopters, mostly Hueys filled with pilots and their families seeking refuge, but also huge CH-47 Chinooks. The unannounced guests had followed the American helicopters out to sea. They were allowed to land and unload, with the carrier deck crews quickly pushing the South Vietnamese helicopters into the water. About 46 ARVN helicopters were dumped into the South China Sea, a necessary move to keep the carrier decks free for operations. Some of the approaching helicopters could not land, so the South Vietnamese pilots ditched them at sea—a maneuver fraught with great peril.

One unscheduled flight involved a small single-engine O-1 liaison plane. On its approach to the *Midway*, the pilot, a Vietnamese major, radioed the carrier's Air Boss, a commander and an experienced aviator in charge of air operations, to request permission to land. The Air Boss suggested he ditch his airplane. The pilot responded that he would need a rescue helicopter standing by since he had his wife and five children on board. *Midway's* captain overheard the exchange and authorized the Air Boss to let the O-1 land, running the risk of collision and fire on his packed flight deck. It was a courageous call. The Vietnamese pilot, with no experience with carrier landings, set his plane down successfully without the assistance of arresting hooks. He and his family then joined the vast assembly of refugees crowded in the hangar deck of the USS *Midway*.

The Saigon rescue effort was part of a larger transfer of more than 130,000 refugees to the United States in the aftermath of the collapse of the South Vietnamese government. *Operation Frequent Wind* had flown 662 sorties to the landing zones in Saigon, the vast majority by Marine aviators (Guilmartin and his fellow Air Force crews flew 82 missions and accounted for almost 20 percent of the evacuees). Tactical fighters had been assigned to provide escort over the evacuation routes, flying off the USS *Kitty Hawk* and the USS *Enterprise*, supported by Air Force aircraft stationed in Thailand. Of all the missions, a tally of 1,422 over Saigon, there was the loss of only three aircraft, all lost at sea. Mixed with these missions were the numerous sorties flown by pilots of Air America during the weeks surrounding the fall of Saigon.

Operation Frequent Wind represented a triumph in the larger context of humiliation and defeat. America's final departure from Vietnam bore haunting similarities to the humiliation of France in 1954, when Ho Chi Minh's army surrounded and defeated the French at Dien Bien Phu. For the evacuees, the helicopter crews had offered—in an apocalyptic moment—a bridge to safety.

GOSSAMER ALBATROSS
HEIRS TO DAEDALUS

ANCIENT GREECE gave birth to the fable of Daedalus and his son Icarus, who were trapped in the Minotaur's labyrinth by King Minos; to escape, Daedalus fashioned feathered wings for himself and his son. The wings were attached to their bodies with wax. Once airborne, the young Icarus became intoxicated with the experience and flew higher and higher. Eventually the heat of the sun melted the wax, his wings slipped away, and he fell into the sea. In the Middle Ages, tower jumpers—using improvised wings—attempted unsuccessfully to match the feat of Daedalus. Throughout history, hubris and danger have been intertwined in the human aspiration to fly as the birds, to achieve transcendence and mobility above the terrestrial realm.

With time, more practical schemes arose to translate the ancient dream of human-powered flight into reality. Leonardo da Vinci became one of the first to study the mechanics of flight, even sketching a human appropriately adorned with wings. In the nineteenth century, George Cayley and Otto Lilienthal endeavored to use birdlike wings to perfect the art of flying. When the Wright brothers flew their engine-powered flying machine at Kitty Hawk, North Carolina, on December 17, 1903, they solved the riddle and inaugurated the air age. The airplane quickly evolved into an effective means for humans to take to the skies.

Still, the ageless interest in human-powered flight did not die away, even if seemingly eclipsed by the airplane. As early as 1912, Robert Peugeot offered a prize for a human-driven flight of 10 meters (33 feet). Later, in the 1930s, soaring enthusiasts in Germany, Italy, and Russia continued to experiment with techniques for human-powered flying machines. In Germany, there were experiments with a glider using bicycle-inspired pedals to provide power. However, the challenge remained: human power was insufficient to launch and to sustain a flying machine.

In 1959, the British engineer and industrialist Henry Kremer stepped forward to offer a cash prize of £5,000 to the first person in the Commonwealth to build a human-powered flying machine that could complete a figure-eight course between two pylons, covering a distance of four-fifths of a kilometer (approximating the distance flown by the Wrights at Kitty Hawk in 1903).

Born in eastern Europe and educated in Switzerland, Kremer had emigrated to Britain after World War I. Among his many accomplishments, the talented Kremer held

(ABOVE)

Paul MacCready (top), designer of the Gossamer Albatross, *and pilot (and power source) Bryan Allen (bottom).*

(OPPOSITE)

Modern synthetic materials and human endurance kept the Gossamer Albatross *aloft.*

The Gossamer Albatross *in flight overhead with sunlight refracted through its Mylar skin. The experimental airplane was an* optimal blend of lightweight materials to achieve human-powered flight over the English Channel.

the patent for a plywood process that was adapted to build the famed de Havilland *Mosquito* bomber in World War II. Kremer's largess, in reality the first of several awards to encourage research in lightweight airplanes, stood in a long tradition of private patronage in aviation: Lord Northcliffe's prize had prompted Louis Blériot to fly the English Channel in 1909; and Raymond Orteig's prize set into motion an intense competition to be the first to fly nonstop from New York to Paris, a race won by Charles Lindbergh in 1927.

The Kremer prize, however, remained unclaimed for 18 years. The exacting standards of the Kremer award were indeed challenging: the airplane had to take off under human power alone, fly the figure-eight maneuver between two pylons separated by a half mile, and then finish the flight at an altitude of 10 feet. This was no easy task.

British designers of experimental lightweight aircraft had failed to win the Kremer prize. Finding the optimal design, lightweight materials, and human propulsion scheme remained elusive. German and Italian designers had adapted pedal-driven propellers to sailplanes in the 1930s, but these planes—though lightweight for their time—were too heavy to take off with human power alone. Some wondered if anyone would ever meet the Kremer standards.

Seeking a breakthrough, Kremer altered the contest rules in 1975, opening the competition to non-Commonwealth participants and raising the cash award to £50,000. This widening of the field prompted teams from several countries to attempt to meet Kremer's challenge, only to end in failure. In the midst of this apparent impasse, a Californian named Paul MacCready decided that he could build a plane capable of winning the Kremer prize. A scientist and head of AeroVironment, a small California engineering company,

A special lightweight propeller was fitted to the Gossamer Albatross.

MacCready brought unique engineering talent, personal optimism, and a flair for innovation to his bid for the Kremer prize. At the time, the Kremer prize was worth £50,000, offering MacCready the potential of securing financial backing for his fledgling company and the means to expand his work with light-airplane designs.

Born in 1925, MacCready displayed an interest in flight from his youth, building model airplanes and earning his pilot's license at the age of 16. He served as a pilot with the Navy's flight training program in World War II.

Graduating from Yale in 1947, MacCready went on to earn a master's degree in physics and a doctorate in aeronautics at the California Institute of Technology. As an adult, he also became a proficient glider pilot, participating in national soaring contests. He won a national championship in 1953 and then an international championship in France in 1955. MacCready's AeroVironment company, established in 1970, ultimately won him widespread recognition for innovation in diverse fields from aviation to alternative energy sources.

For the Kremer competition, MacCready took a simple approach: he wanted an airplane that would be large yet lightweight. He had marveled at the ability of hawks and vultures to remain aloft for hours, elegantly riding the thermals in the sky. Their large wings offered optimal lift and stability in the wind currents.

Accordingly, his new airplane for the Kremer competition, to be dubbed the *Gossamer Condor*, would have a wingspan of 96 feet (later slightly reduced for optimal performance), equal to that of a DC-9 airliner and a dramatic contrast to the typical hang glider with its short triangular configuration. Working with structural designer Dr. Peter

(LEFT)

Pilot Bryan Allen test flies the Gossamer Albatross.

(BELOW)

A bicycle-style mechanism with gears and chain drive allowed Bryan Allen to supply power to the Gossamer Albatross.

Paul MacCready and his team examine a damaged wing of their gossamer airplane at Shafter Airport in California.

Lissaman, MacCready aimed to fashion a featherweight plane with the lavish use of the lightest materials then available, some old, others new: polystyrene foam, balsa wood, aluminum tubing, corrugated cardboard, and DuPont Mylar, a thin transparent covering for the wings. Mylar was not only lighter than the conventional doped fabric used in human-powered craft in earlier decades, it was only four-thousandths of an inch thick and provided an airtight fit. The elegant *Gossamer Condor* with its distinctive canard (the small forward short wing) weighed a mere 70 pounds.

MacCready chose Bryan Allen to be the chief pilot for the *Gossamer Condor*. A biologist by training, Allen's background in bicycling and hang gliding made him an ideal pilot. The physical strain associated with supplying human power for the *Gossamer Condor* required the optimal strength-to-weight ratio: Allen's six-foot frame and 137 pounds fit the profile.

Preparations for the flight were intense, requiring Allen to engage in a demanding program of physical conditioning. A key goal for Allen was to sustain a constant supply of power for the *Gossamer Condor*, even in the extremes of heat and humidity. With his demanding round of bicycling, Allen managed to reach a remarkable level of power output, the capacity to exert .35 horsepower for more than two hours. No less important, Allen spent four months of pilot training at Shafter Airport, near Bakersfield, California, learning to fly the *Gossamer Condor*; he had to master the demanding airplane, in particular the requirement to make coordinated turns and to sustain flight at an altitude of 10 feet. In the history of aviation, Allen assumed the unique place of being both the pilot and the engine for a flying machine.

(TOP)
A takeoff in an early test flight of the human-powered flyer.

(MIDDLE)
The Gossamer Albatross *takes off.*

(BOTTOM)
Landing the lightweight Gossamer Albatross *always posed a challenge to the pilot and flight team, as in this case where a rough landing resulted in wing damage.*

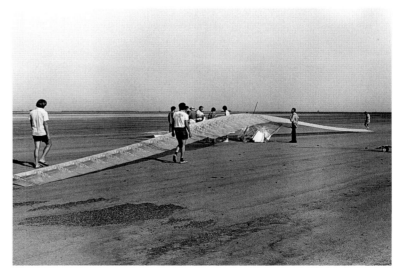

The record-breaking flight of the *Gossamer Condor* took place on August 23, 1977, after some delays to await optimal wind conditions. At 7:25 a.m., Allen set off on the prescribed course, with the red and yellow propeller of the *Condor* moving steadily in the calm morning air. Allen steered around the 1.35-mile figure-eight course in 7 minutes and 27.5 seconds, winning the Kremer prize for the MacCready team. The feat attracted significant media attention, including coverage by *Scientific American, Sports Illustrated, National Geographic*, and even *The Wall Street Journal*.

Aviation enthusiasts viewed MacCready's achievement as a milestone, the realization of the ancient dream of human-powered flight. The *Condor* eventually made its way into the Smithsonian National Air and Space Museum, where it found a permanent home as a pioneering aircraft.

No sooner had MacCready achieved his milestone with the *Gossamer Condor* than Henry Kremer offered yet another alluring prize; this time an award of £100,000 for the first person to steer a human-powered flying machine across the English Channel.

Could MacCready employ his gossamer wings to score another aerial spectacular? The storm-tossed English Channel posed a formidable challenge, as it had done for Louis Blériot in 1909. At the narrowest point, a flight path from England to France would be some 22 miles, and the MacCready team realized that their Gossamer design for the English Channel would have to fly at optimal efficiency and their pilot, again Bryan Allen, would have to marshal an inordinate amount of physical energy to sustain momentum across the wind-swept flight path. As modern-day heirs to Daedalus, the MacCready team was confident that they could win the new Kremer prize.

The Gossamer Albatross *at the start of its historic journey across the English Channel, accompanied by control and rescue motorboats.*

Bryan Allen pedals the Gossamer Albatross *on his way to the French coast. His motive force, even in the face of winds and growing exhaustion, won the day, establishing a new benchmark in flight.*

The new design for the Channel crossing was dubbed the *Gossamer Albatross*. Work began on the new airplane in California in 1978. Inspired by the *Gossamer Condor*, the new *Albatross* was nevertheless a new design, one that took full advantage of state-of-the-art synthetic polymers, a MacCready project that once again enjoyed the sponsorship of the DuPont Company. The *Albatross* was nearly an all-plastic airplane, with metal used only for the pedals, chains, the post for the bicycle seat, and assorted wires and fittings. Aluminum was dropped in favor of carbon-fiber tubes to frame the structure of the new airplane.

The MacCready crew worked diligently to exploit the advantages that came with lightweight synthetic materials, achieving a design weight of merely 55 pounds. The *Albatross* was covered with DuPont Mylar, the durable lightweight skin that could be tightened to create a smooth and taut surface, always a critical step to assure optimal lift. For some of the internal bracing wires, MacCready used cords of Kevlar fiber, which were lightweight, strong, and stretch resistant. Both the landing wheels and the wind screen were also fashioned from modern synthetic materials. The *Albatross* emerged as phenomenally light, sturdy, and capable of long-distance flying.

Working in a former seaplane hangar on Terminal Island, at Long Beach, California, MacCready's 20-member team completed the *Gossamer Albatross* in April 1979, after four months of intensive labor. The *Albatross* was then moved to Shafter Airport for flight testing. At this juncture, the *Albatross* was fitted with a special lightweight propeller designed by Eugene Larabee and three graduate students at the Massachusetts Institute of Technology.

Allen then flew the *Albatross* though a series of demanding tests at Harper Dry Lake in southern California. Aside from the shortened wings and the structural components, there was little difference between the *Albatross* and the *Gossamer Condor*. The design team was elated with the performance of Allen, who performed a duration flight of 69 minutes. This feat prompted a growing confidence that the *Albatross* could make a Channel crossing.

The small cockpit, equipped with its own ventilation system, measured 10 feet by 8 feet, a space adequate in size to allow the pilot to sit upright, as if he were pedaling a bicycle. For the sake of streamlining, Allen's cockpit was encased in plastic, denying him the wind-induced sensation of forward movement. Instrumentation in the cockpit was minimal, including an altimeter, thermometer, and radio. The bicycle-style pedals provided the motive power for the craft. Allen—the human engine—maintained a rigorous training

A control boat and Zodiac inflatable boats stayed close to the Gossamer Albatross *throughout its passage across the English Channel.*

schedule to assure optimal physical capacity for pedaling. He conditioned himself to be able to pedal upright at 1.6 horsepower for short bursts of six seconds. Human and design factors appeared to blend harmoniously in the design of the *Albatross*.

For the 1979 summer competition for the Kremer prize, the Royal Air Force offered to fly the *Albatross* to England at no cost. On April 29, an RAF C-130 Hercules picked up the gossamer-wing aircraft at Nellis Air Force base, outside Las Vegas, Nevada. The MacCready team then established their headquarters at an RAF base in Kent, near the English Channel, in early May. Intensive planning followed, even as the team monitored weather conditions over the English Channel. The projected flight called for a departure from Folkestone, near Dover on the English coast.

The flight of the *Gossamer Albatross* required a highly scripted passage over the 22 miles separating England from France. A marine escort was set up to accompany Bryan Allen as he steered the *Albatross* out over open sea. One large power boat was designated to be the central vessel in the MacCready flotilla; it was equipped with radar and served as the main center for radio communications. Allen was to follow this command boat at a distance of 1,000 feet. In addition, three Zodiac inflatable craft were deployed to move across the surface of the English Channel just beneath the *Albatross*, one under the fuselage, the other two under the wing tips. These speedy escort craft were fitted with 50-horsepower outboard engines and each carried two-way radios and wet-suited divers ready to rescue Bryan Allen, if necessary. In an emergency, the *Albatross* could land on the control boat and be quickly secured with cables. All this careful planning proceeded in collaboration with the Dover

Bryan Allen steers the Gossamer Albatross *to a successful landing on the shores of France.*

port authorities, the English coast guard, and maritime groups such as the Royal National Lifeboat Institution.

The Royal Aeronautical Society, which administered the Kremer prize, dictated that any approved flight be made from the coast of England. And there was also the requirement that the *Albatross* or any competitor craft ascend into the air under its own power. The MacCready team chose a spot that would allow a flight from St. Margaret's Bay, near Dover, to Cap Gris Nez on the French coast, at the narrowest point on the English Channel. Historically, as everyone knew, this narrow expanse of the Channel—even in the summer months—fell victim to storms, shifting winds, and all kinds of unpredictable shifts in weather. Many recalled the D-Day landings at Normandy in June 1944, when bad weather complicated the Allied operations. The MacCready team was well aware of how the weather over the English Channel had frustrated the best laid plans of humans in the past.

Monitoring the relentlessly stormy English Channel had been a frustrating experience for the MacCready team ever since they had set up their operations at RAF base. But, then, on June 11, there was a welcome break in the bad weather reports. That day a stationary high front had moved into place. The much-awaited moment had come, and a decision was made to attempt the flight the following morning.

Preparations continued throughout the night of June 11–12, with the *Albatross* carefully reassembled in the glare of torch lights. Reassuring reports from Cap Gris Nez suggested calm winds holding along the French coast. Crowds soon gathered, as did photographers and newspaper reporters intent on catching the unfolding story.

Taking advantage of the favorable wind conditions, Allen began his takeoff roll in the early hours of June 12. Disaster was only narrowly averted when the *Albatross* suddenly slipped and veered off its takeoff pad, breaking the forward wheel. This damage was quickly repaired, in fact in 10 minutes, by substituting a missing spacer with duct tape. The *Albatross* was airborne at 4:51 a.m., Greenwich Mean Time. A foreboding harbinger then reached MacCready and his anxious associates: a mild easterly breeze had appeared, alerting the crew to the fact that a possible headwind might be awaiting them along the flight path to the French coast.

The mishap with the landing wheel and the news of a possible headwind, however, failed to dampen the excitement of the *Gossamer Albatross* takeoff. Initial progress was excellent, with Allen maintaining a steady passage toward France. Less than 15 minutes into the flight, Allen reported air turbulence. But no real difficulties arose until the *Albatross* reached the one-and-a-quarter-hour mark: at this point the feared headwind was discernible, estimated at four to five knots. This was a sobering development because the *Albatross* had reached only mid-Channel and there were real fears that Allen could not sustain enough lift to reach his landing area at the now distant Cap Gris Nez.

The original projection and training had rested on the confident assumption that it would require a two-hour flight across the English Channel. The power input supplied by Allen's pedaling would provide the means to sustain altitude and forward motion. The headwind made his efforts more complicated, even threatening to compromise the flight. Allen felt the pressure and growing fatigue. Around mid-Channel his water supply was exhausted, which threatened potential dehydration and a possible physical breakdown. The sense of crisis was deepened with the news that the two-way radio link had

broken down, allowing Allen to hear instructions only from his anxious escorts. Allen could communicate with hand signals alone. While pedaling in a steady pattern, Allen's right hand was free to handle the controls and deal with the problem of communication.

With the water supply gone, the headwind, and eventually the appearance of cramps in Allen's legs, a mood of desperation gripped the team. Plans were now discussed to pull the *Albatross* in and declare the flight a failure. In anticipation of such a move, Allen pulled the *Albatross* up to 15 feet to allow the rescue vessel to take position. To his surprise, he discovered that the air at that altitude was less turbulent, allowing for a smooth forward movement. Invigorated, Allen waved off the rescuers and continued his flight toward Cap Gris Nez.

In a short time, the French coast finally came into view, a moment that gave Allen renewed determination to pedal on—the beaches of Cap Gris Nez were close. Still, dangers

loomed: suddenly a tanker moved into the flight path of the *Gossamer Albatross*. This danger quickly passed without a collision or near miss, but the experience only added to the accumulating tension for all, especially Allen, who had to mobilize his residual energy to remain aloft and on course. For most of the flight, he had remained at an altitude of two to six feet, with occasional dips close to the waves. His highest altitude was 25 feet. Only Allen's steady and unrelenting pedaling kept the *Albatross* from falling into the inhospitable waters of the English Channel.

Near exhaustion, Allen reached the French coast at 8:40 a.m. His final passage to the beach took him over an outcropping of rocks. Momentarily the winds threatened to throw the *Albatross* back on the rocks, but Allen triumphantly steered his sturdy craft to the landing zone. Crowds surged forward to welcome the *Gossamer Albatross* to France. Cheers and popping champagne bottles heralded the end of an epic flight.

VOYAGER
NONSTOP AROUND THE GLOBE

TWO DAYS before Christmas, 1986, *The New York Times* headline read: "*Voyager* Succeeds in Historic Flight." For aviation enthusiasts, such a headline signaled a new—and perhaps the final—air milestone for fixed-wing aircraft. A vast global audience had monitored the high-risk journey of the *Voyager* aircraft, piloted by Richard Rutan and Jeanna Yeager, in the first successful nonstop flight without refueling around the world at its widest circumference. The *Voyager* had traversed no less than four great oceans and flown over a diverse array of nations, some welcoming and others openly hostile, in a trajectory that took it over Asia, Africa, and the Western Hemisphere.

Rutan and Yeager had flown through storms, managed to overcome a series of mechanical mishaps, and endured the unique physical and psychological strain of being in the air for nine days. The *Voyager* was a fragile and unforgiving flying machine, a sort of powered glider, what one could describe as a flying fuel tank. Burt Rutan, the younger brother of the pilot, Dick Rutan, had designed the unique aircraft. The story is told that the first sketch of the *Voyager* appeared on a paper lunch napkin in 1980. The aircraft owed its inspiration to Burt Rutan's earlier series of experimental streamlined aircraft made of composite materials—*the Vari-Eze, Vari-Viggen, Grizzly, Defiant,* and *Long Ez.*

The decision to build the *Voyager* was made in 1982, and for the next five years this project took shape, with the Rutans leading a talented team of specialists keen on setting the world's last great air record for heavier-than-air craft. The *Voyager* was a canard design—with a forward elevator—not unlike the 1903 Wright Brothers' *Flyer.* Just like the *Flyer,* the *Voyager* flew only after an exhaustive program of design and testing. The Rutan design called for an aircraft with twin booms connecting the tip of the forward wing (canard) and the main wing to the vertical fins at the rear. The shell of the *Voyager* consisted of a graphite honeycomb composite shell material, which gave the aircraft extraordinary strength and lightness, with a structural weight of merely 939 pounds. The wingspan was 111 feet, slightly larger than the World War II–era Boeing B-17.

The *Voyager* was powered by two fuel-efficient engines mounted in a pusher-tractor configuration on the center fuselage, fore and aft. The *Voyager* cruised at around 115 miles per hour, typically using the aft engine for optimal range. If needed, the forward engine could be run to allow greater speed or to make climbs. For the flight, the *Voyager* was equipped with an autopilot, radar, and a VLS Omega navigation computer, among

(ABOVE)

Dick Rutan and Burt Rutan, pilot and designer of the Voyager.

(OPPOSITE)

The Voyager, *piloted by Dick Rutan and Jeanna Yeager, on its way to establishing a new world record, flying nonstop without refueling around the globe.*

(TOP)

A ground test of the Voyager's *Teledyne Continental engine.*

(BOTTOM)

Jeanna Yeager sorts food and other supplies for the around-the-world flight.

other essential avionics and instrumentation to monitor fuel consumption. The priority for minimal weight dictated that Rutan and Yeager take only the essentials when it came to food and survival gear. Special lightweight parachutes tailored to each pilot were included, along with individual rubber rafts. There was oxygen on board, a vital element for any cruising at high altitude. Jeanna Yeager even bobbed her long hair on the eve of the flight as another weight-saving measure!

The gross takeoff weight of the *Voyager* exceeded 9,000 pounds, largely the result of the huge payload of fuel on board—slightly over 7,000 pounds. The cockpit was small with barely enough room to accommodate a crew of two: they lived and alternated at the controls in a tubelike fuselage two feet wide and three feet high. One pilot flew while the other slept.

Dick Rutan and Jeanna Yeager came from different backgrounds, with each bringing essential and complementary skills to the project. Dick had been born in 1938 and grew up in the 1950s. Early in his youth he displayed a keen interest in all things mechanical, being handy with his two passions—cars and motorcycles. As a youngster, his interest also turned to aviation; he was an avid builder of model airplanes. Later, this same fascination with flight led to a career in the U.S. Air Force, where he won his wings as a fighter pilot in 1967. A stint in Vietnam followed. Dick maintained a close working relationship with his young brother in the design of experimental aircraft, an association that led to their collaboration on the *Voyager* project.

Jeanna Yeager (no relationship to Chuck Yeager) came from Texas. A design drafting engineer by profession, she became fascinated with flying, setting several women's records

*Dick Rutan and Jeanna Yeager lay
out the flight plan for the* Voyager.

in Rutan-designed aircraft. She also participated in the
building of the *Voyager*. Her considerable training in
navigation made her a logical candidate to participate in
the historic flight.

The actual flight of the *Voyager* began with a bumpy
takeoff from Edwards Air Force base in the Mojave Desert on
the morning of December 14, 1986. With Dick Rutan at the
controls, the heavily loaded aircraft, with its fuel tanks topped
off, made a long takeoff run, slowly climbing into the air
with only a thousand feet to spare on the longest runway
in the world.

As the *Voyager* began it slow ascent over Edwards, the
chase plane alerted Rutan that his right winglet was dangling.
This mishap had occurred on the takeoff run when the
wingtip had scraped the runway. A quick check revealed that
there was no fuel leak and the nearly severed winglet did not
interfere with the maneuverability of the *Voyager*. It was then
decided to put the *Voyager* into a sideslip to shake off the
winglet. Rutan executed this maneuver twice before the
winglet broke away. A rough start, but the *Voyager* was
fully operational.

The first leg called for Rutan and Yeager to make the long
flight over the vast Pacific Ocean. Radio contact with mission
headquarters at Edwards provided the outside world with
regular reports on the progress of the *Voyager*. Burt Rutan and
his team at Edwards had a special code to communicate with
the crew. This way they could identify any in-flight trouble
and seek out a remedy with some degree of privacy. Once the
Voyager passed near Hawaii that first night, two friends flying
a Piper Saratoga attempted a rendezvous. Moonlight allowed
the two men to fly near the *Voyager* and establish radio
contact. As the *Voyager* pressed ahead and the Saratoga

banked for a return flight to Honolulu, Dick Rutan remembered the emotion of that moment. The long-distance flying machine was now alone, on its way, and there would be no turning back.

Mother Nature offered a challenge for the next phase of the journey as the *Voyager* moved slowly across the Pacific to Southeast Asia: Typhoon Marge, it was discovered, was moving across the *Voyager's* flight path. The close proximity of the storm posed a threat, but Dick Rutan quickly adjusted the course heading to avoid the storm. Mission control at Edwards carefully monitored the weather along the entire flightpath, which required no small amount of study and daily briefings to the crew.

Rutan and Yeager regularly drank premeasured packets of water; this became a fixed discipline for the entire flight. Dick preferred to mix his water allotment with milk shake mix or pea soup. Given the rigors of the trip, neither pilot could afford dehydration.

During the initial Pacific leg of the flight, Dick did most of the flying, as he would through the entire trip, with Jeanna taking the controls at several critical points in the journey. They could not stand up or freely move about the cockpit area. Even to change positions became a challenge requiring no small amount of effort. And once when Dick moved to the rear of the fuselage to sleep, the *Voyager* underwent a dramatic shift in the center of gravity. All instruments required constant monitoring as they slowly burned off the fuel. There were dangers as well with each transfer of fuel since the aircraft might fall into pitch porpoise oscillations, which could disintegrate the aircraft.

Flying the inherently unstable *Voyager* even with the autopilot required a high degree of concentration. This became a challenge with the passing of time and the exhaustion that came with a long-distance flight covering 24,987 miles. The autopilot had a flashing red light and beeping horn to alert the crew to any trim movement up or down. They had to monitor the "angle of attack" of the *Voyager* for the sake of optimal efficiency. Once out of proper alignment, the aircraft had to be trimmed again. Any severe turbulence required an adjustment of the autopilot. Dick and Jeanna took pains to keep the center of gravity of the *Voyager* in constant balance—failure to sustain the equilibrium could result in a stall in the short time frame of 20 or 30 seconds. One momentary autopilot failure near the Philippines gave the crew a clear indication of the dangers associated with flying the *Voyager*.

The script for the flight called for a southeast heading toward the Malay Peninsula, taking special pains to avoid the hostile air space of Vietnam and Cambodia. Flying night and day, the *Voyager* crew soon displayed the effects of extreme fatigue. Sleep came in short time periods. The cockpit routine—although tedious—was punctuated with one crisis after another. On day four, while entering the Indian Ocean after taking leave of Sri Lanka, there was a concern over a possible coolant leak. Jeanna spotted a few spoonfuls of coolant in the overflow reservoir bottle in the aft section. This leak—if real—could be a mission-ending crisis—"no way to fix it, no way—it's all pressurized," Dick remarked. "If we have blown a seal, that's it." Should they turn back to Sri Lanka? Somehow the problem corrected itself. As they checked and rechecked, the leak did not reappear.

At night, on the approach to Africa from the Indian Ocean, there was another crisis that also turned illusory. Suddenly a light flashed on the canard of the plane. Dick

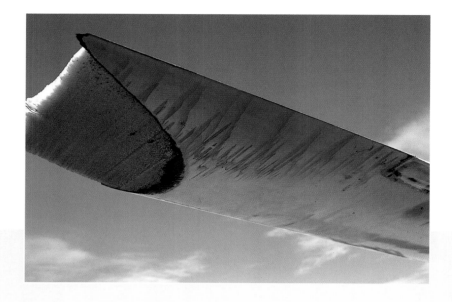

(LEFT)

A winglet, designed to improve the aerodynamics of the aircraft's wing, was damaged on takeoff, but this mishap did not compromise the flight.

(BELOW)

The Voyager's *dawn takeoff run for its historic flight in December 1986.*

peered back and saw what appeared to be a landing light! Since the *Voyager* was off the coast of Somalia—another hostile territory gripped with civil conflict—he feared a fighter plane had come up to either shoot them down or order them to land. Dick hurriedly called mission control to alert them to the impending danger, but his message did not get through. Minutes passed as the crew waited helplessly in the cockpit of the *Voyager* for the fighter to fire a missile or make some move to communicate with them. Then Dick turned the *Voyager* cautiously to the left and looked to see the fighter head on: to his surprise and delight, the light was from Venus, the Morning Star!

The much anticipated passage over Africa brought a new set of challenges. The *Voyager* crew had avoided Somalia intentionally, selecting Kenya as the spot to enter the interior of the continent. There were warnings not to fly into the air space of Uganda or Chad because both countries might greet the *Voyager* crew with a hostile reception.

On day five (December 15), the *Voyager* sped across Kenya on a flight path toward central Africa. At this juncture, the crew encountered a problem with the constant flow of fuel through the 16-tank system of the *Voyager*. There appeared to be an anomaly in the motion of the fuel giving inaccurate readings of the fuel reserves. What became apparent upon checking the fuel tank system was the reassuring fact that the airplane possessed a larger quantity of fuel than first thought—enough fuel to carry the *Voyager* home.

At this point, an exhausted Rutan and Yeager faced the challenge of steering the *Voyager*—at high altitude— through a mountain range and pressing on to the west coast of Africa. Once beyond the Lake Victoria region, as the

Voyager ascended, both Rutan and Yeager hooked up their oxygen units. They flew with both engines supplying power.

They reached the mountainous area in mid-afternoon, the worst time of day to navigate over the middle of Africa. Steep cloud formations—"like a bunch of A-bombs," as Dick remembered them—stood in the path of the *Voyager*. Some clouds extended to 50,000 feet, where the jet stream lobbed off their tops. Below, the heat from the jungle floor fueled updrafts and made the clouds a formidable barrier. Dick guided the *Voyager* through blue holes in the sky, many of which opened to the west. The turbulent ride over the mountains was one of the most dangerous legs in the around-the-world flight.

Days six and seven brought calmer skies as the *Voyager* made its relentless passage over Cameroon to the Atlantic Ocean, flying along the coast of Ghana. Once in the open Atlantic, the *Voyager* moved slowly toward distant Brazil. The Atlantic crossing possessed its own perils with storms forecast all along the flight path. On the approach to the coast of Brazil, Rutan found himself at the controls of the *Voyager* in a thunderstorm. "We got tossed, like a boat in a big wave," Rutan remembered. In this hostile environment Dick successfully flew the *Voyager* out of a near fatal 90-degree bank.

Once the crew passed over Central America on day eight and began the flight northward along the Pacific coast of Mexico, public interest in the *Voyager* intensified, as the media took great pains to cover the final hours of the historic flight.

A new crisis came off the coast of Baja California on the final day, December 23, as the *Voyager* made its approach to Edwards Air Force Base: the shutdown of the aft engine, with 1,200 miles to go to touch down. The fact that the *Voyager*

was so close to home made this last stretch of flying seem
to be a short hop, especially if compared to the distances
already traveled. Suddenly there was an eerie atmosphere
of near silence where once there had been the constant drone
of an engine. After attempts to pump fuel to the aft engine
failed, Mission Control made a firm request to ignite the
front engine—time was becoming a factor. The forward
engine came to life, Dick leveled out the airplane, and soon
the erring aft engine started as fuel began flowing steadily.
The last and most dangerous moment had passed.

Rutan and Yeager landed at Edwards Air Force Base on
December 23—having flown around the world, nonstop,
without refueling, in 9 days, 3 minutes, and 44 seconds!
The *Voyager* team now entered aviation history. In time
the historic aircraft would find its way to the National
Air and Space Museum.

NIGHTHAWK
STEALTH IN MODERN WARFARE

A pilot boards his Lockheed F-117 Nighthawk.

Air-to-air refueling permitted the F-117 Nighthawks and other Coalition aircraft in the Gulf war to carry out missions deep into enemy territory.

THE PERSIAN GULF WAR of 1991 showcased the F-117 Fighter as the leading edge of stealth technology. Difficult to detect, beyond the capacity of the enemy to track, the F-117 flew at night through Iraqi radar nets as a ghostly presence. No Iraqi air defense installation escaped the intruder's penetrating stare. Aptly named the *Nighthawk*, the F-117 could loiter over Iraq—even Baghdad itself—and strike at will with a payload of two GBU-27 laser-guided bombs (2,000 pounds each) or point a laser "designator" at targets for other, more conventional, aircraft to bomb. As the twentieth century drew to a close, the shadowy F-117, with its exotic silhouette, graphite construction, and "fly-by-wire controls," became emblematic of the futuristic air weapon.

The Gulf war lasted from January 17 to February 28, 1991. It arose in the aftermath of Saddam Hussein's invasion and occupation of Kuwait in August of the previous year. The United States led an international coalition of powers to dislodge the Iraqi forces. Air power played a key factor in setting the stage for the ultimate expulsion of Saddam Hussein's army from Kuwait. The Coalition's air campaign against Iraq called for the suppression of the Iraqi air defenses, the disruption of communications, the interdiction of troops and supplies headed for occupied Kuwait, tactical air missions in support of the Coalition's ground forces, the destruction of Iraqi strategic ballistic missiles (SCUDS) and known nuclear, biological, and chemical research facilities, and, ultimately, the physical removal of the Iraqi army from Kuwait. The United States Air Force supplied the largest number of military aircraft—some 807—and led the strategic and tactical air operations. The Air Force was ably assisted by Navy and Marine air units, along with air units drawn from the Coalition powers. All air operations were under a single authority, the United States Central Command (USCENTCOM), headed by Lieutenant General Charles A. Horner.

The 1991 air war over Kuwait and Iraq began with sorties by two F-117 *Nighthawks*, one flown by then-major Greg Feest. His remarkable mission on the night of January 17 signaled the beginning of the Gulf war, for certain, but—one must add—it also demonstrated how stealth technology had redefined the nature of air warfare.

For Major Feest and all F-117 pilots, the Gulf war offered the first real test of this new technology. Would it work? Had the enemy already forged countermeasures to negate the stealth weapon? Would the crucible of combat vindicate the enormous

An apocalyptic scene in the Gulf war: clouds of black smoke from oil wells set ablaze by retreating Iraqis.

(TOP)

U.S. Air Force ground crews arm a GBU-27 laser-guided bomb prior to loading on an F-117 Nighthawk.

(MIDDLE)

A Nighthawk *is towed from its reinforced shelter.*

(BOTTOM)

The Nighthawk *presents a unique silhouette on takeoff.*

investment of the U.S. Air Force in the so-called Black Jet? Feest knew that the *Nighthawk* was not invisible; it was, strictly speaking, just a "low observable" flying machine of unique design. His crew chief offered Feest the last words prior to going airborne: "Kick some ass!" As it turned out, it would be Feest who would drop the first bomb in Operation Desert Storm, the campaign to expel Saddam Hussein from Kuwait.

Flying in formations of two aircraft each from an air base in the Arabian Peninsula, the F-117s were at the cutting edge of the Coalition's air armada. Major Feest and his wingman, Captain David Francis, flew at the tip of the aerial sword in strict radio silence. Their first task was to rendezvous with a KC-135 tanker at a prearranged time and altitude. This critical maneuver, even at night, proved to be smooth and without mishap. Once both *Nighthawks* had their fuel tanks topped off, they headed north toward Iraq. Happily for Feest, the night was pitch black, without any moonlight to allow a visual sighting of the F-117 intruders.

It was now 2:30 a.m., and Feest became the first to cross the Iraqi border. His target was a bunker, southwest of Baghdad. This facility was a crucial command link between forward Iraqi radar sites and Saddam Hussein's air defense headquarters. If it was destroyed, the Iraqi capacity to wage an effective air defense operation against Coalition forces would be sharply diminished.

Feest, on the approach to Baghdad, quickly switched to the stealth mode and found his target on his infrared display in what he later described as "a highly sophisticated video game." His attack on the Iraqi installation had to be swift and unerring: in 30 minutes, if all went well, he would be back at his air base in Saudi Arabia. As he approached the

(ABOVE)

*An Iraqi tank explodes after a
direct hit. Hundreds of destroyed
Iraqi tanks littered the desert
landscape during the Gulf war.*

(LEFT)

A flight of Nighthawks *of the 49th
Fighter Wing from Holloman Air
Force Base in New Mexico.*

A Nighthawk pilot shows a slogan adapted from a television commercial, to demonstrate the effectiveness of stealth aircraft.

Each Nighthawk *pilot took this identification with him on combat sorties over Iraq.*

target area, Feest looked out the window and saw only a few lights on this extremely dark night. Laser on, he tracked the target. Once the display confirmed Feest was in range, he pushed the "pickle button," the weapons bay opened, and a 2,000-pound laser-guided bomb headed for the target. Feest kept the crosshairs on the target as the bomb moved relentlessly toward its intended point of impact. The bomb image appeared at the bottom of the display just before it hit the Iraqi site and exploded. The time: approximately 2:51 a.m. The air war was underway.

The so-called video game now took on an ominous air. Feest quickly moved his *Nighthawk* in a new heading for his second target in western Iraq. At that instant, the sky filled with tracers, antiaircraft fire, and flak. The sudden attack of the F-117 had stirred a hornet's nest. Feest watched warily as several SAM missiles were launched to seek out and destroy the invaders. While much of the antiaircraft fire was random and misdirected, the SAMs passed by the *Nighthawk* to the front and to the rear—at the same altitude! This defensive fire, however, was unguided. The Iraqi defenders had filled the skies with fire in the vain hope of hitting the stealth aircraft.

One of the peculiarities of modern air warfare over Iraq was the simultaneous broadcast of the battle scene to the outside world on television. What Feest observed from the cockpit of the F-117 *Nighthawk* that night also appeared in living rooms in America. There was no lag in time; there was no intervening filter to process the action, or, in the case of any American losses, to frame the action in some positive fashion. This was real time. People at home, and certainly the Iraqis, understood the remarkable stealth technology that allowed Feest and other F-117 pilots in the Gulf war to enter

A Boeing KC-135R refuels a Nighthawk while a second F-117 awaits its turn.

A Nighthawk deploys its drag parachute to reduce its ground speed while landing.

Iraq's air space, attack strategic targets, and return home undetected.

Flying his F-117 into position, Feest fired his second bomb and then headed home. His wingman was a mere one minute behind him. The initial stealth attack had worked flawlessly. Upon reaching the Saudi border, Major Feest went through his "destealth" procedures. The mission now required a linkup with a KC-135, hovering in the dark sky to replenish the F-117's fuel for the final leg home. Once he determined the tanker was on station, Feest broke the radio silence and called his wingman, David Francis. Several seconds passed without a response, giving Feest a keen sense of apprehension that his wingman had not made it. Then Francis's voice came across the designated radio frequency, announcing that he was close by and ready to refuel.

It took two hours for Feest and Francis to fly from the tanker rendezvous to the home Khamis Mushiat air base. They landed in the dawn's early light.

The night sortie of Major Feest was not an isolated event. Behind him came an awesome air contingent of stealth and conventional aircraft, including Apache AH 56 helicopters. Over the subsequent weeks of the Gulf war, the Coalition established total air supremacy, allowing for a systematic application of strategic and tactical sorties against the hapless Iraqis.

Saddam Hussein had built modern hardened shelters for his aircraft. They were designed to absorb the worst the Americans could throw at them, even nuclear weapons. Nonetheless, the F-117's 2,000-pound bombs proved to be more than adequate to destroy these sites. These bombs, with delayed fuses, penetrated the hardened steel and concrete canopy of the shelters and then wrought huge destruction once they exploded. The Air Force ordnance was a lethal accompaniment to the stealth technology.

The Coalition's high-tech weapons were not restricted to the Air Force raids on Baghdad. Offshore, the U.S. Navy launched cruise missiles from the cruiser USS *San Jacinto* stationed in the Red Sea. The initial Tomahawk cruise missiles were fired at 1:30 a.m.; these "smart" weapons followed a 700-mile trajectory to their targets at a speed of 450 knots. Three other ships—USS *Bunker Hill*, USS *Missouri*, and USS *Wisconsin*—participated in the coordinated action.

The fabled F-117 was part of the "black" program responsible for the development of stealth technology— the same hidden research and development effort that later produced the B-2 stealth bomber. The program was extremely expensive, but represented one of the Air Force's most advanced weapon systems, a capability useful in both the Gulf war and the Kosovo air action of 1999. The F-117 also represented the handiwork of Ben Rich and Lockheed's famed "Skunk Works."

Stealth, in reality, was the ultimate expression of camouflage—a technique that could be traced back to World War I when aircraft were painted to make them less visible to the enemy. For the F-117, the design embodied the concept of "low observables," using faceting techniques to reduce the capacity of enemy radar to detect the aircraft. For the computer-generated shape of the F-117, the more familiar curves and contours of the typical aircraft were abandoned in favor of flat panel sections meeting at sharp angles. These peculiar contours reflected enemy radar waves away from the aircraft rather than sending a "return," which would provide the enemy with the aircraft's position. No less important for

*A Nighthawk pilot stands next to
his stealth F-117 fighter.*

the F-117, and especially the B-2 bomber, was the use of
radar-absorbing materials. The F-117 used magnetic iron and
ferrite materials encased in a special polymer. The F-117, as
Feest and other pilots acknowledged, was not invisible, but
was extremely difficult to detect and shoot down.

The F-117 is a single-seat fighter, designed to operate at
night and in the worst weather with the aforementioned
GBU-27 laser-guided bombs (a payload of 4,000 pounds).
Equipped with two F404-F1D2 turbofan engines, the
F-117 possesses a range of 1,100 miles. But, as the Gulf war
illustrated, the stealth fighter required refueling to reach
many of its "high value" targets. The Lockheed F-117
mirrored the high-tech warfare preferred by the United
States as the first century of flight closed.

Even as stealth technology continued to evolve in
the 1990s, there were disturbing hints that antistealth
techniques were close at hand. There was growing evidence
that improved and integrated network sensors could detect
radar-evading aircraft. In the Kosovo air campaign one
F-117 was shot down, another damaged. There is one theory
that when the F-117s repeatedly flew the same routes into
Yugoslavia they unwittingly made themselves vulnerable to
enemy air defenses. The debate as to whether this event was
a consequence of luck or rudimentary countermeasures, or
perhaps a combination of both, will haunt military planners
for years to come.

The story of Major Feest and his F-117 suggested in 1991
that modern air warfare still had a place for the pilot. Feest
and his fellow flyers stood in a long tradition of military
pilots going back to World War I. Still, he flew in a sky filled
with missiles and smart weapons—a harbinger for automated
wars in the twenty-first century.

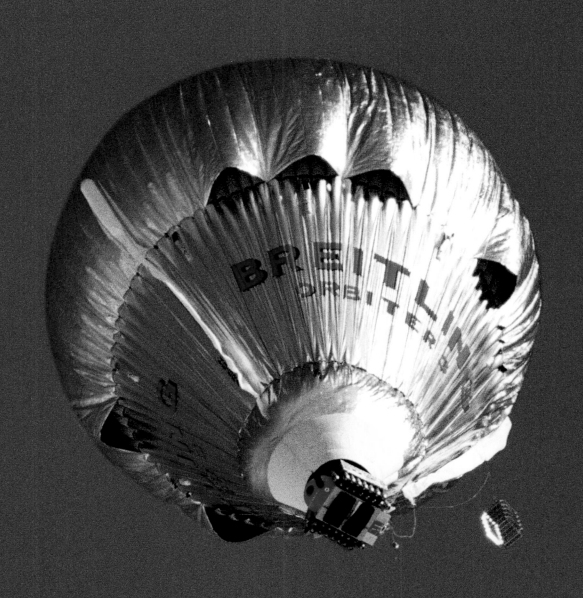

BREITLING ORBITER
AROUND THE WORLD IN A BALLOON

CHATEAU D'OEX, Switzerland, March 1, 1999. Four hours remain in the countdown for an around-the-world flight in the balloon *Breitling Orbiter 3*. Up to this time, no one had ever successfully circumnavigated the planet in a lighter-than-air balloon. Bertrand Piccard later remembered his apprehension: "This likely would be my last chance for a shot at flying around the world. My last two attempts had failed—one after six hours, one after nine days—and our sponsor, the Breitling watch company, had told us that there would be no *Orbiter 4*."

For Piccard and his copilot, Brian Jones, the *Breitling Orbiter*'s attempt to fly around the world nonstop was part of an intense competition. Such an improbable flight—the last major record for lighter-than-air craft—had inspired a number of talented aeronauts in recent decades to make an attempt, often with lavish funding and using the latest technology. In fact, Richard Branson, the founder of Virgin Atlantic Airlines, had been forced to ditch his balloon off Hawaii in a celebrated flight the previous December. Even as Piccard and Jones prepared to launch the *Breitling Orbiter*, Andy Elson and Colin Prescot were already aloft somewhere over India attempting to be the first to achieve the around-the-world milestone. The Budweiser Cup and an award of $1 million awaited the winner of the competition.

The silver-colored *Breitling Orbiter* stood 180 feet tall when fully extended and filled with helium (529,000 cubic feet volume). Don Cameron of Bristol, England, had designed the 9.2-ton balloon for a nonstop circumnavigation of the globe. The pressurized gondola capsule represented a state-of-the-art design, being constructed of carbon fiber and Kevlar. The capsule was small—8 feet in diameter, cylindrical in shape, and 18 feet in length. The layout of the capsule consisted of two pilot stations at one end, a single bunk, a toilet, and a storage compartment. The capsule came equipped with the latest instrumentation, radios, and survival gear.

Piccard and Jones brought diverse backgrounds and talents to the Breitling project. Piccard, the captain, came from a family with deep roots in ballooning; his grandfather, Auguste Piccard, a physicist and inventor of the pressurized cabin, was the first person to reach the stratosphere in a balloon in 1931.

"When I first experienced the thrill of hang gliding," Piccard observed, "I discovered something that I had not learned at school." For Piccard, hang gliding and other sports

(ABOVE)

Bertrand Piccard and Brian Jones during the epic flight of Breitling Orbiter 3. *"We took off as pilots, flew as friends, and came back as brothers."*

(OPPOSITE)

Before the Breitling Orbiter 3 *lifted off on March 1, 1999, there had been 21 failed attempts to fly a balloon around the world.*

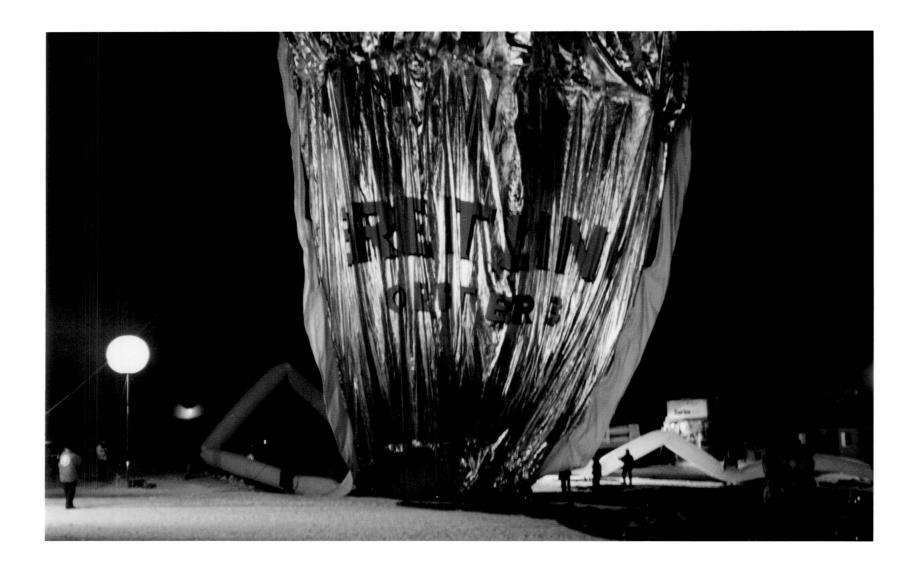

such as parachuting, surfing, and skateboarding, to name a few, created self-reliance and a quick response time to challenging situations. During a balloon race over the Atlantic, Piccard encountered other challenges—seeking out wind currents and developing the patience to accept whatever speed these currents offered a balloonist. When not engaged in sports such as ballooning, Piccard pursued a career in psychiatry in Switzerland.

Jones, by contrast, was an Englishman with a long record of service in the Royal Air Force. He learned to fly at the age of 16. Later, his interest in ballooning prompted him to seek out a commercial ballooning license and instructor's rating in the late 1980s. At the time of his appointment to the position of copilot, he had accumulated over 5,000 hours of

flying, 1,200 hours of it in balloons. Not only did Jones bring technical expertise to the historic flight of the *Breitling Orbiter*, he possessed considerable experience with the Breitling project in the years 1997 and 1998, when the earlier, failed attempts had been made to complete the around-the-world circuit.

As with any undertaking of similar scope, the Breitling project team recruited a number of key specialists. Meteorology, of course, was an essential element in assuring the success of the *Orbiter*—so many failed attempts in the past had been scuttled because of adverse weather. One could not control the weather, but accurate predictions of conditions across the planet were essential. Luc Trullemans and Pierre Eckert provided this expertise as team

(OPPOSITE)

Inflation of the Breitling Orbiter 3 *was one of the most difficult and critical phases of the flight.*

(RIGHT)

Just after take off from Château d'Oex in the Swiss Alps on March 1, 1999.

meteorologists at the control center in Geneva, Switzerland. Many technicians—often nameless to the public—shaped and controlled the unfolding drama. From the design of the balloon, to the weather forecasting, to flight coordination, these team members were central to the success of the historic flight. Everyone knew how difficult any balloon flight around the planet would be—even with forgiving weather and reliable equipment.

As aeronauts, Piccard and Jones stood in a long tradition going back to the Montgolfier brothers who, in 1783, first flew a hot air balloon fashioned with linen cloth and lined in paper. These brothers, Joseph and Etienne, demonstrated their remarkable feat before Louis XVI and Marie Antoinette at Versailles. J. A. C. Charles, an English physicist, soon took the principle of lighter-than-air flight in a new direction with his experiments with hydrogen gas–filled balloons.

The boldness of these early balloonists quickly established a series of milestones, beginning with the flight of J. F. Pilatre de Rozier and Marquis d'Arlandes over Paris in November 1783. While this epic flight covered five miles at an altitude estimated at 300 feet, there were even bolder and higher risk aerial treks to come, in particular the crossing of the English Channel by Jean- Pierre Blanchard and Dr. John Jeffries on January 7, 1785.

Ballooning fascinated Ben Franklin, among others, and the generations that followed in the nineteenth century. In the American Civil War (1861–1865) and the Russo-Japanese War (1904–1905) there were experiments with the use of balloons for reconnaissance. In the twentieth century, lighter-than-air technology would go in several directions, giving birth to the shortlived era of passenger-carrying

(OPPOSITE)

To conform to Chinese regulations, the Breitling Orbiter 3 *was required to fly below the 26th parallel, across India to the Pacific Ocean.*

dirigibles and scientific research as exemplified in the work of Bertrand's grandfather, Auguste Piccard.

The high-tech *Breitling Orbiter* stood in sharp contrast to its predecessors. Built at a cost of around $2 million, the *Orbiter* appeared well-equipped to realize the old dream of riding the wind currents around the earth. Flying at altitudes of 30,000 feet in their pressurized gondola, Piccard and Jones enjoyed many creature comforts—a tiny kitchen, a bunk for sleeping, a washbasin, even a hot water heater. Electric power came from 20 solar panels, three feet in width and 18 inches tall, suspended on a line below the gondola. Safety equipment, even parachutes, added to a sense of security. Two radar transponders alerted the ground team to the altitude, position, and identity of the *Orbiter*. The GPS (Global Positioning System) offered precise data on the balloon's position and speed at any time. The Montgolfiers and early aeronauts would have marveled at the design and performance of the *Breitling Orbiter*.

Jones later remembered vividly the preflight silver *Breitling Orbiter,* with its red gondola image at dawn, as "a colossal exclamation point" in the sky. The day of the departure, March 1, 1999, was cold. Several thousand onlookers had gathered in the small town of Chateau d'Oex, Switzerland to see Piccard and Jones off. There was some anxiety about the enthusiastic crowd just prior to the takeoff. They had moved too close to the *Orbiter*: if the heavy Mylar of the envelope had split, it could have fallen on them, and the 32 propane tanks might have ruptured and exploded. Both pilots were relieved as the *Orbiter* broke free from its tether.

The passage out of the Alps posed some dangers as well. Once the *Orbiter* reached around 1,000 feet, it showed the effect of hitting an inversion layer, the point where the cold air hovering over the ground meets the warmer air in the upper layers of the Alpine sky. Once the *Orbiter* encountered this inversion layer, it ceased to climb. Such a turn of events over flat terrain would normally have aroused no concern, but Piccard and Jones were in the Alps, seeking a route out. Any long delay at this altitude might put the *Orbiter* in a drift toward a mountain side, with catastrophic results. To generate lift, Bertrand ordered one bag of sand cast over the side. Jones then poured a 33-pound bag of sand ballast down a plastic escape tube to lighten the *Orbiter*, even as Piccard ignited the propane flame to warm the hot air cavity and the helium cell above. It worked. The *Orbiter* began to climb, the first crisis passed.

On March 1–2, the *Orbiter* followed a flight path that moved across the Swiss Alps, over Italy and the Mediterranean to Morocco. For this leg of the journey, they kept an altitude above 20,000 feet. Once they reached the skies over Morocco, the intrepid balloonists set a course east over Africa to the Middle East. This trajectory—if the weather remained favorable—would take the *Orbiter* over India, southern China (permission granted in advance), the vast Pacific Ocean, the United States, the Atlantic Ocean, and finally a landing in Africa. They anticipated 20 days aloft.

Teamwork became a vital concern for both men. While Piccard was in command, he preferred to work by consensus with his easy-going partner. "By talking together all the time," Piccard recalled, "we got rid of the need to have one chief and one person obeying orders. There was Brian, there was myself, and there was Both of Us—and Both of Us was the one who always did the right thing." Their routine called for eight hours of sleep (each taking one-half night shifts). They alternated sleeping in the gondola's sole bunk.

(TOP)

The Breitling Orbiter 3 *gave Piccard and Jones many dramatic vistas while in flight.*

(BOTTOM)

View of the cockpit of the Breitling Orbiter 3.

Crossing the Sahara left an indelible impression on both men. At night there was the spectacular sight of the moonlight on the sand of the Sahara, which stretched to the horizon with countless stars in the firmament above. At dawn, the same Sahara turned a dark red hue. For Piccard this grand vista reminded him of earlier pioneers—Jean Mermoz, and Antoine Saint-Exupery—who once flew commercial air routes for L'Aeropostale over these sands from France to Dakar, in Senegal.

On March 4, they decided to drop four empty auxiliary propane cylinders over Mauritania. These tanks could not be released automatically, so one member of the crew needed to make an EVA, or extravehicular jaunt, outside the gondola. Jones performed this maneuver first, at 10,000 feet, followed by Piccard. They had descended to this lower alttiude to deice the gondola. Piccard dislodged the icicles with an axe. Both men found their time in the EVA work to be exhilarating, to be above the Sahara in clear skies and fresh air.

Always a captive of the shifting wind patterns, the *Orbiter* soon found itself in a political crisis—or, at least, on the threshold of one. The preset flight plan called for a passage over the Middle East, but in no way did they wish to enter the prohibited air space of Yemen. While Libya and even Saddam Hussein's Iraq had displayed open interest and best wishes for the *Orbiter* crew, Yemen was another matter. On March 4, the *Orbiter* began to drift toward Yemen, to the alarm of the control team in Switzerland. No effort to deviate from the flight path seemed to work. Patrick Schelling, the controller, then made repeated calls to the control tower in Yemen's capital requesting clearance. The man on duty asked in broken English, "What is the balloon's destination?" When told by Schelling that this was an around-the-world trip, he

(TOP)

Sunrise viewed from the frozen porthole of the Breitling Orbiter 3.

(MIDDLE)

Bertrand Piccard uses his Swiss Army knife to remove ice from the control panels.

(BOTTOM)

Suspended solar panels provided electric power for the Breitling Orbiter 3.

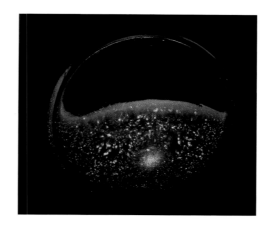

only repeated the question. The man in the tower in Yemen stated that he lacked the authority to grant a clearance. Schelling kept the conversation going until it was clear that there were no plans in Yemen to disrupt the flight. Everyone expressed relief when the *Orbiter* cleared Yemen air space.

On March 9, the *Orbiter* crew learned that Andy Elson and Colin Prescot—both friends and rivals—had ditched at sea, ending their attempt to be the first to make a nonstop balloon flight around the planet. This event had been confirmed by fax. Now the sole obstacle would be nature herself—could the *Orbiter* still make the long journey ahead across Asia, the Pacific, the United States, the Atlantic Ocean, and Africa? The odds were that they would suffer the same fate as Elson and Prescott and the many others who had attempted this elusive milestone.

By March 8, they were over India at 16,000 feet, where they could see the distant Himalayas on the horizon. Pressing on, they reached Iwo Jima in the Pacific on March 11. They passed over the island at 24,900 feet. The anticipated flight path across 8,000 miles of ocean, however, was suddenly changed. The meteorological team, Luc and Pierre, decided that the changes in the weather dictated a shift southward, to pick up a jet stream that they predicted would take shape in three days! This proposed change startled Piccard and Jones, who remembered that this was the same area where Richard Branson had been forced to ditch a few months before. The revised plan called for an additional thousand miles to the journey. Reluctantly, Piccard and Jones accepted the confident orders of their weathermen.

This same area in the South Pacific, as Jones remembered, had been the place where Steve Fossett had crash-landed his balloon into the ocean in 1998. Violent winds and hail had

ruptured the envelope of his balloon at an altitude of 28,000 feet. His descent had been a hair-raising event. Fossett had turned his propane burners on full power to retard the fall, and then laid down flat on his bunk, hoping the impact of hitting the water would not kill him. Fossett survived, and he later would make a single nonstop flight around the world in 2002. But Piccard and Jones had ample reason to wonder what might await them in the skies of the South Pacific.

On March 15, the *Orbiter* crew learned that they had broken the long-distance record for a balloon. This news came at dawn, while they were at an altitude of 32,000 feet above the Pacific Ocean. They had exceeded Steve Fossett's old record of 14,236 miles. Morale and confidence waxed with this important milestone.

Three tedious days passed as the *Orbiter* moved slowly over the Pacific, North America, and the threshold of the West Indies. The *Orbiter* passed Haiti on March 18, at 36,100 feet. While the balloon was at its ceiling, on course, and at cruising speed, there was growing concern with a steady drift southward. To correct the situation, Piccard and Jones had to vent helium to descend to a more favorable altitude and heading. At this juncture of the flight, there was concern over any excessive burning of propane. The maneuver worked. They were back on course, but with only 40 hours of propane-burning left.

The passage over the Atlantic was swift, at 80 knots. As they approached Africa, they had regained an altitude of 36,000 feet, which brought an intense cold to the interior of the gondola. Outside, Piccard later reported, the temperature was 58 below zero Fahrenheit. By March 20, they had reached the coast of West Africa. For the ground

control team in Switzerland and a growing audience across the globe, there was a solid expectation that Piccard and Jones were on the verge of a new record, one that had eluded so many over the years.

Where to land once the *Orbiter* reached Africa? The option of Mali or Mauritania was not appealing because of the remoteness of the interior and land mines scattered across the landscape. Algeria was no less a turn off; the government there had been very cool and uncooperative toward the flight. Libya was welcoming, but why not press on to Egypt? Moreover, why not a dramatic landing at Giza near the ancient pyramids?

Before dawn on March 21, 1999, over the Libya-Egyptian border at 32,000 feet, Piccard and Jones initiated their descent, falling at around 300 feet per minute. The *Orbiter* also began to lose speed. They had to land in the first two hours of daylight, otherwise the balloon would find itself tossed about by the strong desert winds. The Breitling team sent an airplane to intercept the *Orbiter* and assist with the complicated and always dangerous landing of a balloon. The *Orbiter* hit the ground with a thud, bounced up some 300 feet, and then settled down on the desert floor.

Jones later described the dramatic landing: "Bertrand cried, check the time! Check the time! It was a few seconds after 0600. Quickly I retrieved the laptop, which had shot off the desk and flown across the cabin, and at 0601 faxed to control: The Eagle has landed. All OK. Bloody good. B." Piccard summed up his feelings by saying, "I am with the angels." He added that he had felt an "invisible hand" guiding this most remarkable flight of a balloon around the globe.

INDEX

ILLUSTRATION CREDITS

l = left, r = right, t = top, c = center, b = bottom

Abbreviations: AMNHL- American Museum of Natural History Library; **DH**- Dirck Halstead; **EL/NASM**- Eric F. Long, National Air & Space Museum; **JO**- Joe Oliva/ Jetpix.com; **LC/NASM**- L'Aérophile Collection, National Air & Space Museum; **LC/NSM**-Loomis Collection, National Soaring Museum; **MG**-Mark Greenberg/ Visions; **NASM**- National Air & Space Museum; **NGS**- National Geographic Society Image Collection; **NMPFT**- National Museum of Photography, Film & Television/ Science & Society Picture Library; **VH**- Von Hardesty Collection.

1 VH. **2/3** JO. **5** Don Monroe. **6** EL/NASM (SI 2001-134). **8** Trevor Collens, © Marathon Racing, Inc. 2002. **9** NASM (SI 77-11793). **11** NASM (SI A-43352). **12** NASM (SI 86-147). **13t** USAF/NASM (SI A-4507-A). **13b** NASM (SI A-4485-C). **16** EL/NASM (SI 2001-11460). **17** NASM (SI 90-9558). **18/19** EL/NASM (SI 2001-116). **20t** NASM (SI 89-4710). **20b** NASM (SI A-38618-A). **21t** NASM (SI A-52375). **21b** NASM (9A00625). **22** NASM (SI A-26767-B). **23t** EL/NASM (SI 2001-1127). **23c** NASM (SI 93-15834). **23b** NASM (SI 85-3311). **24/25** NASM (SI 86-9865). **26** NASM (SI 00180888). **27l** NASM (SI 2002-21703). **27r** NASM/Bella Landauer Sheet Music Collection. **28** EL/NASM (SI 99-40420). **29** VH. **30/31** EL/NASM (SI 94-2184). **32tl** LC/NASM (2001-11724). **32tr** NASM (00010506). **32b** NASM (SI93-9132). **33** Roger Viollet/NASM. **34** LC/NASM (SI 2001-11632). **35tl** LC/NASM (SI 2001-11687). **35tr** LC/NASM (SI 2001-11630). **35b** LC/NASM (SI 2001-11633). **36** NASM (SI 95-2260). **37t** LC/NASM (SI 2001-11725). **37b** NASM (SI 98-20587). **38t** NASM (SI 82-8732). **38b** NASM (SI A-44401-C). **39t** LC/NASM (SI 2001-11722). **39b** VH. **41** Old Rhinebeck Aerodrome. **42** James Dietz/ NASM (SI 90-2792). **43, 45, 46, 47** all Igor I. Sikorsky, Jr. **48/49** NASM (SI 83-16525). **50t** NASM (SI 90-2091). **50b** Igor I. Skiorsky, Jr. **51, 52t** VH. **52b** Alexander Nicolsky. **53** all Igor I. Sikorsky, Jr. **54/55** EL/NASM (SI 94-2188). **55t** NASM (SI90-2138). **56,** Alexander Nicolsky. **58** EL/NASM (SI 99-40421). **59** USAF/NASM (SI A-3853). **60/61** Mark Avino/ NASM (SI 86-12094). **62t** NASM (SI A-42477). **62b** NASM (SI 84-6288). **64t** NASM (SI 76-13317). **64c** NASM (00046543). **64b** NASM (SI 76-13287). **65t** NASM (SI 94-5782). **65b** NASM (SI 90-8279). **66t** NASM (SI 85-12311). **66c** NASM (SI 2001-1053). **66b** NASM (SI 85-12308). **67t** NASM (SI 91-3049). **67c** NASM (SI 85- 12301). **67b** NASM (SI 96-15991). **68** NASM (SI 73-7510). **69** NASM (00119714). **70t** NASM (SI 81-12161). **70b** NASM (SI A-19984-F). **71t** US Navy/ NASM (00097380). **71b** NASM (SI84-6290). **72** EL/NASM (SI 2001-6536). **73** NASM (SI 86-13507). **74/75** EL/NASM (SI 2001-137). **76** NASM (SI 82-11546). **77t** NASM (SI94-7993). **77b** EL/NASM (SI 2001-4158). **78l** Marjorie French/NASM (SI 77-8848). **78tr** NASM (SI A-42065-A). **79** EL/NASM (SI 2001-1352). **80t** NASM (SI83-2469). **80c** NASM (SI A-12720-B). **80b** NASM (SI A-12785-E). **81tl** NASM (SI A-19864-M). **81c** NASM (SI 2001-10539). **81b** NASM (SI 89-4021). **82t** NASM (SI A-746-C). **82b** NASM (9A00627). **83** NASM/Bella Landauer Sheet Music Collection. **84/85** EL/NASM (SI 2001-6534). **86** NASM (SI 98-15068). **87** VH. **88t** NASM (SI2001-10532. **88b, 89** VH. **90, 91, 92, 93, 94, 95, 96, 97, 98, 99** all courtesy Ron Davies. **101** NASM (SI 92-15623). **102, 103, 104/105, 106, 107** all NMPFT. **108** VH. **109, 110, 111, 112, 113t,** all NMPFT. **113c** Hulton Archive/ Getty Images. **113b** NMPFT. **115** NASM (SI 72-10187). **116** NASM (SI 83-97). **117** NASM (SI 83-99). **118t** NASM (SI 99-15416). **118b** VH. **119t** NASM (9A00655). **119c** NASM (SI 99-15418). **119b** NASM (SI 99-15529). **120t** NASM (9A00624). **120b** NASM (SI 99-15420). **121** NASM (SI 2001-10527). **122t** NASM (SI 90-7010). **122c** VH. **122b** NASM (SI 99-15422). **123** NASM Film Archives **124t** NASM (SI 99-15419). **124b** VH. **125t** NASM (SI 99-15439). **125b, 126** VH. **126/127** (NASM (SI 99-15471). **128, 129, 130, 131, 132, 133, 134, 135,** all VH. **136t** Pearson Air Museum. **136b** Leonard Conkling. **137, 138, 139, 140** all VH. **142, 143, 144t, 144c** all LC/NSM. **144b** VH. **145t, 145c** LC/NSM. **145b** NASM (9A00634). **146/147** VH. **148, 149, 150, 151** all LC/NSM. **152t** NASM (SI 78-19121). **152b, 153t, 153b** Von Hardesty and Fred Beck. **154** VH. **155** AMNHL. **156, 157** NGS. **158/159** NASM (SI 2001-10534). **160, 161, 162, 163** AMNHL. **164tr** VH. **164c, 164b, 165, 166** all AMNHL. **167 tl, 167b** NGS. **167tr** AMNHL. **168** EL/NASM (SI 98-15874). **169, 170, 171t** VH. **171b** NASM (SI98-20692). **172t, 173b, 173** VH. **174t** NASM (SI A-46594-F). **174b, 175** VH. **176** NASM (9A00629). **177** courtesy Thomas S. Britton. **178** White Sands Missile Range. **179, 181** VH. **182** NASM (SI 81-12615). **183** NASM (SI A-2013). **184** NASM (SI 98-15403). **184/185** EL/NASM (SI 2001-1353). **186t** NASM (USAF-32543AC). **186b, 187t, 187c** VH. **187b** NASM (SI79-14868). **188** NASM (9A00628). **189** NASM (9A00626). **190/191** NASA Dryden. **192** NASM (SI 2000-9697). **193t** NASM (SI A-5179-G). **193c** NASA Dryden. **193b** NASM (SI A-5231). **194t** NASM (SI71-2699). **194b** VH **195, 196t, 196b** NASA Dryden. **197** NASM (SI 82-2111). **198** DH. **199** John J.Guilmartin Jr. **200, 201, 202, 203t** all DH. **203b** John J. Guilmartin, Jr. **204/205, 206, 207, 208, 210** all DH. **213t** John J. Guilmartin Jr. **213b** DH. **214, 215, 216/217, 218, 219, 220, 221, 222, 223, 224/225, 227** all Don Monroe. **228** MG. **229** Doug Shane. **230, 231, 233, 234/235** all MG. **234t** Doug Shane. **236** Jeffery Vock. **237t, 237b** MG. **238/239** Carol Berson. **239** MG. **240** JO. **241** NASM (9A00614). **242** NASM (9A00601). **243t** NASM (9A00598). **243c** NASM (9A00613). **243b** NASM (9A00612). **244/245** JO. **245** NASM (9A00610). **246** JO. **247** Col. Gregory Feest. **248t,b, 250/251** JO. **252, 253, 254, 255, 257, 258, 259, 261** all Breitling SA. **264** AMNHL.

ACKNOWLEDGMENTS

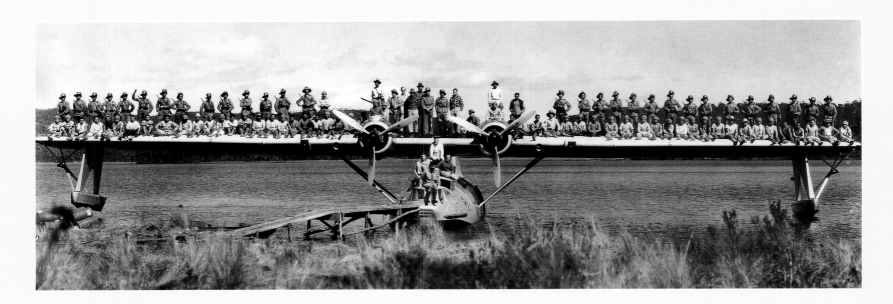

THE MULTIFACETED work behind *Great Aviators and Epic Flights* involved a large number of people over time. The genesis of the project goes back to the year 2000, when the idea was first proposed by the author as a fitting way to capture a sense of the rapid advance of aviation in the twentieth century. Patricia Jamison Graboske, Head of Publications for the National Air and Space Museum, played a key role in getting the project under way and, in particular, seeking out Hugh Lauter Levin as a potential publisher for the large-format, illustrated volume. Graboske's constancy and timely coordination played a key role in bringing the complex project to fruition.

Fashioning a narrative for 18 separate historical episodes and then seeking out appropriate illustrations for each story became a formidable challenge for several talented and highly motivated people. Lawrence DiRicco, a museum volunteer, worked at the epicenter of the project, providing baseline research and expertise on aviation history. Charles O. Hyman oversaw the complex process of collecting photographs and illustrations for the book, dealing as well with a thicket of permissions problems. The book's designer, Kevin Osborn, brought an infectious enthusiasm for the project, and we acknowledge with profound appreciation his creative work. Two museum photographers, Eric Long and Mark Avino, sent our way a number of excellent photographs of aircraft in the National Air and Space Museum; we also appreciate Eric's many labors on our behalf to copy a number of rare historical photographs. Archivists Melissa Keiser, Dan Hagedorn, and Kristine Kaske deserve special praise for their unrivaled knowledge of archival resources at the museum. As archivists, they provided a constant stream of ideas and expert advice, not to mention many key historical images and illustrations. Mark Taylor, another museum archivist and a specialist with documentary films, assisted us with the recovery of still images from a documentary film related to the historic Banning and Allen flight. Ann Monroe Jacobs provided an essential baseline of research on photographs, and we acknowledge her contribution to the project.

Several curators in the Aeronautics Division of the National Air and Space Museum offered consultation and editorial expertise to the project: Tom D. Crouch helped to shape the concept of the book, although he should in no way be held responsible for our final choice of stories; Peter Jakab weighed in with welcome advice and suggestions on chapters dealing with early flight; Ron Davies aided us in many ways, in particular the development of the *Graf Zeppelin* chapter; and John Anderson provided many insights on supersonic flight and modern aircraft design and systems. Joe Guilmartin, history professor at Ohio State University, generously offered consultation on the Saigon rescue of 1975, an event in which he played a significant role as an Air Force helicopter pilot. Museum specialist Carl Bobrow provided expertise for the preparation of the Igor Sikorsky chapter and assisted us as well with the photo research phase of the project. No less important, Gene Eisman, a museum volunteer, offered in a timely and enthusiastic way his considerable skills as a reader and editor for the text. We thank these advisors for their unfailing willingness to assist us and to answer technical questions.

For all of us working on the project, there was a keen and abiding appreciation for the professionalism of our publisher, Hugh Lauter Levin. A long-time friend of the museum, Hugh Levin has demonstrated an interest in aviation. He gave us time, resources, and encouragement to make the book a reality. Ellin Yassky, our director at Hugh Lauter Levin Associates, deserves special praise for her constancy and administrative skills; as the project evolved, she provided critical support and her own creative ideas for the book. Deborah Zindell, editor at Hugh Levin, brought skill and efficiency to the preparation of the text, and we appreciate her role as well.

Finally, I would like to acknowledge the support, patience, and occasional editorial consultation of my wife, Patricia Hardesty. Her role, if informal, was no less important, even critical, in bringing the book to final form.

Von Hardesty
National Air and Space Museum